Library of
Davidson College

Writing Another's Dream
The Poetry of Wen Tingyun

Writing Another's Dream
The Poetry of Wen Tingyun

Paul F. Rouzer

Stanford University Press
Stanford, California   1993

Stanford University Press
Stanford, California
© 1993 by the Board of Trustees
of the Leland Stanford Junior University

Printed in the United States of America

CIP data are at the end of the book

Stanford University Press publications
are distributed exclusively by
Stanford University Press within
the United States, Canada, and Mexico;
they are distributed exclusively by
Cambridge University Press throughout
the rest of the world.

"César" by Paul Valéry from "Album de
vers anciens" in *Poésies*, © Editions
Gallimard, 1978. Reproduced by
permission of Editions Gallimard.

For Stephen Owen

Acknowledgments

THIS BOOK IS a reworking of a dissertation I wrote at Harvard University; like so many books produced under these circumstances, it has had a lengthy gestation period and countless midwives; I apologize in advance for anyone whose assistance I may have forgotten.

My greatest gratitude must go to my advisor, Professor Stephen Owen, whose advice, criticism, and friendship have made writing it a real pleasure. I have considered myself particularly fortunate for having found a teacher who combines kindness and humor with rigorous standards.

I also extend my thanks to many of my teachers and colleagues who have in one way or another contributed to the intellectual development of this book as well—notably Peter Bol, Michael Fuller, Judith Zeitlin, K'o Ch'ing-ming, Cheung Suk-hung, and Kang-i Sun Chang. I offer special thanks to Burton Watson, who reviewed the entire manuscript and aided me with his insights.

The contributions of a number of my graduate students (Edward Walsh, Jo-wen Tung, Charles Laughlin, Maryanne Cartelli, and Kris Torgeson) have been essential; their discussion of an early version of this book has assisted me greatly.

Chapter 3 was published in slightly different form in the 1989 issue of *Chinese Literature: Essays, Articles, and Reviews*. William H. Nienhauser offered his own comments on this particular part, for which I am grateful. The editors at Stanford University Press, Helen Tartar and John Ziemer, have been particularly kind to a fledgling writer and must receive special thanks as well.

Finally I thank my wife, Jennifer Carpenter, whose diligent re-reading of drafts, skeptical criticism, and moral support have been essential for the book's completion.

P.F.R.

Contents

Note on Translation and Abbreviations xi
Chinese Dynasties and Selected Reigns xiii

ONE Fraudulent Verses 1
TWO Words for the Singing 27
THREE Watching the Voyeurs 69
FOUR Patterns of History, Failures of History 95
FIVE Small Ambitions 170

Appendix: A Note on the Tonality of Wen Tingyun's Seven-Character Yuefu 215

Reference Matter
    Notes 223
    Bibliography 241
    Index of Titles 247
    Index of Subjects 253

Note on Translation and Abbreviations

MUCH INK HAS been spilled on what constitutes a "correct" translation of a Chinese poem. Though compelling arguments have been made for various approaches, ranging from the radically literal rendering to the artistically gifted imitation, I very much doubt that any method of translation will suffice to capture the nature of Chinese poetry. However, in a study such as this, discussion and analysis may to some extent compensate for the loss of spirit that results from the heinous perpetration of translation. If the reader unacquainted with the quality of the originals may guess at their original beauties through my readings, then my task will have been partially accomplished.

I have nonetheless paid some attention to felicity of expression and to the poetic rhythm of the originals. Generally speaking, I have adhered as closely as possible to Waley's practice: roughly one stressed syllable per Chinese character. This has resulted occasionally in some changes from the syntax of the originals; I can only apologize for this by claiming that a more literal rendering would result in constructions so clumsy and convoluted they would betray the grace of the originals.

Wen Tingyun is a highly allusive poet and often the full equal of Li Shangyin in obscurity. I have avoided paraphrasing in translation to make Wen's meaning clearer, because that would give the impression that he is a more lucid writer than he is. Instead, I have explained difficult lines and allusions in the notes that follow the poem. I apologize in advance for the inconveniences this may cause for my reader, but Wen is not a convenient poet.

In translating seven-character lines, I have divided the translated line at the caesura and indented the second half of the line. Again, this was a practical solution to the imagistic density of Wen's style. The line numbers shown in the margins are those of the Chinese text, not of the translation. Unless otherwise noted, all translations are my own. In quotations from other English-language sources, I have silently converted Wade-Giles to pinyin.

The following abbreviations are used in the text and notes:

LHSJ	Li He, *Li He shi ji*
QTS	*Quan Tang shi*
QTWDC	*Quan Tang Wudai ci*
WFQ	Wen Tingyun, *Wen Feiqing shi ji jian zhu*
YFSJ	Guo Maoqian, *Yuefu shi ji*
YTXY	Xu Ling, *Yutai xinyong*

Chinese Dynasties and Selected Reigns

Dynasties

Eastern Zhou 東周	ca. 770–256 B.C.
Spring and Autumn 春秋	722–468 B.C.
Warring States 戰國	403–221 B.C.
Qin 秦	221–207 B.C.
Han 漢	206 B.C.–220 A.D.
Former (Western) Han 前漢	206 B.C.–A.D. 8
Later (Eastern) Han 後漢	A.D. 25–220
Three Kingdoms 三國	220–65
Jin 晉	265–420
Western Jin 西晉	265–317
Eastern Jin 東晉	317–420
Southern Dynasties 南朝	420–589
Liu Song 劉宋	420–79
Southern Qi 南齊	479–502
Liang 梁	502–57
Chen 陳	557–89
Sui 隋	581–618
Tang 唐	618–907
Five Dynasties 五代	907–60
Song 宋	960–1279
Northern Song 北宋	960–1126
Southern Song 南宋	1127–1279

Chinese Dynasties and Selected Reigns

Yuan 元	1260–1368
Ming 明	1368–1644
Qing 清	1644–1911

Tang Dynasty Emperors

Gaozu 高祖	618–26	Dezong 德宗	779–805
Taizong 太宗	626–49	Shunzong 順宗	805
Gaozong 高宗	649–83	Xianzong 憲宗	805–20
Zhongzong 中宗	684	Muzong 穆宗	820–24
Ruizong 睿宗	684–90	Jingzong 敬宗	824–27
Empress Wu 武后	690–705	Wenzong 文宗	827–40
Zhongzong 中宗 (restored)	705–10	Wuzong 武宗	840–46
		Xuanzong 宣宗	846–59
Ruizong 睿宗 (restored)	710–12	Yizong 懿宗	859–73
		Xizong 僖宗	873–88
Xuanzong 玄宗	712–56	Zhaozong 昭宗	888–904
Suzong 肅宗	756–62	Aidi 哀帝	904–7
Daizong 代宗	762–79		

Writing Another's Dream
The Poetry of Wen Tingyun

ONE

Fraudulent Verses

BY THE MIDDLE of the Tang Dynasty, it had become the goal of a substantial number of educated young men to find powerful patrons in government, to pass the civil service examinations that were administered in the capital, and, subsequently, to dedicate their lives to public service and to politics. To fulfill this ambition, they trained themselves in the literary arts, especially poetry; skill in such matters guaranteed their opportunity to participate in the social and political order. Literary talent, however, had to be accompanied by a certain degree of moral seriousness. Unfortunately, at the beginning of his career, the young and talented Wen Tingyun 溫庭筠 (polite name Feiqing 飛卿; ca. 812–ca. 866) attracted attention for his unconventional behavior. One piece of gossip reveals an early disaster.

Wen had a considerable reputation for literary composition. Immediately after passing the local examinations, he went traveling along the Yangzi and Huai rivers. The Imperial Representative for Yangzi 楊子, Yao Xu 姚勖, rewarded him richly; Wen was still young, however, and whenever he obtained money, he would squander most of it in the brothels. Xu was infuriated by this and drove him away with a bamboo staff; it was for this reason that Wen failed to pass the examinations.

Wen's older sister was the wife of Zhao Zhuan 趙顓. Each time her brother failed the exams, she would gnash her teeth over Yao Xu's conduct. One day there was a guest at the district office, and she happened to ask who it was. The servants answered that it was Yao Xu; thereupon she broke in upon the matters being conducted in her husband's office and, weeping loudly, seized Yao Xu's sleeve. Xu was considerably startled. She clung tenaciously to his sleeve and could not be pulled away, although he remained ignorant of the cause.

After a time, Madame Wen said, "My little brother was young and was only sowing his wild oats. These human desires are common to all—how could he deserve a beating for them? Up until now, he has been unsuccessful. This must be because *you* caused it to be so!" Xu broke into a loud laugh and after some time managed to get away from her. He returned home enraged, and because of this incident he took sick and died.   (*WFQ*, p. 258, quoting *Yu quan zi* 玉泉子)

Although we cannot be sure that this soap-opera vignette is true, the relish with which it is told reflects the ambivalence of later Chinese toward writers like Wen. On the one hand, we see him as a ne'er-do-well who steadfastly refused to take his future seriously; on the other hand, we may have a certain secret admiration for him and a desire to forgive his iniquities. Although Yao Xu was perhaps justified in his treatment of his protégé, most of us side with Madame Wen in the end.

This varying tone of praise and blame aptly characterizes the ambiguities of Wen's career. He never passed the higher examinations, but he continued to participate in them; he never held important office, but he kept up a search for patrons who might find him one; he was accused of writing only for an ephemeral popularity or for money, yet the beauty and ease of his compositions won admiration from everyone; he frequented brothels instead of government offices, but he used his experiences to write sensitively of the demimonde. Wen, like the doomed emperor Li Yu 李煜 (937–74) or the swaggering artist Tang Yin 唐寅 (1470–1524), was the sort of semi-legendary figure whom the Chinese have publicly condemned and secretly embraced.

Traditional literati, who were always willing to see poetry as the product of personality and society, might find Wen's life typical of his times. Ever since the debates on Tang poetry that arose in the late Song, and which emerged in one form in Yan Yu's 嚴羽 (fl. 1200) famed periodization of Tang poetry in his *Canglang shihua* 滄浪詩話, ninth-century literature has been seen as a product of an age of decay and dissolution—and yet an age that produced a seductive and highly aesthetic writing as well, most critics' condemnation of it to the contrary.[1] Readers of Wen's poetry (*shi* 詩) could find there the same attraction and repulsion they felt in examining the life of the poet or the events of his age. Poetry at its most proper was a serious communication of morally acceptable experiences; the following poem, however, obviously reflects its author's dissipated life.

Recalling True Pearl Pavilion 懷真珠亭

Its pearl screens and silver hooks 珠箔銀鉤對彩橋
   faced the decorated bridge;
In years gone by, at this spot 昔年於此見嬌饒
   I looked on Jiaorao.
Under a fragrant lamp I gazed sadly 香燈悵望飛瓊鬢
   at Feiqiong's tresses;
4 And under a cool moon, an earnest plea 涼月殷勤碧玉簫
   came from Biyu's flute.
The screen leaned against an old window, 屏倚故窗山六扇
   a mountain in six leaves;
Willows drooped over chill steps, 柳垂寒砌露千條
   dew on a thousand branches.
Now ruined walls that have endured the rain, 壞牆經雨蒼苔徧
   gray moss everywhere—
8 And I pick up, left from that time, 拾得當時舊翠翹
   an old tailfeather from a kingfisher.
   (*WFQ*, *j*. 4, pp. 102–3)[2]

  Title/ An alternative title is "Passing by Old Haunts" 經舊游. "True Pearl" may be the name of a courtesan.
  2/ Jiaorao may be Dong 董 Jiaorao, the beautiful girl described in a Later Han 後漢 dynasty (25–220) song by Song Zihou 宋自侯 (*YFSJ*, p. 1034). Here, obviously, it is an elegant designation for a courtesan.
  3/ Feiqiong means "Flying Jasper," a fairy maid-in-waiting to the Taoist goddess Xi Wang Mu 西王母, the "Queen Mother of the West"; a courtesan is meant here as well.
  4/ Biyu is "Green Jade," the concubine of Prince Runan 汝南王 of the Jin 晉 (265–420) dynasty. He praised her beauty in a famous ballad (*YFSJ*, pp. 663–64). Here, she is an elegant substitution for a courtesan-musician.
  5/ The free-standing screen (used to close off sections of rooms) is decorated with paintings of mountains, which stretch across its different leaves.
  8/ Kingfisher feathers were used as hair ornaments by women.

As the poet passes this old pavilion, probably once part of a brothel, he envisions the time he spent there before it fell into decline. Not only does Wen thumb his nose at the poetic tradition by writing on a frivolous theme, but he parodies in a mild way a serious convention. Poets often wrote on visits to historically portentous locations, such as old battlefields or palace ruins. Wen relocates the poetic subgenre to the ruins of a house of ill-repute and pulls from the wreckage not some memento of past imperial glory but a reminder of sensual pleasure. It is a classic Tang theme reinterpreted by a roué.

The appearance of Wen's less savory occupations in his poetry might be enough to condemn his works as dangerous reading, at least by official arbiters of taste. However, a more important and subtle argument was often used to denigrate his poetry and that of the Late Tang. Post-Song authors of "poetry conversations" (*shihua* 詩話) saw ninth-century poetic output as largely superficial, too eager to please, and incapable of expressing the great truths of the self and of the world. In the long run, this critical emphasis was most damaging to Wen's posthumous reputation, because it implied a moral distaste for his works as well as his personality. To elucidate what I mean by a moral attack on the literature itself, I compare two regulated poems: the first by the High Tang master Wang Wei 王維 (699?–761?) and the second, on a similar theme, by Wen Tingyun himself.

Written Offhand While Living in the Mountains 山居即事

Alone, isolated, I shut my brushwood door; 寂寞掩柴扉
Mid the great vastness I face the sinking rays. 蒼茫對落暉
Cranes nest everywhere in pine branches; 鶴巢松樹遍
4　Human visitors are few by my overgrown gate. 人訪蓽門稀
Tender bamboos hold in fresh pollen; 嫩竹含新粉
Red lotus lets fall its old garment. 紅蓮落故衣
By the ford, lantern lights are lit, 渡頭燈火起
8　While every water chestnut gatherer heads for home. 處處採菱歸
　　(QTS, j. 126, p. 1277)

Early Autumn, Dwelling in the Mountains 早秋山居

With the mountains near, I feel the cold early; 山近覺寒早
By my grass hut the frosty air is clear. 草堂霜氣晴
Trees grow bare; there's sunlight in my window. 樹彫窗有日
4　The pool is full; its waters, still. 池滿水無聲
When fruit falls, I see gibbons pass. 果落見猿過
Leaves are sere, so I can hear deer pass by. 葉乾聞鹿行
Worry over plans are calmed by my silk-stringed zither: 素琴機慮靜
8　Clear sounds that idly accompany the creek at night. 空伴夜泉清
　　(WFQ, j. 7, p. 151)

On an initial reading, both poems may strike us as beautiful and effective examples of regulated verse. Yet few traditional readers would find Wen's poem equal to Wang's.

Both poets write of a life of retirement in the countryside. The skilled reader will understand the situation: conventional, but conventions hold true when the situations they describe are the shared experiences of the literate community. The poet who gives voice to Taoist or Buddhist sentiments of reclusion may in real life be a prominent statesman or an ambitious, patronage-seeking youth, but that would not prevent his sentiments from being true at the time of writing. A reclusion poem could give the poet an opportunity to express his place in society, to claim his own political position, to assert the purity of his aspirations, or to emphasize his commitment to Buddhist practices. The poem might be playful or solemn in tone; but the content must *ultimately* convey something important.

Wang Wei fulfills the tradition's expectations perfectly. In the first couplet he locates himself within the poem, in the second and third he gives details of the scene, and in the closing couplet he presents an image that is meant to linger in our thoughts and let us recreate his state of mind. His poetic juxtapositions are simple but powerful: the numerous cranes (a symbol of the Taoist immortals) are placed against worldly human visitors, who have grown few. Bamboo and lotus can refer to the recluse himself—the former flourishes even in cold weather, and the latter grows clean and pure, although its roots are anchored in mud. Wang thus suggests his own spiritual renewal amid such surroundings. The last image hints perhaps at Buddhist concepts (the lamps are an emblem of consciousness amid the darkness of the world) and of the natural return of man to his rightful place. Other more facile poems might give an explicit emotional response at the end; it is a mark of Wang's much-admired style that he can simply point to the landscape to convey a sense of depth. No matter where he looks, the landscape tells him of the rightness of his place in nature and his newfound peace of mind.

Wen's poem too is, stylistically speaking, exemplary regulated verse. As in Wang's, the opening couplet sets the scene; the middle, parallel couplets give details of what the poet sees; and the final couplet suggests an emotional response. Moreover, the language is simple, direct, and transparently easy to understand. But a late traditional reader would soon feel that this is not "great" poetry. This may partly be because of the prejudices such a reader brings to a poem when he knows who has written it, but there are other factors as well. The first sign of the poem's "weakness" occurs in the second couplet. Here the poetic voice gives a subtle causal explanation for the bright window and the still water: both are signs of the season: the increasingly bare branches, the change of the water level due to the movement from spring and summer months to the increasing dormancy of autumn and winter. Perhaps the contrast between the glitter of the air and the glitter of the pool is too pretty; we are so distracted by the scene that we cannot trace the possible correspondences between it and the state of the poet's mind.

The virtuosity of the third couplet is even more distracting. Visual phenomena contrast with aural ones as the poet wittily organizes the fauna in his vicinity. We abruptly catch the bright flash of falling fruit and the shadows of monkeys behind them, and we hold our breath as we strain to hear the rustle of hooves on paper-thin leaves. And, of course, dry leaves and falling fruit, like the pool and branches, are insignia of autumn, the topic of the poem.

The poet makes one final attempt at seriousness in line seven, when he claims that his plans and worries for worldly success are tamed and exorcised by the zither he plays (strumming the zither at night is a poetic convention of gentlemanly self-expression), but he fails in the last line, when he merges the strumming with the sound of the nearby stream. The poet suggests that he is one with nature—but it is an artful and artificial way of making the suggestion.

Make no mistake. This is a skillful piece of work, filled with cunning juxtapositions of light and sound. But it is also, traditionally speaking, a bad poem, artistically and perhaps morally. The poet does not speak from the heart/mind (*xin* 心). His subject is his own ability to write a beautiful poem; the poem's items, instead of suggesting possible correspondences between the poet's sentiment (*qing* 情) and the world (*jing* 景), signify themselves and nothing more. It is a poem that chronicles a simple love of surfaces.

The dislike of surfaces is an essential element in the traditional aesthetic theory of China. The reader of poetry maintained a personal relationship with the poets of his culture. He believed that if the poet wrote truly of his feelings and experiences in his work, his audience would be able to reconstruct the biography and even the personality of the man. Thus, the reader knows well that authorial intent is the central tenet of the rules of reading; in fact, as has been pointed out, the Chinese tradition goes one step further in identifying poem with poet. The "intention" (*zhi* 志) of the poet is not so much creative inclination as inevitable, spontaneous expression; he cannot help but express his situation and state of mind at that moment of time. Hence, the belief that poetry is authentic autobiography (or, rather, diary, since it is produced during life, and not at its end, when fading memory and ulterior motives might transform the "truth").[3]

Although a modern, Western reader might object to the supposed infallibility of the poem as window into the poet's inner self, it is this very attempt to recreate the emotionally charged circumstances of the literary act that has helped to delineate the "greatness" of the poets of the Chinese canon. Du Fu 杜甫 (712–70) above all has gradually become the product of his readers' perceptions of him as they attempt to trace the feelings and biographical hints ostensibly exposed in line after line of his verse. This may result in a circular process, in which biography and poetry explain each other. William Hung, whose biography of Du Fu is a thoughtful critique of such speculation and yet a superb product of it, inadvertently reveals the paradox.

> Three centuries after [Du's] death, scholars began in earnest to collect his works, to edit them, and to provide them with commentaries. They began to study the incidents of his life in the light of his poetry and to understand his poetry in terms of his life and time. Thus the admiration of the man came from the fascination of his poetry, and the admiration of the poetry was further strengthened by the more detailed knowledge of the poet's life.[4]

This process of biographical reconstruction is rarely the work of one critic or historian; the framework for a Tang poet's life may be built over centuries, with each new reader adding one tentative brick to the work of his predecessors. After a millennium, few notice how delicate the entire edifice is and how many conclusions are drawn from an initial handful of facts and hypotheses. This does not mean that the biographical research of centuries of scholars is largely worthless, for we must always keep in mind that Du Fu himself wrote in a tradition that believed that poetry was nonfictional. Rather, the work of such critics has been essential in *defining* Du Fu's greatness—not because it creates a man from his poetry, but because it illuminates the ever-vital relations between life and art.

The biographical reading of poetry became increasingly prevalent after the Tang; by the Qing, the general assumptions underlying literary composition came to have the unbending qualities of laws. The promise of spontaneous self-expression that guaranteed communication with poetic predecessors became also a poetic straitjacket; it was demanded of the poet that he be serious and that he be scrupulous in the observation of generic conventions and content. If he is frivolous or displays a self-conscious craftsmanship in his work, he is guilty not only of bad poetry but of betrayal of the readers' trust.

The critic Xue Xue 薛雪 (1681–1763?) encapsulates this critique of Wen's work by contrasting "cleverness" (*minjie* 敏捷) with true "beauty" (*mei* 美).

Wen [Tingyun] of Taiyuan could compose eight verses while clapping his hands eight times; in this way he arrived at [lines like]:

> Silk windtossed on fragile willows,
>   evening on the level bridge;
> Snow dots the cold plum,
>   spring in the little garden.

From beginning to end the emotion [*qing*] and scene [*jing*] have no bearing on each other; it's basically a couplet for inscribing on a garden kiosk.

> The seductive airs of a Little Su
>   bewitch Xiacai city,
> While a great poetic talent resembles
>   Sima Xiangru at Linqiong.

His use here of allusion is random, confused, and makes no sense; it is difficult to discuss or analyze. Surely this is employing cleverness in order to please the reader?[5]

Xue may be unfairly citing mediocre examples from Wen's work, but surely his criticism that Wen fails to infuse his landscapes with his own personal sentiment could be leveled at the fine autumn poem we have read. If a poet's motive is merely to please the reader rather than to communicate some inner truth about the self, then the "honesty" of poetry is in jeopardy. Poems are moorless and float away from the poet and his biographical circumstances; they become (in Chinese terms) "difficult to discuss or analyze." This is a more serious crime than writing a biographically clear but morally questionable poem; that at least is understandable, if unfortunate.

Later readers would believe with some justification that Wen's biographically ambiguous poems were just as much a product of his decadent life and age as his more explicitly erotic ones. The Late Tang poets were often accused of spending too much time on parallelism and craft to the detriment of spontaneous self-expression. This tendency was often traced to Jia Dao 賈島 (779–843), the talented monk-poet and member of the Han Yu 韓愈 (768–824) circle. Few writers discussing Jia's work have failed to allude to the following anecdote.

When Jia Dao first went to the capital for the examinations, he happened to hit upon a couplet of poetry while he was riding a donkey:

> The birds roost in trees by the pool,
> A monk knocks on a gate under the moon.

At first he chose the word "push," but later he took a liking to "knock." He rehearsed both in his mind, undecided, reciting the line aloud from the back of his donkey. From time to time he put forth his hand and imitated the gestures of knocking and pushing. At this time Han Yu held a position in the Board of Public Office in the capital, and Jia inadvertently blundered into his retinue. Han's servants seized him and brought him before their master. Jia then proceeded to explain the lines he had composed, and so forth; Han held his horse still for a long while, then finally said to Jia, "'Knock' is better."[6]

Apocryphal or not, the anecdote illustrates Jia's sensitivity to the best word in the best place. Such self-conscious artfulness in some Mid-Tang and most Late Tang poetry seemed dishonest to later readers: Wang Fuzhi 王夫之 (1619–92) for one condemns Jia Dao for not knowing whether the monk pushed or knocked.

> "A monk knocks on a gate under the moon" is only a random guess or a false speculation, as though speaking of another's dream. Even if you make the description vivid, how could it ever affect the heart? Those who know this will know that brooding over the choice of "push" or "knock" is only speculating on the behalf of some other person.[7]

Wang's criticism here, though negative, summarizes precisely a major characteristic of Wen Tingyun's verse: an ability to stand outside of the self and to "speculate on the behalf of some other person."

For a later imperial reader, then, Wen's poetic vices could be summarized as twofold. First, when he wrote of morally dubious experiences, he brought into question the important role poetry was meant to play in society. Second, and more important, as a historical actor he was often "unreadable" for later generations. Frequently he left behind only the poem (a morally ambiguous aesthetic artifact) or, at most, an image of a sophisticated versifier manipulating language for pure entertainment. Poetry of surface, when written by men like Wen, is not just empty; it actually *conceals* the immoral mind that frames it. It is deceptive and fraudulent.

Of course, this is judging Wen's works not by his own personal standards but by the calcified laws of composition that grew up after his death. The frequent choruses of disapproval and the constant use of Wen's poems as examples of poetic and moral turpitude suggest that his work posed a real and attractive danger to readers and poets of the later tradition. Apparently the critics and theorists saw it (and Late Tang poetry in general) as the most seductive alternative to what had become the "proper" exercise of the poetic art. This view lingers even today in China; when one modern scholar attempts to salvage Wen's reputation as a poet, he does so (predictably) by claiming that the poet's ballads (*yuefu* 樂府) are in fact political satires on the court of his day.[8]

These prejudices make a rereading of Wen's literary works a compelling enterprise, because they suggest that an important body of poetry (not just Wen's, but the poetry of the Late Tang in general) has been neglected through the applications of standards created after it was written that do not necessarily apply to a Western reader. On the other hand, they tell us that Late Tang poets may possibly have been operating on creative assumptions that the later mainstream tradition not only discarded but saw fit to attack. Relatively free of the moral constraints of the tradition, we can look at Wen's work (and that of other Late Tang poets) on its own terms. We may even find it easier to do so than a traditional reader would— for, in spite of our difficulty in bridging language and cultural distances, we are comfortable with two concepts that might still seem strange to late classical Chinese: (1) that a poem can be read as a product of an age and a personality without relating it explicitly to events in the poet's life; and (2) that a writer may still produce fine work despite his moral failings. To re-evaluate will lead us not simply to a new appreciation of a neglected Tang master; it will enable us to revise our history of Chinese poetry and poetics. This study will address these issues in the light of individual readings and interpretations. First, however, we must ground ourselves in the few facts known about the poet's life.

Although many traditional Chinese have based their reading of Wen's poetry on his personal reputation, much of that reputation is based on hearsay and contradictory evidence. The biographical pickings are slim indeed; he merits brief notices in both Tang histories, although the two accounts limit themselves to a few minor details.[9] With the aid of these, and a few stories found in unofficial sources dating from the Late Tang and Song, traditionalist scholars of this century (in particular, Xia Chengtao and Gu Xuejie) have attempted an outline of his life.[10] Although a reasonable reconstruction, by no means can their accounts be accepted as indisputable.

Wen's birthdate has been set as early as 798 and as late as 824; until recently, 812 was an accepted estimate, but recent scholarly debate has widened the possibilities.[11] Although he may have claimed to be the descendant of several prominent ministers, evidence suggests that he belonged to a family of minor gentry dependent on the examination system for social advancement. The dynastic histories list him as a native of Taiyuan 太原, in modern Shanxi; but the predominance of southern scenes in his poetry suggests that he either was born in the eastern Yangzi valley or moved there early in his life.

Almost every detail we have of his career seems to have been collected (or fabricated) to emphasize his role as black sheep. For example, one source claims that he changed his personal name from Qi 岐 to Tingyun after he "was humiliated by a relative by marriage in the Jiang Huai region."[12] We are meant to believe that the incident became common knowledge and that Wen hoped to escape social disapproval by changing his name. Some scholars believe that the humiliating incident was the beating he received from Yao Xu, but we have no evidence that Yao was a relative by marriage. Moreover, the whole idea of a name change for Wen is odd, since his brother's name was Tinghao 庭皓, which suggests that the brothers always shared the character *ting*.[13]

Biographical anecdotes, though possibly spurious, may at least indicate aspects of Wen's character. His precocious talent obviously impressed his contemporaries (the dynastic histories also note his skill in music, which would prove important in his poetry).[14] He had also acquired by an early age an indifference to accepted codes of conduct. Yao Xu may represent the first in a long line of alienated patrons—and at a time when a successful government career depended on the patronage of high-ranking officials, the young poet's chronic failures later on may in no small part be attributed to his inability to earn the confidence and respect of the elite bureaucracy.

On shaky evidence from two autobiographical poems, we can guess that Wen had traveled to the capital, Chang'an, to take the metropolitan examinations by the late 830's.[15] Illness may have prevented him from participating once or several times, and he seems to have failed at least once (if not twice) by 839. It is likely that he married at this time as well; there is a reference in one of these poems to a wife. Wen was later to father at least two children: a son, Wen Xian 憲, who passed the examinations late in life; and a daughter, who married Duan Anjie 段安節, the author of an early work on musical poetry, the *Yuefu zalu* 樂府雜錄 (Anjie was also the son of Wen's friend and fellow poet Duan Chengshi 成式). After this period, however, no reference to his family can be found in Wen's poetry.

Around 840, he sought support and patronage from the important Tang minister Li Deyu 李德裕 (787–850), who may already have had some connection with the Wen clan. It is unlikely that Li gave him any major assistance, since Wen continued to fail the exams through the reign of Wuzong 武宗 (840–46), the period of Li's ascendance at court. In fact, Wen continued to fail repeatedly for the next ten years.

It is tempting to attribute Wen's failures to the petty factionalism that racked the central bureaucracy during the mid-800's; certainly Chinese readers have believed that Wen's contemporary, Li Shangyin 李商隱 (813–58), never achieved high office because of the animosity of the powerful Linghu Tao 令狐綯, partisan of the Niu

Sengru 牛僧孺 clique, who was insulted when Li married the daughter of a member of Li Deyu's party.¹⁶ We must be cautious in making such assumptions about Wen, however. True, the effects of political infighting may have penetrated to the lowest levels of officialdom; certainly talented examinees could become pawns in the struggles of various factions to obtain long-term dominance at court. Nevertheless, Wen seems to have done an admirably thorough job of insulting almost every important minister who might have helped him. Moreover, any official willing to assist Wen would have had to champion him as an extraordinary poetic talent and not as a potential official of high moral probity. With such patrons, Wen would probably have remained a sort of literary companion who could be brought out at parties to compose sophisticated *vers de société*. This may account for one important aspect of Wen's surviving verse—its emphasis on wit and on describing lively social occasions.

Even if Wen was associated at some time with the Li Deyu clique, this connection must have ended by the late 840's. The dynastic biographies inform us that Wen became fast friends with the "corrupt scions of great ministers' families." This included Linghu Gao 縞, the son of Linghu Tao; the latter managed to achieve the post of chief minister during the 850's under Xuanzong 宣宗 (r. 846–59). This possibly Falstaffian role was bound to displease Linghu senior, although a few anecdotes suggest that the latter did support Wen during these years. Gossip has it that Wen repaid his support with contempt.

Xuanzong loved to sing lyrics to the "Pusa man" tune; the Minister Linghu Tao "borrowed" some of Wen's splendid compositions [to this melody] and put them forward secretly [as his own]. He commanded Wen not to expose this action, but Wen leaked it to someone; Linghu consequently became alienated from him. Wen also has a line that reads: "In the Chancellery sits a military man...," which was meant as a dig at the minister's lack of learning....

Once Linghu Tao sought Wen's help in identifying a literary allusion. Wen said, "This is from the *Zhuangzi*, which is hardly an obscure book. If Your Excellency has leisure, it would be suitable for you to take some time and study [the works of] antiquity." Tao was even more furious. He memorialized that Tingyun was talented but lacking in proper behavior, and so he never passed the examinations.¹⁷

Although once again we cannot be sure of the accuracy of these stories, the fact remains that Wen failed to benefit substantially from Linghu's brief ascendancy at court.

In 855, Wen evidently involved himself in another scandal. Several sons from prominent families who had failed the *jinshi* 進士 examination were given the opportunity to take the special *hongci* 宏詞 Palace Examination. One of them, Liu Han 柳翰, son of the governor of the Chang'an district, managed to obtain the set topic for the prose-poem composition (*fu* 賦) the examination required and had Wen write it for him in advance. Liu passed, but the deception became known to the other students, and news of it reached the court. The Censorate was ordered to investigate, and several officials were dismissed or exiled.[18] Roughly at this time, Wen was also disqualified from the examinations by the chief examiner, Shen Xun 沈詢, who suspected that the poet had been helping his fellow examinees in the examination room. Wen petitioned in protest, but his behavior had provoked the rancor of several high-ranking officials, who despised him for "selling his writings."[19] Gu Xuejie suspects that these incidents, perhaps exacerbated by other actions as well, resulted in Wen's first exile, as commandant of Fangcheng 方城 in modern northwest Hubei. Since Wen had never passed the examinations, the assignment of this unimportant and distant office was likely intended to get him out of the capital, where he was sowing discord among the young examinees. It was during this period perhaps that he came under the protection of Xu Shang 徐商, who was at that time military governor of the Shannan-East 山南東 circuit. Xu made Wen a local inspector, although the poet probably spent most of this period in the attractive provincial capital of Xiangyang 襄陽, where he was joined briefly by his younger brother, Tinghao.

Several years later, Wen apparently grew restless and headed for the southeast; disappointed by his lack of success, he may have felt the need to return to the warm and pleasant country of Jiangnan ("South of the Yangzi"), where so many of his poems are set. By this time, Xuanzong had been succeeded by Yizong 懿宗 (r. 859–73), who eased Linghu Tao out of power and made him military governor of Huainan 淮南. When Wen reached the Huainan capital of Yangzhou 楊州, he snubbed his old patron and refused to visit him; evidently he was bitter over Linghu's failure to promote him in the 850's. Instead, Wen spent most of his time in Yangzhou brothels. One evening (probably in 863) he violated the curfew and received a beating from a military guard; as a result he lost several teeth and was severely disfigured. Wen immediately went to Linghu and demanded the guard's arrest. Once Linghu had interviewed the guard, however, he became convinced that his actions were justified and released him. Shamed and infuriated, Wen returned to Chang'an, where he wrote to various prominent statesmen, explaining his actions and complaining of the injustice he had suffered.

Upon returning to the capital, Wen found that his other major patron, Xu Shang, was now one of Yizong's most important ministers. Yizong apparently made Wen an assistant professor of the Imperial Academy, an institution responsible for educating future examinees.[20] Wen's tenure may have been short, however, because Xu retired from office in 865, and the dynastic histories claim that Wen incurred the hostility of the minister Yang Shou 楊收, who exiled him yet again. We do not know if Wen ever returned from exile, or precisely when he died; we do know, however, that his brother Tinghao wrote an epitaph for him (dated in one source to 866) and that Tinghao himself died in a revolt in 868. Consequently, 866 is the most likely year for the poet's death, with 867 and 868 as distinct possibilities.

This biographical sketch must remain tentative, mainly because the principal sources contradict themselves; for example, the accounts of Wen's exiles are inconsistent. The anecdotes I have related must be accepted with caution as well, although they probably do illustrate the poet's character in some way. Other stories must be rejected; for example, there is insufficient evidence to prove that Wen really carried on a love affair with the famous courtesan-poet Yu Xuanji 魚玄機 (ca. 844–68), as popular tradition suggests. No extant poems by Wen mention her, and Yu's two poems addressed to him are not amorous enough to provide conclusive proof.[21]

Wen's refusal to limit himself to any particular genre or meter attests to his interest in the artifice and craft of poetry. With over 340 surviving poems, his collection is comparable in size to that of other important Mid- and Late Tang figures: Li He 李賀 (791–817; ca. 230 poems), Li Shangyin (ca. 600 poems), and Du Mu 杜牧 (803–52; ca. 520 poems).[22] He was the only Late Tang poet to write a substantial number of "ballads" or *yuefu* (over seventy), and he produced a number of long and allusive extended regulated poems (*pailü* 排律) and a dozen or so "old style" poems (*gushi* 古詩). The remainder, an impressive body of regulated verse (*lüshi* 律詩), vary widely in style and content. Many of the poems in seven-character lines are complex and allusive, relying on virtuosic parallelism for their effect. Poems in five-character lines are usually simpler and more straightforward in their language, if not in their meaning. The most prevalent subjects are traveling and parting, visits to historical sites, Buddhist and Taoist monks, and reclusion.

With this variety, evaluating Wen's work in the context of the Late Tang becomes difficult. Although later critics often used his poetry as representative of Late Tang style, Wen transcends the verse of most minor ninth-century poets in scope and skill; only his occasional regulated verse may be compared fruitfully. On the other hand, he bears only a limited resemblance to his two greatest contemporaries, Du Mu and Li Shangyin, even though Li and Wen were "equal in fame" in their own lifetimes and the two of them were often linked in the term "Wen-Li" to describe the Late Tang style.[23] It may be that a certain similarity in Wen's and Li's careers encouraged their contemporaries to associate them: both were precocious, possessed a marvelous ease in composition, and were singularly unfortunate in their official careers.[24*]

The best approach is not to compare Wen's work as a whole to the work of any other single poet but to take his poems by generic and subgeneric groups and locate them within poetic developments of their time.[25] As we shall soon see, Wen's *yuefu* show interesting affiliations to the song lyrics (*ci* 詞) of the Tang and played an important role in Wen's increasing interest in *ci*. His regulated verse, on the other hand, may be placed against a series of developments both intellectual and literary: an increasing disillusion with the political order, a growing attraction to the charms of purely social verse, a fascination with elaborate conceits, and, conversely, a gradual retreat from the rigorous demands of "serious" art. But even though Wen's poetry in each genre has its own distinctive qualities, there is obviously a single creative intelligence behind all of them. Although we may not be able to read Wen the way a Chinese poetry lover reads Du Fu (as a man reacting to events) we can sense a personality in search of a more objective and aesthetically distanced art, a personality fascinated by the attractions that language holds for a poet, and a personality in flight from the dangers and disasters beginning to overtake his age and his social class.

Each of these themes will preoccupy us in its time. As an introduction to these important issues, a few representative poems will suffice.

Wen's *yuefu* do betray aspects that make it easy to understand the moral condemnation of later readers. They are lush and difficult, sensuous in their use of language, and often explicitly erotic. Their inspiration varies, from the court poets of the sixth century to popular songs and the more complex works of Li He.

Song of Wu Garden　　　　　　　　　　　　　　吳苑行

Brocade pheasants fly in pairs,　　　　　　錦雉雙飛梅結子
　the plums bear fruit;
Distant green in level spring　　　　　　　平春遠綠窗中起
　rises up within the window.
River of Wu, a pale painting—　　　　　　吳江澹畫水連空
　its waters stretch to the sky;
4 While a three-foot-wide ornamental screen　三尺屏風隔千里
　blocks off a thousand miles.

The little garden has gates　　　　　　　　小苑有門紅扇開
　with their red doors open;
Heaven-silk and dancing butterflies　　　　天絲舞蝶俱徘回
　flutter and tarry.
Brocade window, carved balustrade　　　　綺戶雕楹長若此
　are as long-lived as this:
8 Spring light, year after year　　　　　　　韶光歲歲如歸來
　returns—just so.
　(*WFQ*, *j.* 1, p. 21)

Title/ Wu is the ancient name for the Yangzi Delta region. Wen is playing on the associations of the area with royal splendor and decadence, particularly of the court of the Warring States era kingdom of Wu 吳. If the poem describes a screen painting (see discussion below), then the painting may be specifically of this ancient royal court.

6/ Heaven-silk: the catkins of willow trees.

Throughout his work, Wen is fascinated by the line dividing art and nature. Here we can never quite be sure whether he describes a real garden or merely a painting of one. The belief that a painting can be transformed into some inhabitable reality occurs in Yu Xin's

庾信 (513-81) poem series "On a Painted Screen" 詠畫屏風詩 and was explored in several of Du Fu's works.²⁶ Here, Wen imperceptibly merges a screen scene with a possibly real outside without clarifying the boundary for us. Is the Wu River of line three like a painting, or is it a painting in reality? And if the screen cuts us off from the vista of line two, is the second stanza nothing more than a description of the painting? This ambiguity gives the closing couplet particular complexity. Wen could, like so many other poets, be commenting on the unchanging qualities of the seasons, or he could be saying that this painting of the seasons perfectly realizes what spring should be. It was the deliberate complexity of verses such as these that made Xue Xue suspect Wen of merely piling up luxurious details without considering the meaning; for a literal-minded reader, a poem like "Song of Wu Garden" can seem confusing.

In Wen's regulated verse a penchant for a lush poetic density emerges as well, although many poems eschew these qualities for a deceptive clarity and rely instead on a virtuosic parallelism and refined couplets to dazzle the reader. Wen's most famous poem aptly illustrates this point.

Setting out Early from Mount Shang 商山早行

At dawn I rise, stirring my carriage bells. 晨起動征鐸
This traveler goes on, grieving for his home. 客行悲故鄉
Cry of the cock, moon on the thatched inn; 雞聲茅店月
4 Tracks of someone, frost on the plank bridge. 人迹板橋霜
Oak leaves fall on the mountain road; 槲葉落山路
Orange blossoms brighten the post-station wall. 枳花明驛牆
And so I long for my Duling dream; 因思杜陵夢
8 Ducks and geese fill the curving pool. 鳧雁滿回塘
    (*WFQ, j.* 7, p. 155)

Title/ Mount Shang is in modern Shaanxi, east of Shang district near the Hubei border.

7/ Duling was the tomb of the Han Emperor Xuan 宣 (r. 73-49 B.C.), located southeast of Chang'an. By the Tang it was a popular site for outings from the capital. Wen is most likely traveling away from the capital, perhaps on the way to exile, and so expresses his sadness at leaving it.

It is the second couplet that has been admired by critics, and indeed the play of aesthetic content is almost endless. It evokes what the traveler happens upon as he sets out: the rooster's crow, the moon, and the frost are signs of early morning. The moonlight on the inn becomes more concrete as we compare it with the frost on the bridge. Both are pale marks of nature set against the constructions of human beings. The rooster's cry and the tracks of people are indications of invisible presences: he cannot see the rooster, and the people who preceded him are now out of sight. The images also hint at the poet's melancholy state of mind, for both are signs of transience: the rooster marks the passing of another night, and the tracks of those who went before will melt as the day progresses—so does human life itself fade away. But consider the relations between the first part of each line and the second. In line four, this is clear: the tracks can be seen in the frost on the bridge; the frost makes their existence possible. But what about the third line, which now asks us to find a similar relation between cock-cry and moonlight? If we imagine the cock-cry as a "mark" on or in the moonlight (both intangible, as compared to the fragile tangibility of tracks and frost) we have subtle and striking synaesthesia. All in all, it is no wonder that the couplet was admired. Although its words are simple and none are used in unusual or syntactically strange ways, their interrelations are complex indeed.[27]

Nor is the third couplet unsuccessful: it sets dark leaves on a horizontal and twisting road against white flowers on a vertical and flat wall. It also acts with the second couplet to create a unifying chiasmus: stationary edifices (inn and post station) bracket paths of movement (bridge and road) to simulate one day's travel. Yet the reader cannot help but be slightly disappointed by it, after the level of expectation created in the second couplet. Moreover, the theme of expressive melancholy is to some extent lost while the cleverness of Wen's writing comes to the fore. This, then, is the danger of virtuosic parallelism: it demands that a poet sustain a level of extraordinary poetic power in every line and then find ways to unite those lines in a coherent emotional effect still greater than the power of each individual image. Few poets could succeed; and many Late Tang poems disintegrate into lovely and quotable fragments.

However, in many of Wen's seven-character regulated verses, virtuosic parallelism goes hand in hand with dense, sensuous imagery. The effect is much more unified, even if individual couplets do not have the flashy distinction of those in "Setting out Early."

Written Offhand on a Forest Pavilion　　　　　　偶題林亭

Moon kiosk, breeze pavilion　　　　　　　　　　月榭風亭繞曲池
　　surround the winding pool;
Plaster walls curve and turn,　　　　　　　　　　粉垣回互瓦參差
　　roof tiles in jumbled rows.
A sheet of white penetrates the curtains,　　　　侵簾片白搖翻影
　　shadows shaking and turning;
4　Melancholy red falls on the mirror,　　　　　　落鏡愁紅寫倒枝
　　image of branches inverted.
Ducks with fantail feathers,　　　　　　　　　　鸂鶒刷毛花蕩漾
　　blossoms that float and drift;
Egrets curl up their feet,　　　　　　　　　　　鷺鷥拳足雪離披
　　then their snow disperses.
When Old Man Shan is drunk,　　　　　　　　　山翁醉後如相憶
　　if he should remember me
8　Mid feathered fans and clear cups,　　　　　　羽扇清尊我自知
　　then I shall know his thoughts.
　　　　(*WFQ, j.* 4, p. 83)

Title/ An alternative title is "On a Friend's Poolside Pavilion" 題友人池亭.

3/ This line describes the pavilion, giving the effect of light and shadow on the curtains trembling in the breeze.

4/ This probably describes leaves or blossoms falling on the water of the pool, which reflects the branches of poolside trees. They are "grieving red" because they are leaves that indicate autumn or the flowers that will soon fade (line five suggests the latter, since blossoms have fallen into the pool); this can also be the reflection of a woman wearing rouge, who grieves because she detects the signs of aging in her reflection.

6/ Egrets possess white plumage, so their departure from the pool resembles snow scattering.

7–8/ Shan Jian 簡 was a fourth-century aristocrat who became governor of Xiangyang. One of his favorite haunts was a garden pool owned by the Xi 習 family; there he would drink heavily, later leaving completely drunk.[28] Wen is probably reminding the owner of the pool (whom he jokingly compares to Shan) of the parties they had at the pavilion in the past.

The language here is considerably more elaborate. Although both this and "Setting out Early" avoid what the Chinese call "empty words" (*xu ci* 虛辭: grammatical particles, connectives, and prepositions) except in openings and closings, the vocabulary of the five-character poem is plain enough to give a clear mental picture. In "Forest Pavilion," however, descriptive binomes make the images richer but less distinct: *huihu* 回互, "twisting, turning"; *cenci* 參差,

"uneven"; *dangyang* 蕩漾, "rocking, floating"; *lipi* 離披, "dispersing, separating." These impart a mood rather than a precise scene. Wen also draws specific attention to detail (the egrets' feet and the ducks' tail feathers, for instance) or to illusion (reflections in the pool). The result is hazier, more atmospheric, closer to "Song of Wu Garden." Except for the last couplet, whose plain, hypotactic language seems somewhat out of place, humans are absent, remaining only through an observing eye. Although the poem does give an overview of the scene, it is not a scene occupied by a poet whose sentiments must be conveyed to the reader. Rather, it is a polite if complex depiction of a friend's pleasure garden, with a witty signature at the end.

It is this last characteristic that defines what I shall call "objectivity" in this study: namely, the removal of the poet's *explicit* presence from the scene he describes. In Wen's work, several factors may have encouraged such a tendency: first, quite simply, he may have wanted to suppress his own personality as far as possible, since he must have depended on complimentary social verse to keep himself popular among his patrons; second, as a poet famous for his skill and wit, he may have preferred to create an image of himself as "word magician," operating behind the scene to create striking effects. The poem's purpose is to titillate aesthetic sensibilities.

A poem can titillate erotic sensibilities as well:

Carefree Wanderings 偶遊

A twisting lane slants down 曲巷斜臨一水間
   to a stretch of water;
The little gate remains unopened 小門終日不開關
   all day long.
Like a small canopy of red pearls, 紅珠斗帳櫻桃熟
   the cherries have grown ripe;
4 With gold tails like folding screens, 金尾屏風孔雀閒
   the peacocks idly wander.
Her cloud coiffure often diverts 雲髻幾迷芳草蝶
   the butterflies from their fragrant grass;
Her forehead-yellow is limitless 額黃無限夕陽山
   like hills in evening light.
"With you I'm surely paired 與君便是鴛鴦侶
   just like mandarin ducks;
8 So don't seek to go back and forth 休向人間覓往還
   out there in the human world."
   (*WFQ, j.* 4, pp. 95–96)

Title/ Literally, "random wandering." This sometimes refers to the directionless pleasure seeking of the libertine, and so the title also implies frivolity, especially in romantic affairs.

5/ That is, butterflies are confused and mistake her hair for some flowery growth—an elaborate erotic compliment.

6/ Women coated their foreheads with yellow powder; high foreheads were admired and were often compared to hills.

7/ Closing an erotic poem with the words of the woman described is a convention of palace poetry; see Chapter 3. Mandarin ducks were symbols of conjugal fidelity.

8/ "The human world" is often used to describe the world of mortals in Taoist parlance. Here the woman compares her rooms to a Taoist heaven in an attempt to dissuade her lover from departing.

As with "Recalling True Pearl Pavilion," the traditional reader would find this poem frivolous or even immoral in content. We can see how Wen's tendencies toward objectivity and lush descriptive language naturally move him toward a sort of voyeuristic eroticism, in which a woman is described in fetishistic detail from a seemingly dispassionate distance. We will explore this aspect of Wen's work at greater length later.

Finally we may note how these qualities of Wen's poetry emerge in specific subgenres. Wen was particularly fond of the *huaigu* 懷古, or poems describing a visit to an old site of historical significance—the same subgenre we noted him parodying earlier. The following, though written in his "simpler" style, reflects Wen's love of wit, his eye for detail, and his knowledge of historical allusion.

Written on the Shrine to the Bamboo Valley Spirit　　題竹谷神祠

Green-gray, this evening of pine and bamboo;　　蒼蒼松竹晚
A single path enters the overgrown shrine.　　一徑入荒祠
Through ancient trees a breeze blows on my horse;　　古樹風吹馬
4　By empty galleries the sun shines on banners.　　虛廊日照旗
Smoke and ash where the dawn libation took place;　　烟煤朝奠處
Wind and rain when he returned at night.　　風雨夜歸時
Alone and sad, the Xiang River traveler　　寂莫湘江客
8　Looks in vain on Jiangdi's stele.　　空看蔣帝碑
　　(*WFQ, j.* 7, p. 156)

Title/ "Bamboo Valley Spirit" was another name for the spirit of Marquis Jiang Ziwen 蔣子文 (also called "Lord Jiang," *Jiangdi*; see line eight). Originally a late Han official who died in battle with rebels at Zhongshan 鐘山 (near Nanjing), he was deified, and a temple to him was erected at the place of his death. Under

Emperor Wu 武 (r. 502–50) of the Liang 梁, Jiang Ziwen was entreated to provide relief from a severe drought. When no rain resulted, the angry emperor threatened to burn down Jiang's temple and image; just when he was about to set fire to the wood, a sudden storm came up that shook the palaces and halls of the capital. Emperor Wu apologized and withdrew his threat.[29]

7/ Evidently, Wen arrived at Zhongshan after traveling from Hunan, the general area of the Xiang River valley.

In describing this brief brush with the numinous, Wen accentuates the mysterious and vague. No people are described, only the signs of their presence. Sun and wind penetrate this seemingly abandoned structure and hint at the god's immanence. The third couplet, although evidently a description of the sacrifices at the temple, is also an allusion to Emperor Wu's sacrifice to Jiang. Knowledge of this anecdote enables both Wen and the reader to feel the god in the evening shower, to see the ashes of sacrifice and the wind and rain as cause and effect without identifying them as such explicitly. While gloomily effective in the context of the scene, it is also the type of witty reference that flatters the educated reader and separates the connoisseur of poetry from the novice.

Wen, like most of his poetic contemporaries, visited Buddhist and Taoist temples frequently. This was a conventional theme among Late Tang poets, who used the occasion to express religious sentiments that they may have ceased to take seriously. Although Wen's seriousness as a Buddhist disciple is obscured by the flash and wit of his verse, he nonetheless plays with conventions and images and imparts a certain freshness to them. As such, these gentle poems illustrate why he was the Late Tang poet *par excellence*.

Matching Zhao Gu: "Written on the Peak Temple" 和趙嘏題岳寺

Faint echoes of scattered bells, 疎鍾細響亂鳴泉
   a wildly roaring stream.
The visitor has looked out from on high 客省高臨似水天
   into a sky like water.
Blue mountain mists come in the darkness, 嵐翠暗來空覺潤
   so one can only feel the damp;
4 Lingering briskness in the stream-water tea 澗茶餘爽不成眠
   keeps one sleepless.
A Yue monk stands in the cold 越僧寒立孤鐙外
   beyond the solitary lamp;

A mountain moon in autumn
    faces a myriad trees.
Zhang's and Bing's zeal for office
    was weak indeed;
8 Beyond Lord Yuan's window
    there are lotuses in the pool.
    (*WFQ, j.* 8, pp. 170–71)

岳月秋當萬木前
張邴宦情何太薄
遠公窗外有池蓮

Title/ Zhao Gu (fl. 850's) was a noted poet of Wen's generation (for his collected poems, see *QTS, j.* 549–50, pp. 6339–80). This is the only indication of an association between the two. Although the Qing commentators on Wen's poetry and Gu Xuejie (p. 221) both identify the peak (*yue*, a term usually applied to China's five sacred peaks) as Mount Hua 華 in the west, the Yue monk in line five suggests that Mount Heng 衡 in the southeast is more likely.

2/ Reading *sheng* 省 in its occasional sense as *ceng* 曾 ("once before").

7/ Zhang is Zhang Liang 良, the major military advisor of Gaozu 高祖 (r. 206–179 B.C.), the first emperor of the Han; after establishing Gaozu on his throne, he went into retirement. Bing is Bing Han 漢, also of the Han period, who refused to accept more than a moderate salary as an official.

8/ Lord Yuan is Huiyuan 惠遠, the noted Buddhist monk and philosopher of the fifth century. He grew lotuses in the pool outside his residence on Mount Lu 廬.

The visual focus of this poem is difficult to determine; although the general assumption of the Chinese reader is that a poet always describes his own experiences, several factors obscure that possibility here. First, the poem "matches" another poem on the same subject by Zhao Gu; this discourages a reading that would emphasize the devotional, meditative aspects. Instead, we focus on the role of the poem as a form of social intercourse. Second, although it ends in a sort of intellectual realization of the value of reclusion, the poem is detached and objective in tone. Perhaps Wen meant it to be read as a representation of Zhao's experiences at the temple as interpreted by Wen.

The first couplet, though effective, is to some extent conventional: the blending of the sounds of the temple with the sounds of nature is a commonplace, as is the visitor looking out from a high building of the temple complex. Nor is the description of passing the night at the temple (lines three to six) unusual in this sort of poem. Yet the power of this description is considerable. In lines three and four, unable to sleep due to the lingering effects of the tea, the visitor waits for dark to fall. It is a couplet in which the effects of nature impinge on his *physical* state, not necessarily on his emotions: the mountain mists bring a slick clamminess, the tea (made from the roaring stream of line one) keeps him on edge and sharpens his perceptions. It is as if the surroundings were preparing him for the midnight epiphany of the third couplet, in which the lamplit monk is embraced by the moonlit trees: a brilliant image of the religious man's austerity, his rectitude, and his unity with the surroundings. Like the trees, he "stands in the cold," confronting autumn and night, lit by his own personal moon.

Wen now moves on to the philosophical closing. If Zhao is the protagonist in the scene, Wen suggests that it is Zhao who is capable of these extraordinary insights and visions. It is thus Zhao who learns his lesson from them: namely, that, like Zhang and Bing, he must be indifferent to the seductions of office. In the last line, Wen compares Zhao to Huiyuan's lotuses: symbols of detachment from the world, displaying clean leaves and blossoms while planted in mud and dirty water. He may be commenting on Zhao's "lofty" poetic style as well, as exemplified in the original on which this poem is modeled. It may even be that Wen created the scene completely out of his imagination—that he was not even at the temple when he wrote the poem.

"Written on the Peak Temple" reveals a complex combination of techniques and interests. While falling clearly within the conventional subgenre of temple-visiting poem, it still draws attention to its own art. Wen is the skilled craftsman in the middle couplets, carefully preparing the scenes for maximum effect; he is vague as to the poetic subject, preferring to remain a dispassionate observer; and when he does give a personal response, he produces a generalized lesson from the scene in a thoughtful, intellectual manner. Although a Chinese reader raised on Du Fu and Wang Wei might read this little verse as hollow hypocrisy, we may see it as a fine arabesque that manipulates the expectations of the tradition. This, as we shall see, marks almost all of Wen's poetry, whether *yuefu* or occasional regulated verse, whether erotic lyric or Buddhist meditation.

Although this brief examination of a few of Wen's verses may serve as a broad introduction to his work, we have only begun to explore Wen's qualities as a highly individual poet and his representative nature as a Late Tang poet. In the following pages, I preface readings of Wen's poems with examinations of the poetic background that would have influenced him. An investigation of Tang song-writing art will lead us to a reading of his erotic *yuefu* and his *ci*; a look at Late Tang poetry's use of historical themes will provide a frame for his historical songs and his *huaigu*; and the predominant trends of Late Tang social verse will suggest fruitful ways of viewing his occasional poems. Wen is a poet of considerably greater quality than later criticism suggests, but this emerges only when we have the patience to put his verse in its proper artistic context.

TWO

Words for the Singing

LIKE ALL LYRICAL poetry traditions, that of the Chinese had its roots in music and song. The seminal text for Chinese poetics, Mao's Great Preface 毛詩大序 to the *Classic of Poetry* 詩經 demonstrates the close relation between music and poetry; portions of it were adapted, almost verbatim, from an account of music's affective power found in the *Record of Rites* 禮記.[1] This influence indicates that at some time early in the development of Chinese literature, theorists began to attribute the emotive strength of music to the lyrics that accompanied the music (that is, to the poetry itself). This was the important counterpoint to the belief in spontaneous expression of emotions in poetry—that someone who hears a poem will be moved spontaneously and, if the poem is virtuous in intent, will thereby internalize the principles of correct conduct.

In the first several centuries of Chinese literary history, song-poetry is often associated with this educative ideal. The Han interpretation of the *Classic of Poetry* emphasized the role of the texts in imparting normative modes of behavior to those who studied them.[2] The Han also witnessed the founding of the Yuefu 樂府, or the Music Bureau, one of whose duties was to collect popular folk songs and present them to the throne as samples of public opinion. These Han folk songs (which came to be called *yuefu*) have always received respectful attention in the Chinese tradition, which interpreted them as untutored and spontaneous manifestations of the people's character. As texts, they were valued for their honesty of expression and simplicity of language.

By the end of the Han, however, educated members of the elite were composing poetry in imitation of the Han *yuefu*. Although the degree and kind of imitation are still debated, it is fairly safe to assume that both the content of the songs and their music were equally attractive to the individual poet. Other, more complex motivations for imitation might emerge as well. At times, for example, dissatisfaction with the legitimate model (a real folk song could be a "gem in the rough," aesthetically and morally not quite the ideal Confucian representation of *das Volk*) might lead to rewriting by a more sophisticated interpreter. Later, as poetry became increasingly associated with cultivated aristocratic circles, *yuefu* could also supply a series of interesting tropes and themes on which court poets could improvise in their artistic games. A huge gap separated a Han *yuefu* and its sixth-century imitation: the former was a genuinely musical lyric, the latter an unsingable and sophisticated example of an individual's poetic talent. Both kinds of poetry, however, break with the mainstream Chinese poetic tradition in that they often use fictional personae—that is, it is not assumed that a *yuefu* narrator is the poet.[3]

The history of *yuefu* is further complicated by shifts in musical styles. Whenever a musical tradition associated with a kind of song lyric died, there were always new musical developments to replace it. New, authentic song lyrics reflecting the most advanced trends in music coexisted with unsingable literati imitations of older, now defunct traditions. Some of these new songs were genuine folk lyrics; others were "popular" in nature, reflecting a complex urban life-style in which scholars as well as merchants and prostitutes participated. Although many authors continued to write morally serious *yuefu* and could rely on the hermeneutic tradition to make such poems autobiographical (for example, a poem written in the voice of a conscripted soldier could be read as the author's attack on the military policies of his emperor), other educated poets could imitate new pop songs whenever they simply wanted to write something gay and amusing. All of these poems—ancient folk songs, more recent pop songs, morally serious imitations of ancient ballads, and sophisticated literati experiments with new styles—are called *yuefu* by Chinese writers; anyone browsing through the main anthology of *yuefu*, Guo Maoqian's 郭茂倩 *Yuefu shi ji* 樂府詩集 (ca. 1060), will easily note the amazing variety.

Wen Tingyun wrote his own *yuefu* within this complex context, and the issues that inevitably emerge from the definition and development of *yuefu* as a genre (degrees of fictionality, musicality, and poetic form) emerge again and again in his own works and those of his contemporaries. Exploring this context will provide an essential introduction to the appreciation of his art.

Music and Poetry in the Tang

In discussions of prosody, most scholars classify *yuefu* under the broad category of "old-style verse" or *gushi*—a catchall for any poetry not organized by the strict rules of tonal prosody governing regulated verse. However, the move toward regulation in the Tang was a gradual process; even regulated poems of the eighth century often "violate" the rules, and it was not until late in imperial history that the system of tonal regulation used today was articulated.[4] It would be more accurate to say that regulation was a *tendency* of poetry in the Tang and that the degree of regulation in a poem depended largely on the suitability of the poetic content. Social verse (first of the courts, later of everyday polite interactions) encouraged tonal proprieties, because even mediocre poets could write passable poems if they followed the rules. Thus, the full set of requirements of regulated verse developed first in that particular area. On the other hand, poets who attempted to recapture the moral earnestness of the early *shi* poets of the second and third centuries would deliberately flout tonal rules in order to recreate a sense of rugged antiquity. *Yuefu* poetry was something in between these two options; it could not be restricted either to social verse or to morally serious self-expression. Certainly imitations of Han ballads would fall into the second category and would eschew tonal regulation; however, when a poem was meant to be sung to contemporary melodies, the qualities of tonal regulation would bring a euphonious quality to the words that would enhance its suitability for singing.[5]

The most widespread kind of tonally harmonious song lyric was the quatrain; indeed, the quatrain was the predominant song form of the Tang. Quatrains themselves first appeared in the Six Dynasties period (222–589) as a kind of folk song. The Eastern Jin 東晉 (317–420) and Liu Song 劉宋 (420–79) witnessed the emergence of popular quatrain songs that explored romantic themes, usually in a woman's persona. True to the dynamics of the *yuefu* genre, aristocratic poets of the Southern Qi 南齊 (479–502), Liang 梁 (502–57), and Chen 陳 (557–89) adapted them to their own ornate and courtly language, a language that soon became associated with the "palace style" (*gongti* 宮體) particularly fashionable in the Liang. One chapter of the principal palace-style compilation, *New Verses from the Jade Terrace* 玉臺新詠, consists entirely of quatrains, both anonymous folk examples and contemporary imitations. The Tang popular song inherited the style of the Six Dynasties quatrains, which had delineated to a great extent the sensuous content thought appropriate in song lyrics—dramatic representations of maids longing for their faithless lovers, of girls washing silk or gathering lotus, or of palace ladies bemoaning the loss of the emperor's favor; atmospheric descriptions of the fertile Chinese south and the luxurious life-style associated with it were popular topics as well. Later, after the reunification of south and north under the Sui 隋 (581–618), evocative portrayals of the frontier and of military life also became widespread, more because of their exoticism than because of their moral significance.

Musically speaking, Tang quatrains were sung to the new tunes that arrived from Central Asia in the seventh century and that soon displaced almost all native musical traditions. Together, they became the primary form of popular song in the cities of the Tang empire, coexisting with the "serious," non-musical *shi* tradition, as well as with the non-musical imitations of earlier *yuefu*. Metrically speaking, quatrains soon developed a tendency toward tonal regulation. Although some scholars have argued that the "new-style" 近體 or "tonally correct" quatrain was invented by halving an eight-line regulated verse,[6] it seems more likely that it resulted simply from the application of new tonal rules to the already existing genre. Song quatrains maintained a consistency of content throughout their development, from their early, unregulated days to the flowering in the Tang. A brief glance at three examples illustrates this.

Anon. (fourth century): *Song of New Green*　　　　青陽歌曲

Blue-green lotus covers the green water,　　　　青荷蓋綠水
Hibiscus sends forth fresh red.　　　　芙蓉發紅鮮

Below, lotus with roots combined; 下有並根藕
Above, lotus with the same heart. 上生同心蓮
    (*YTXY*, p. 484)

Xiao Yan (Emperor Wu of the Liang, 464–549): 蕭衍(梁武帝):
Autumn Song (first of four) 秋歌四首之一

Embroidered sash with knots of mingled joy, 繡帶合歡結
Brocade robe with pattern of twined branches. 錦衣連理文
Cherishing passion, she enters in moonlit night; 懷情入夜月
Full of smiles, she leaves with the morning clouds. 含笑出朝雲
    (*YTXY*, p. 504)

  1/ Reading variant *jie* 結 for *ju* 炬. The sash is probably ornamented with a decorative pattern of joined leaves representing the *hehuan* 合歡 or "mingled joy" tree, whose double leaves fold together at night and thus came to symbolize sexual fulfillment.
  2/ Twined branches signify joined lovers.
  4/ The last line evokes the famous sexual encounter between a king of Chu 楚 and the Goddess of Mount Wu 巫, described in Song Yu's 宋玉 *Gaotang fu* 高唐賦.[7] As the deity left the king, she said, "In the dawn I am 'morning cloud,' in the evening, I am 'moving rain.'" Hence, "clouds and rain" became a commonplace euphemism for intercourse.

Li Bai (701–62): *In the Qingping Mode (third of three)* 李白:清平調
    三首之三

The Famous Flower and the State-Toppling Beauty 名花傾國兩相歡
  delight in one another;
They always win the regard of 常得君王帶笑看
  the ruler with a smile.
Unknotting the endless resentment 解得春風無限恨
  that comes in the spring wind,
North of Aloes Pavilion 沈香亭北倚闌干
  she leans upon the rail.
    (*QTWDC*, p. 33)

  1/ The Famous Flower is the peony. The phrase "city-toppling beauty" or "state-toppling beauty" originates with Li Yannian 李延年 (ca. 140–ca. 87 B.C.), who described his sister, Lady Li, in a song:

> One glance [from her] topples a man's city;
> Another destroys his kingdom.[8]

Lady Li later became the favorite of the Han Emperor Wu 武 (r. 140–86 B.C.). It is generally believed that Li Bai was comparing Lady Li to the Tang emperor Xuanzong's 玄宗 (r. 712–56) favorite consort, Yang Guifei 楊貴妃.

Although impossible to introduce into this translation, the first poem employs several different terms to describe parts of the same water plant, the *lian* 蓮 or lotus. *He* 荷 are the leaves that spread over the water; *furong* 芙蓉 are the blossoms; *ou* 藕 are the roots that stretch down to the riverbed. The "heart" (*xin* 心) of the lotus may be the seed or the calyx of the blossom. Moreover, as is typical for these folk quatrains, several puns are employed to reveal the inner meaning of the poem. "Root" is a pun for "pair of lovers" 耦. "Lotus" is a pun for "cherish" 憐; thus, "lotus with the same heart" can mean "requited love." We are probably meant to read this quatrain as a song sung by a girl out gathering lotus; she is either coyly dropping hints to her lover or bemoaning her own unhappiness in comparison with the lotus's "connubial bliss."

The next two poems are more distanced, erotic descriptions of women, although Li's illustrates the Tang style's mixture of emotion and scene. As the song quatrain moved from the countryside to the court, it developed not only a more sophisticated content but also greater tonal euphony: both Xiao Yan's and Li Bai's poems are strictly regulated.[9]

This is not to say, of course, that all quatrains were songs; an important (and more famous) non-musical tradition evolved concurrently and is best represented by works like Wang Wei's *Wang Stream Collection* 輞川集 (*QTS*, *j*. 128, pp. 1299–302). Such poems grew out of court social verse and were more conscientious in following the rules of tonal regulation. These two traditions of quatrain writing and the inclusiveness of the term *yuefu* make the task of delineating precisely the qualities of sung quatrains difficult. There are essentially two approaches to the problem: an impressionistic one, which describes the qualities of content and diction that seem appropriate to songs; and a technical one, which examines the actual evidence for song performance in primary sources.

The latter task has largely been accomplished by Ren Bantang 任半塘, who has compiled an anthology of poems that can be conclusively linked to specific Tang melodies. His *Musical Poetry of the Tang* 唐聲詩 begins with a complex investigation into contemporary lists of song tunes, especially those found in the *Account of the Imperial Music School* 教坊記, a late eighth-century description of Xuanzong's court music establishment. Ren examines all available Tang poems that have titles identical or similar to the tune titles and evaluates them by a stringent set of criteria to prove their status as song lyrics. All the resulting *shi* are written in even lines of five, six, or seven characters, are two to twenty lines in length, and display some tendency toward tonal regulation.[10]

Ren's tunes, unlike later *ci* tune patterns, are not distinguished from each other by their different tonal requirements, line lengths, and rhyme schemes (although Ren generally requires a consistency in these areas among all the examples of one lyric); rather, they are distinguished simply by their different melodies, now lost. Ren suspects that much of the confusion in classical scholarship over Tang song writing stems from attempts to compare it to *ci* composition techniques as they existed after the Song dynasty.[11] If we think in terms of different melodies rather than of different metrical patterns, we can understand why so many Tang tune patterns are metrically indistinguishable from each other; although all are essentially even-lengthed, partially regulated *shi*, they were sung to different melodies.

Not surprisingly, the majority of Ren's examples of sung poems are indeed quatrains: out of 156 tune patterns identified, 49 are five-character quatrains, and 49 are seven-character. Next in number are eight-line poems that come close to metrically correct *lüshi* (23 five-character and 9 seven-character). In Ren's anthology, the quatrains cover all the themes we would expect from the musical quatrain tradition; many of them are by poets from the Mid-Tang or even Late Tang.

Fu Zai (fl. early ninth century): *Song of Ganzhou*[12]　　符載:甘州歌

In the moonlight, Chang'e goes without eyeblack;	月裏嫦娥不畫眉
She robes herself only in clouds and mist.	只將雲霧作羅衣
Unaware, her dream follows the dark phoenix away;	不知夢逐青鸞去
She returns, concealing her face, still grasping a sprig of flowers.	猶把花枝蓋面歸

1/ Chang'e is the goddess of the moon; she flew there after stealing an elixir of immortality from her husband.
2/ This is probably a reference to Nongyu 弄玉, who accompanied her lover Xiao Shi 簫史 to heaven on the back of a phoenix.
4/ A metaphor for the moon shining through the branches of a tree.

Nie Yizhong (fl. 871): *Crows Cry at Night*[13]　聶夷中：烏夜啼

All the birds go home to their branches;　衆鳥各歸枝
Only these crows refuse to nest.　烏烏爾不棲
They must know the grief I feel;　還應知妾恨
They caw on purpose before my green window.　故向綠窗啼

The first example here summons up the sensuality of erotic description; although an elegant description of the moon, it probably evokes a court beauty as well. The second falls back on the tradition of a woman bemoaning her loveless condition.

Ren is particularly interested in proving that the *predominant* music-lyric tradition in Tang times involved *shi* and not *ci*. He argues that *ci* did not arise because of the need to alter *shi* to fit certain melodies; rather, they evolved as a minor artistic phenomenon, concurrently with the Tang sung *shi* tradition he describes.[14] For him, *ci* are simply defined by their tune-patterns, which have uneven line lengths; he uses the accepted classical term "long and short lines" (*changduan ju* 長短句) to describe them. His genre definitions are thus strictly formalistic and relatively unimportant for our purposes. Certainly by Wen Tingyun's time, songs by literati with uneven line lengths were (for whatever reason) increasingly prevalent but had yet to emerge as a genre different stylistically and thematically from the even-lined *shi* lyrics.[15] Ren may emphasize a genre difference in order to define and trace an artistic trend, but it would seem that in most cases the true distinction drawn by Chinese poets and musicians of the time was what kind of poem did or did not make for a good song. Ren's work is most useful in leading us to a consideration of that issue; by reading his anthology we can move on to an impressionistic analysis of the aesthetic qualities desired in sung poetry, especially quatrains.

One of the most important qualities that emerges in sung poetry is the vague, generalized import of its conventional images. While the mainstream of Tang regulated verse was building up a complex method of conveying meaning based on the juxtaposition of descriptive images in parallel couplets, the song style relied on the modal associations of things and events. If, for example, Du Fu mentions the moon in a parallel couplet and matches it against rain, the reader must see the importance of the juxtaposition for the poet at that particular place and time. Mention of the moon in a song lyric, however, evokes a certain generalized emotion that everyone feels when thinking of the moon: in a frontier song, it may mean the isolated chilliness of the desert; in a love poem, it may betoken the austere and withdrawn beauty of a court lady. This vague modal use of poetic language further separates the poem from its author and makes it universally adoptable by musicians and singers.

By dealing only with poems that can be proved to have been sung to specific tunes, Ren avoids the issue of compositional intention. We cannot know if a song lyric was written as a non-musical poem and later adapted to music by the poet or by musicians; we cannot even know if a poem was sung to more than one tune. Ren does admit that the body of poetry that could be sung was a larger one than he can determine with his criteria, but once outside his guidelines we must depend on guesswork. We do know that the interchange between musical and non-musical worlds was relatively fluid. Musicians could raid the body of a poet's work for poems or even sections of poems that would make good songs. Ren notes, for instance, the appearance of half of a regulated poem by Wang Wei as a song quatrain attributed to Zhang Hu 張祜 (fl. mid-eighth century); even more unusual is the extraction of four lines from a twenty-line *pailü* court poem of Wang's to form the lyrics to another song.[16] In turn, the aesthetic qualities of song must have exerted an influence on poets, whether they were deliberately writing song lyrics or not. It seems likely that a poet could call on the romantic themes and style of popular song when his need for self-expression demanded it. Thus, a poet like Wang Changling 王昌齡 (ca. 690–ca. 756) or Wang Zhihuan 王之渙 (688–742) can write a quatrain that gives his personal reaction to a specific event, and yet write it in a quatrain style that depends on the generalized emotional evocation and economy of expression that characterize songs. It in turn may actually become a song lyric, and its words take on an applicability that transcends a specific poet or a certain moment.[17]

Another quality of the musical quatrain is its open-endedness; though short, its evocative powers create the possibility of constructing larger aesthetic frameworks through the playing of a number of songs in a single performance. Ren notes the existence both of suites 大曲, in which several poems were sung to different tunes, and the poem sequence 連章, in which lyrics were sung to the same tune, in the manner of stanzaic songs. Of the latter, he gives examples of series that describe the months of the year or the watches of the night.[18] Again, Ren's distinction here is not as important as his observation of linked-poem performances in general. We have hints of these from contemporary sources; for example, in his preface to a set of five "Willow Branch Songs" 楊柳枝, Xue Neng 薛能 (fl. 846) describes a banquet he held, at which courtesans danced to performances of this particular tune. "None of the lyrics they sang were worth listening to, so I myself wrote five quatrains to be set to this new 'Willow Branch' melody."[19]

It would not be unreasonable to assume under these circumstances that a certain aesthetic pleasure was derived from listening for the transition from one song to the next, and that some artistic judgment was required in arranging the order of a performance. This in turn may have had an influence on the increasing popularity of the quatrain sequence in the Late Tang; we find in any number of poets' works not only sets of songs (such as Xue Neng's) but also groups of poems that view different aspects of the same thing or event or examine it from various points of view. Although many of these sequences were probably never meant to be sung, their authors may have intended to impart a poetic effect that they had first noticed in song performances. Few critics have chosen to read quatrain sequences as artistic wholes, but a consideration of one such sequence (by an author who must have known the popular music world well) will reveal an interesting underlying coherence.

Du Mu: *Passing by Huaqing Palace*   杜牧：過華清宮絕句三首

I

   I gaze back from Chang'an: embroideries in folds.   長安回望繡成堆
   On the peak, a thousand gates open, one after another.   山頂千門次第開
   One horseman in red dust; the consort smiles: 一騎紅塵妃子笑
4 No one else knows that it's the lychees that have arrived.   無人知是荔枝來

II

Mid the green trees at Xinfeng
   a brown dust stirs;
Several riders from Yuyang;
   investigators return.
One song—"The Rainbow Robe"—
   across a thousand peaks;
8 She'd dance to bits the central plain
   and only then come down.

III

In every land, pipes and songs
   were intoxicated with peace;
Palace and court against the sky
   split the brightness of the moon.
Mid clouds, a frenzied drumming
   as Lushan dances;
12 Wind crosses the piled-up peaks,
   carries down the sound of laughter.

新豐綠樹起黃埃
數騎漁陽探使回
霓裳一曲千峯上
舞破中原始下來

萬國笙歌醉太平
倚天樓殿月分明
雲中亂拍祿山舞
風過重巒下笑聲

(QTS, j. 521, p. 5954)

Title/ Huaqing Palace was located near the warm springs at Lishan 驪山, east of Chang'an; it was a favorite resort for the Emperor Xuanzong and his favorite, Yang Guifei. Du Mu's sequence refers to the events leading up to the An Lushan 安祿山 Rebellion (begun in 755), started by an ambitious military commander in northeast China who had previously been one of Xuanzong's most trusted men. For a further discussion on treatment of this theme, see Chapter 4.

4/ Because Yang Guifei loved lychees from southern China, Xuanzong made use of a relay system of horsemen to bring her the fruit before it could spoil. The incident is often cited as an example of Xuanzong's excesses in his later years.

6/ Xuanzong suspected that An Lushan was planning a revolt from his home base at Yuyang (near modern Beijing) and sent several officials to determine his motives. An Lushan bribed them and they returned to court, where they reassured the emperor of An's loyalty.

11/ In spite of An Lushan's obesity, he was supposedly light on his feet and often danced for the amusement of the emperor.

Rather than writing a long, cohesive poem on the Huaqing Palace and on the fall of Xuanzong, Du Mu here breaks his poetic vision into half-seen, half-heard images. Each poem is an intense moment of sensual experience, as befits the special qualities of the song quatrain. The reader is left to fill in the gaps; not only by fleshing out the actual scene, but by reading in the moral and tragic implications as well. Du Mu need never mention the An

Lushan rebellion, since our own recognition of each scene's eventual aftermath will add depth and poignancy to the poem's seeming simplicity.

The three poems are best read, however, as a set. The images reinforce each other, and we can even perceive a certain progression from one quatrain to the next. With each poem we are brought closer and closer to catastrophe: the dust stirred by the lychee-bearer in the first poem becomes the dust stirred by the bribed officials in the second. Yang Guifei's smile in the first poem becomes the unbridled and dissipated hilarity of the third. In the first, we have the cause of the rebellion, the wastefulness and decadence of the ruler telescoped into one incident; in the second, we have a hint of rebellion (though one vouchsafed us in hindsight, i.e., An's schemes, which are left unexposed by the messengers) and the growing anarchy caused by Yang Guifei; the last line is a powerful restatement of the half-dead metaphor *qingguo* 傾國, "a beauty who overturns the state."[20] Finally, Lushan joins in the dance, but "riotously" (*luan* 亂), the word used for disorder and rebellion. Note too that, when read as a sequence, the poems possess a frame: at first, Du Mu looks up toward the hillside palace from Chang'an and recreates the scenes of the past; by the end, in the night, the ghostly laughter drifts down to him on the wind as he sees the palace towers dark against the moon. Thus, Du Mu has created a single vision out of fragmentary modal images intensified by the structure and form of the quatrain he uses. It seems not unlikely that in this he was influenced by song aesthetics rather than by the more literary quatrains of regulated social verse: note, first, the vivid imagery that characterizes the songs we have been discussing, and, second, the shifts of mood and scene that certainly were important in the performance of a series of songs. The sequence form allows Du Mu to broach themes of deep historical significance while keeping to the light, sensually rich style he has chosen to adopt.

Interestingly, the use of song aesthetics draws our attention away from the high moral themes toward an appreciation of beautiful language and imagery for its own sake—the superficial "aestheticization" often seen as a characteristic of the Late Tang. Like Li Bai, who described Yang Guifei in song before the rebellion, Du Mu cannot help but admire her and her story, tragic though it turns out to be. It is, in part, his willingness to bring morally serious historical meditation into the realm of the light lyric that marks him as a voice of the Late Tang.

From Quatrain to Stanza

The popularity of the quatrain has a further consequence in the Tang: it seems to have encouraged the development of stanza divisions in long "old-style" (*gushi*) verse. Wang Li notes that this is particularly evident in the seven-character form, which, unlike five-character *gushi* and *yuefu*, was a relatively recent innovation and had no strong connections with traditions of "authenticity" and the values associated with antiquity. Rather, seven-character poems had connotations of novelty and freshness and were thus available for technical experimentation. Early in the Tang we can note an increasing tendency to change rhymes every four lines in seven-character *gushi*; initially this was evidently done for the sake of liveliness and variety, for the rhyme changes seem to have little effect on the poetic content itself. By the High Tang, however, we have many poems that are, metrically speaking, linked quatrains with a heavy tendency toward tonal regulation. The rhyme scheme for each stanza is usually *aaba*, and the laws of tonal balance are almost always followed within a line, often within couplets, and occasionally within quatrains. One further characteristic of the form is the tendency to alternate level-tone rhymes with deflected-tone rhymes.[21]

In these poems, the effect on poetic content varies widely. Most typical, perhaps, are *gushi* songs like the following meditation on the old capital of the state of Wei 魏 by Gao Shi 高適 (716–65).

Song: Old Daliang　　　　　　　　　　　　古大梁行

The ancient walls a boundless green,　　　　古城蒼茫饒荊榛
　　thick with thorns and brambles.
I drive my horse to the overgrown city;　　　驅馬荒城愁殺人
　　it grieves me to the quick.
The King of Wei's palaces and halls　　　　　魏王宮觀盡禾黍
　　turned all to millet fields;
4　Lord Xinling's guests and retainers　　　　信陵賓客隨灰塵
　　follow the way of ash and dust.

I recall that in the past this was a mighty town,	憶昨雄都舊朝市
with its old palaces and markets;	
Canopied carriages shining bright,	軒車照耀歌鐘起
where songs and sounds of bells rose up.	
The show of troops, armor-clad,	軍容帶甲三十萬
three hundred thousand men;	
8 The camp sites for the nation's fate	國步連營一千里
stretched across a thousand miles.	
How can we even speak	全盛須臾那可論
of its brief moment of splendor?	
High terraces, curving pools—	高臺曲池無復存
not a single one left.	
All I see in the ruins	遺墟但見狐狸迹
are tracks of foxes;	
12 On the ancient site, nothing remains	古地空餘草木根
but the roots of grass and trees.	
In an evening sky all flutters and falls,	暮天搖落傷懷抱
I'm stricken to the heart;	
I lean on my sword, sing of grief,	倚劍悲歌對秋草
face the autumn grass.	
Knight-errants still pass on	俠客猶傳朱亥名
the tales of Zhu Hai's fame,	
16 Passers-by still recall	行人尚識夷門道
the road to Yimen.	
White jade disks, yellow gold,	白璧黃金萬戶候
nobles possessed of a thousand households:	
Jeweled blades and swift steeds	寶刀駿馬填山丘
now fill the mounds and hills.	
That era's grown cold now,	年代淒涼不可問
we cannot seek after it.	
20 In our travels we only see	往來唯見水東流
the water flowing east.	

(QTS, j. 213, p. 2217)

4/ Lord Xinling was a nobleman of the Warring States, famous for his hospitality toward men of talent.

8/ This meaning of 國步 is derived from the *Classic of Poetry*, Mao no. 275.

15/ Zhu Hai was a famous knight-errant who helped Lord Xinling gain control of Wei's army and come to the aid of Zhao, at war at the time with Qin.

16/ Yimen was the gate at which Lord Xinling met Hou Ying 侯嬴, an advisor who later helped Xinling when he came to Zhao's assistance.

Here the rhyme changes (-*īn* in the first stanza, -*iə̆* in the second, -*ə̄n* in the third, -*aŭ* in the fourth, and -*ōu* in the fifth) help the reader trace the progress of Gao's thought.²² The first section emphasizes the present; the second, the glories of the past; the third is the present scene of desolation; the fourth and fifth are Gao's personal reaction and meditation on transience. These section divisions have, however, not yet affected the structure to a significant degree; even though the quatrains do compartmentalize the stages in the course of the poem, they lack distinction individually. For example, the second would make no sense read individually, and the fifth would seem hackneyed out of context.

Gao's poem is very much part of a *gushi* tradition, and tonal regulation is not exact, though significant; most lines are tonally correct, as are a few couplets. When a stanzaic *gushi* poem enters the realm of social verse, however, its sections come to resemble occasional regulated quatrains.

Meng Haoran (689–740): *Matching Magistrate Lu's "Seeing off Zheng the Thirteenth on His Way back to the Capital"; The Poem Was Also Sent to Him*	孟浩然：和盧明府送鄭十三還京兼寄之什
A place to climb and look out on the scenes of former times;	昔時風景登臨地
Today, a parting banquet for capped and gowned officials.	今日衣冠送別筵
Drunken we sit and pour for ourselves the wine of Pengze;	醉坐自傾彭澤酒
4　Thinking of going home, a long gaze at a sky of white clouds.	思歸長望白雲天
At Dongting, but one leaf— shocked autumn comes so soon.	洞庭一葉驚秋早
Empty, unused, I sigh in vain as I linger on the river isle.	濩落空嗟滯江島
Send word to our colleagues in power at court:	寄語朝廷當世人
8　When again shall we see the roads of Chang'an?	何時重見長安道
(*QTS*, *j*. 159, pp. 1629–30)	

3/ The Eastern Jin poet Tao Qian 陶潛 (365–427) was famous for his series of poems on wine; he briefly served as official of Pengze before he gave up an official career for farming and drinking.
5/ Dongting Lake, in Hubei.
6/ "Empty and unused" is a cliché derived from the first chapter of the *Zhuangzi*; it describes a huge gourd grown by the philosopher Huizi that went to waste because of its awkward size. Zhuangzi accuses Hui of not making the best use of it. Meng is thus bemoaning the fact that he is out of office.

The first four lines, a perfectly regulated quatrain (except for the slightly errant rhyme scheme: *abcb*), would make an impressive poem by themselves: line four is a characteristic closing line for an occasional High Tang quatrain, with its emotional response hidden beneath the understated act of "gazing afar." The second stanza is a fine quatrain as well, regulated save for its deflected rhyme and a violation in the sixth character of the second line. And yet another model, that of eight-lined regulated verse, is followed as well. Despite the inappropriate rhyme-scheme, the poem obeys the pattern expected of regulated octets: the opening couplet sets the scene, the second and third elaborate, and the fourth gives an emotional response.

The most interesting and original use of stanza divisions occurs in poems that are part of the musical quatrain tradition or influenced by it. Here, stanzas are independent, and the breaks between them determine the way we read the poem. In fact, distinctions between stanzaic poems and sequences of quatrains can become blurred. For example, Ren Bantang notes that a twelve-line song by Li He, "Moduo louzi" 摩多樓子, possesses a perfect quatrain structure; since a Li Bai song of this title consists of a single quatrain, Ren concludes that Li He's "poem" is actually a sequence of three separate verses. Elsewhere, he shows that 2 six-character quatrains by Liu Changqing 劉長卿 (ca. 710–ca. 787) are, judging from other poems to the same tune, probably one eight-line poem. Finally, in the case of two songs by Wen Tingyun, "Tangtang" 堂堂 (seven-character, eight lines) and "Damo zhi" 達摩支 (seven-character, twelve lines), Ren admits that only the lack of concrete evidence to the contrary (i.e., the survival of other poems to the same tune with a different number of lines) prevents us from splitting them into two poems and three poems respectively.[23] A good example of the full effect of song style on stanza formation is Cui Hao's 崔顥 (d. 754) "Seventh Night Song" 七夕詞.

In Chang'an city, a moon like bleached silk;	長安城中月如練
In every household this evening they take up needle and thread.	家家此夜持針線
In fairy skirts and jade pendants, vainly she knows	仙裙玉佩空自知
4 In heaven and the world of men they can never meet.	天上人間不相見
At Changxin Palace, deep shadows; the night turns to stillness.	長信深陰夜轉幽
On jade steps to golden rooms a few fireflies drift.	瑤階金閣數螢流
Lady Ban tonight feels an endless grief;	班姬此夕愁無限
8 She sees the Weaving Girl and Herd Boy at midnight, by the river.	河漢三更看女牛

(*QTS*, *j*. 130, p. 1326)

Title/ "Seventh Night": on the seventh day of the seventh lunar month, the two astral lovers, the Herd Boy and the Weaver Girl, could be reunited for a brief time; their constellations are separated by the Milky Way ("the Heavenly River").

2/ It was a custom on the Seventh Night to hold competitions in which participants attempted to thread needles by moonlight; those who were successful were guaranteed good luck.

7/ Lady Ban is Ban Jieyu 婕妤, a favorite of Emperor Cheng 成 (r. 32–6 B.C.) of the Han. When she was replaced in his favor by Zhao Feiyan 趙飛燕, she voluntarily retreated to the Changxin Palace to live with the Empress Dowager. Because the poem "Lament" 怨詩 (*YTXY*, pp. 14–15) attributed to her mourns her loss of favor, she is frequently alluded to in poems on abandoned consorts.

The generalization of description and emotion characteristic of the musical quatrain also gives these two quatrain stanzas an independence as separate poems. In fact, only the change in rhyme from level to deflected tones suggests that this is one poem, not two.

We read a stanzaic poem differently from the way we read an undivided one. Stanza forms in both the West and in China have their roots in the repetitions of music and emphasize a reading/hearing process that moves by separate stages and pauses after every completed thought. What is still fairly rudimentary in Gao Shi's poem becomes more pronounced in a poem as close to musical lyric as Cui Hao's; and by the ninth century, the process reaches fruition, particularly in the works of Li He and Wen Tingyun.

Li He wrote little in the *lüshi* form, concentrating instead on "old-style" poems and ballads (which may be called either *yuefu* or *gexing* 歌行, "songs").[24] Perhaps his affinity for song forms of all kinds can be explained by his own connections with the Tang music establishment—he was a famed songwriter and held the rank of "harmonizer of pitch pipes in the Court of Imperial Sacrifices."[25] Although we may never know how many of his surviving poems were actually sung, there seems little doubt that his propensity for writing in song genres must have come from his familiarity with and appreciation for music.

The rhyme changes in Li's poems may often be attributed simply to a desire for variety; his stanzas vary greatly in length and indicate an interest in structural experimentation. For instance, a few poems are written in rhyming couplets. However, quatrains predominate over any other form: out of 106 poems with rhyme changes, 33 fall into quatrain stanzas, and 26 use quatrains to a greater or lesser degree. Many of the quatrain songs are Li He's most famous works; the following may be taken as an example.

The Terrace of Liang 梁臺古意

The terrace and pool of Liang's prince
    rise up in mid-air; 梁王臺沼空中立
The sky-river's water at night
    flows down into them. 天河之水夜飛入
Before the terrace, mortised jades
    form dragons and serpents; 臺前鬭玉作蛟龍
4 Green bamboo's powder sweeps the sky,
    grieving in the wet dew. 綠粉掃天愁露濕

He struck the bells, drank his wine,
    shot his arrows at heaven. 撞鐘飲酒行射天
Gold tigers on his creased robe
    were spitting bloody spots. 金虎蹙袋噴血斑
Dawn after dawn, dusk after dusk,
    he lamented the churning seas, 朝朝暮暮愁海翻
8 So with a long robe he tied down the sun
    and took pleasure in the year. 長繩繫日樂當年

Hibiscus congeals in red,
    turning an autumn hue; 芙蓉凝紅得秋色
Orchid faces leave the spring,
    weeping, gazing longingly. 蘭臉別春啼脉脉

On the reedy isles, the traveling geese	蘆洲客雁報春來
bring news of spring's return;	
12 Lonely and desolate, the stagnant pools	寥落野湟秋漫白
spread their white in autumn.	

(LHSJ, p. 269)

Title/ The Prince of Liang would seem to be Prince Xiao 孝 of the Han, who constructed a palace and garden in Henan.
2/ Sky-river: the Milky Way.

Although no single four-line group has the completeness of vision that marks the Du Mu quatrains, they resemble them in the independence of the imagery in each stanza. We must struggle to find the reason for the sequence of images and must interpret the purpose of each stanza in Li's poetic argument.

First, the terrace is described, not as Li He sees it now, but as it must have been once. The poet carefully excludes humans, however, and speaks only of human artifacts: the terrace, the pool, the jade ornaments, the bamboo garden. The second quatrain centers exclusively on the Prince of Liang, his pride, his gestures, and his emotional response to the passing of time; note that he is not named, and we ourselves must identify him in order to make sense of the poem. Finally, we leave the terrace altogether and confront disjointed, fragmented images of nature that have no coherence as a realized scene: seasons fly by (autumn, spring, autumn) and proclaim the cycles that the prince strives to escape. Like another Li He protagonist, the King of Qin (*LHSJ*, p. 53), the Prince of Liang becomes a powerful mythical substitution for Li himself; yet the Chinese poetic convention of mourning the passing of time here becomes historical or even cosmic, bursting the limitations of any one lifetime. Li He can achieve this effect by the juxtaposition of stanzas, devoid of comment—man's things, man's aspirations, the cycles of nature. As Du Mu did in his quatrain sequence, Li has taken the rich imagery and diction of song lyrics and has made them address a serious theme.

Li also employed song-style quatrains in poems on the immortals.

Dreaming of Heaven　　　　　　　　　　　　　　　夢天

| Old hare and cold toad | 老兔寒蟾泣天色 |
| weep heaven's colors; | |

> Cloud pavilions half-open,
>   their walls slanted and white; 雲樓半開壁斜白
> Jade wheels crush the dew,
>   dampening their rounded light; 玉輪軋露濕團光
> 4 Phoenix pendants meet together
>   on cassia-scented lanes. 鸞珮相逢桂香陌
> Yellow dust and clear waters
>   below the three mountains; 黃塵清水三山下
> The hour changes, a thousand years pass
>   like galloping horses. 更變千年如走馬
> Afar they gaze on China,
>   nine specks of mist— 遙望齊州九點烟
> 8 And the one surge of ocean water
>   as though poured from a cup. 一泓海水杯中瀉
>   (*LHSJ*, p. 28)

1/ Both hare and toad were animals said to inhabit the moon.
3–4/ Jade pendants are synecdoches for the immortals, as the wheels are for their carriages.
5/ The three mountains are the islands of the immortals, located in the eastern seas.
7/ Tradition held that China was originally divided into nine districts.

Li He imagines a dreamer flying off and visiting the immortals; the two stanzas reflect perfectly the trajectory of his visit. First he flies upward, past the moon to the cloudy habitations of the divinities; there, he observes their congregations. Then, with them, he turns and looks down—and sees his own world reduced to trivialities. The stanza break marks an important turning point in narrative and emotional content.

The other major Tang poet to have adapted stanzaic form is Wen Tingyun; the number of his longer *yuefu* is particularly striking, since Late Tang poets in general seem to have given up on the genre except for the writing of simple quatrain-length songs. Wen's *yuefu* are also surprisingly homogeneous, much more so than Li He's: out of a total of seventy-five songs, ten are "Willow Branch" lyrics (i.e., regulated, seven-character quatrains); forty-seven are seven-character songs of eight lines or longer; fourteen are five-character songs of six lines or longer; and only four have irregular line lengths. When we look at stanza formation, consistency is even more evident: of the forty-seven seven-character songs, thirty-seven fall precisely into quatrain stanzas, with each stanza following the expected rhyme scheme of *aaba*; of the remaining ten, six are written in quatrains with only one aberration (e.g., a six-line stanza or a separate couplet). As we might expect, the five-character poems show a less marked tendency toward quatrain divisions—only five out of fourteen. Nevertheless, forty-eight out of sixty-five long *yuefu* are basically quatrain-stanza songs. This would seem to indicate that Wen essentially thought in terms of quatrains when he wrote *yuefu*.

The seven-character songs also display a predominant trend toward tonal regulation that surpasses Li He and most other authors in the genre; although Wang Li has pointed out that a certain tonal regularity can be expected in such poems, Wen carries this trend even further (see Appendix). In fact, the individual stanzas of his seven-character songs fulfill Ren Bantang's requirement for sung poetry, even though we have no extrinsic evidence to prove that they were sung.

Two examples of Wen's work should demonstrate that he was influenced not only by the quatrain song tradition but also by Li He's sophisticated developments of it.

Lotus Bank Song 蓮浦謠

Ringing oars sound noisily, 鳴橈軋軋溪溶溶
   stream water flows on.
A bank of mist over abandoned green, 廢綠平烟吳苑東
   east of Wu gardens.
Water clear, lotus enchanting— 水清蓮媚兩相向
   the two are face to face.
4 In this mirror she sees her grief; 鏡裏見愁愁更紅
   grieved that the flower is redder.

On white horse with gold whip 白馬金鞭大隄上
   he stands on the Great Bank;
Evening comes to the Western River, 西江日夕多風浪
   many waves stirred by the wind.
The lotus-heart has dew drops 荷心有露似驪珠
   the shape of black pearls;
8 Though not completely round, 不是真圓亦搖蕩
   they still roll about.
   (*WFQ*, *j*. 1, p. 5)

4/ The lotus serves as a mirror of youth; the lotus gatherer is upset because the lotus is ruddier than she—that is, that her own youth is waning.

7–8/ The dew drops are shaken loose because of the rising tumult of the waves.

To evoke the atmosphere of the Southern Dynasties, the time when lotus-gathering songs were first written, Wen uses a variety of place-names and scenes associated with the eastern valley of the Yangzi River. Wu was both a Warring States kingdom located there, and a post-Han kingdom eventually destroyed by the Jin dynasty; Great Bank was the name of an embankment near Xiangyang, to the west in Hubei. The "Western River" is often used to describe the Yangzi as it flows through the eastern provinces of China.

Although this song possesses many of the refinements of Wen's Late Tang style, it also repeats many of the gestures, images, and tropes found in Six Dynasties *yuefu*: the comparison of the lotus gatherer to the lotus, the lover or potential lover watching from the bank, and the pun at the end (which plays on the associations of *yuan* 圓, "round," "fulfillment"; this last line could be paraphrased as "Her heart is restless because they are not truly together"). The first stanza ends with the recognition by the reader that the woman is grieving at the passing of her beauty. The use of a "reflection" to expose that grief shows a poetic wit typical of Wen: the reader and the woman become conscious of this grief simultaneously, and the reader is asked implicitly to make the link between woman and flower—both beautiful, both destined to fade. The woman, of course, could see these same signs of her aging in the water itself (which would be a true, literal mirror of her appearance rather than a metaphorical one).

We move from her self-absorption in line four to the horseman in line five; the change of attention coincides with the stanza break. This intruder, like us, is an observer of the scene; if he is her lover, he may be a cause for an anxiety on her part as well: if she is aging, how can she hope to keep him? This anxiety, meanwhile, seems to create a reaction in the natural world (the rising wind and waves, the lateness of the day), which forces an end to the excursion and, symbolically, to their love. Lotus-gathering poems usually end with some gesture of return and of the day ending; here, the man's arrival seems to force a conclusion. Across the stanza break we have experienced a drastic change of mood and an increasing complexity of imagery.

A more ambitious *yuefu* by Wen shows the influence of Li He's "Dreaming of Heaven."

Dawn Immortal Song 曉仙謠

The Jade Consort summons the moon 玉妃喚月歸海宮
   to return to Sea Palace.
Moonlight, pale white, 月色澹白涵春空
   soaks the spring air.
The Silver River is about to turn, 銀河欲轉星朧朧
   the stars fade.
4 Jade waves and piled hills 碧浪疊山埋早紅
   bury the early red.

Dew on palace flowers 宮花有露如新淚
   like recent tears;
The thick plants in tiny gardens 小苑叢叢入寒翠
   enter the chill mist.
The water clock emptily echoes 綺閣空傳唱漏聲
   through splendid chambers;
8 In netted galleries, too early to read 網軒未辨凌雲字
   the words "Transcending Clouds."

Far off, the pearl curtains: 遙遙珠帳連湘烟
   mists along the Xiang.
Crane-feathered fans, frost-white: 鶴扇如霜金骨仙
   the metal-boned Immortals.
The jade flute song ends, 碧簫曲盡彩霞動
   bright auroras drift.
12 They look down upon the nine regions: 下視九州皆悄然
   all is still.

The King of Qin's daughter rides 秦王女騎紅尾鳳
   the red-tailed phoenix;
Astride the void, she turns her head: 乘空回首晨雞弄
   the morning cock crows.
Fog blocks the wild and swirling dust 霧蓋狂塵億兆家
   of a million million homes;
16 Where worldlings are still dreaming dreams, 世人猶作牽情夢
   snared in their desires.
   (*WFQ*, *j*. 1, pp. 7–8)

1/ Jade Consort: a type of Taoist transcendent being or *xian* 仙 (here translated as "immortal," by convention).[26] The Sea Palace is probably located on Penglai 蓬萊, one of the isles of the immortals in the eastern seas. Most of the poem is seen from the immortals' perspective as they watch the sun rise on the Chinese continent.

4/ The immortals' islands and the waves of the sea still conceal the approaching dawn.

8/ The galleries of the immortals' palaces are hung with a wide-meshed gauze. Evidently, the galleries are also decorated (as in mortal palaces) with signs that name the different rooms. This gallery has an appropriately Taoist name.

9/ The curtains of the palace begin to merge with the mists of the human world. The Xiang River is associated with the river goddesses described in two of the Nine Songs 九歌 in the *Chu ci* 楚辭.

10/ Immortals had feathers that enabled them to fly; they could also turn themselves into cranes, or ride them.

12/ The King of Qin's daughter is Nongyu; see the note to line 2 of Fu Zai's "Song of Ganzhou" above.

Wen luxuriates in Taoist lore as he gives a resplendent account of the dawn, as the sun rises behind the immortals' abode on Penglai. The process comes in stages, reflected by each stanza. The first is cosmic, as the stars and moon give way to the approaching daylight. The second centers on the early effects of dawn on the immortals' palace, as the poem closes in to observe various details. The third stanza moves back again, as the immortals watch dawn strike the land of ordinary men; their own music of the night ends, and the magic aurora of dawn begins to move forth. Finally, as Nongyu rides forth on her phoenix and the heavenly cock sounds (the cock whose crowing causes all earthly roosters to answer), we have a full vision of the earth, darkened by the dust and passions of another day. Like Li He, Wen allows himself to take a cosmic view on events, and he shifts perspective suddenly and magically. Moreover, the stanza breaks simulate to some extent his participation in the immortals' world; he can jump from scene to scene without the limitations of human locomotion and vision. Here the song lyric aesthetic—rich language, ambiguity, colorful flashes of imagery—gives him the style he needs to evoke the supernatural.

Occasion and Imagination

How does Li He, and Wen after him, exploit song style in *yuefu* of even greater length and ambition? We may begin to address the question by comparing two poems of similar themes, both on musicians and their performances. When Wen wrote a poem about his musician friend Guo, he very probably had Li's famous poem on the harpist Li Ping in mind; even if he did not, surely later readers would note the similarities between the two texts.

Li He: *The Ballad of Li Ping and His Harp* 李憑箜篌引

    Silk of Wu, wutong of Shu
        open up in the high autumn sky. 吳絲蜀桐張高秋
    In empty hills, congealing clouds
        crumble down, stop their flow. 空山凝雲頽不流
    The Xiang ladies weep on bamboo,
        the White Girl grieves. 湘娥啼竹素女愁
4   Li Ping plays his harp
        in the center of the land. 李憑中國彈箜篌

    Kun Mountain jade shatters,
        the phoenixes cry out. 崑山玉碎鳳凰叫
    The lotuses weep dew
        and fragrant orchids smile. 芙蓉泣露香蘭笑
    Before the twelve gates
        the cold light melts. 十二門前融冷光
8   The twenty-three strings
        move the Purple Emperor. 二十三絲動紫皇

    Nü Wa smelts her stones
        to fill in Heaven's gaps; 女媧煉石補天處
    But the stones crack, sky startles,
        and autumn rains leak through. 石破天驚逗秋雨
    In dreams he enters divine mountains
        to instruct the Holy Crone; 夢入神山教神嫗
12 Old fish jump the waves,
        gaunt sea serpents dance. 老魚跳波瘦蛟舞

    Wu Gang, sleepless,
        leans on the cassia tree. 吳剛不眠倚桂樹
    Dew drops fly aslant
        and soak the chill hare. 露腳斜飛濕寒兔
       (*LHSJ*, p. 3)

Title/ Ye Congqi notes two different musical instruments called the *konghou*. Only one of them has twenty-three strings; it is of northern origin and is held vertically, like the Western harp. However, one may note that the other version of the *konghou* was supposedly invented during the reign of Emperor Wu of the Han as an instrument for use in the worship of the spirits. Considering the supernatural effects of Li Ping's own playing, perhaps Li He was thinking of this as well.

    1/ Silk from Wu reputedly made the best music strings, and wutong wood from Shu made the best body.

    2/ Reading variant *shan* 山 instead of *bai* 白.

    3/ The Xiang ladies were daughters of Yao and consorts of Shun; they are associated with the divinity or divinities described in two of the Nine Songs of the

Chu ci and are said to dwell in the Xiang River. Their tears shed at Shun's death stained the bamboo growing on the riverbank. The White Girl played an unbearably sad tune for the Yellow Emperor, whereupon he broke her fifty-string zither in half.

7/ Chang'an had twelve city gates.
8/ The Purple Emperor was one of three supreme Taoist divinities.
9/ Nü Wa, a primordial goddess of China, repaired the sky after a demon had damaged it.
11/ The *Sou shen ji* 搜神記, a fourth-century collection of outré anecdotes, mentions a divinity by this name who appeared during the reign of Emperor Huai 懷 (r. 307–13) of the Jin; she was a talented player of the harp.
13/ *Gang* 剛 is the generally accepted correction of text *zhi* 質. Wu Gang lived on the moon, where he occupied himself with the Sisyphean task of chopping down its cassia tree.
14/ Again the hare refers to the hare in the moon.

Poems describing musical performances were not unusual in the Tang, and they were still common in the Mid and Late periods.[27] The style and content of these poems can vary considerably, but they share several characteristics: on the one hand, they can stress the aesthetic and emotional reactions of the listener; on the other hand, they may attempt to describe the sound of the music itself. In the former case, we can see an aspect of the "reaction to stimulus" (*ganxing* 感興) model for Chinese poetic writing; the listener responds to music as he would to a landscape or to parting from a friend. Moreover, these responses themselves can be expressed in different ways: if the musician is a friend of the poet's, then certainly the great paradigm of friendship, Bo Ya 伯牙 and Zhongzi Qi 鐘子期, must lie below the surface; by hearing the music, the sympathetic listener understands not just the music but the musician as well.[28] In several other noted cases, performances have produced nostalgia and a mourning for a past historical glory, as in Bai Juyi's 白居易 (772–846) "Pipa xing" 琵琶行 (*QTS, j.* 435, pp. 4821–22). In these situations, poetic attention focuses on the author's feelings.

In attempting to describe a musical piece, a poet may rely on explicit metaphor (often synaesthetic):

Sweetly, the words of boy and girl:	昵昵兒女語
Kind or harsh, they use intimate names;	恩怨相爾汝
Abruptly, he changes to a lofty air;	劃然變軒昂
Brave soldiers on the way to the battlefield.[29]	勇士赴敵場

or:

Hibiscus leaves fall; 芙蓉落葉秋鸞離
  autumn phoenixes part.
The King of Yue rises at night 越王夜起遊天姥
  and wanders on Tianmu Mountain.³⁰

Of course, common allusions to mythical or historical musicians may be expected. But in all musical performance poems, whether emotive or descriptive, we can see a common goal: a desire to recreate the experience, to find a poetic equivalent for the music. The main difference is one of emphasis. Does one simulate the mental impressions that constitute the subjective musical experience of the individual listener, or does one analyze the qualities of the performance in a more objective way, describing the musician's techniques, style, emotional motives, and the *concrete* effects of his playing on his listeners?

Li He blurs this distinction from the very beginning in his tribute to Li Ping; lines one to three introduce the music (with the musician first appearing in line four); yet we cannot clearly find the source of these images. Are lines two and three meant to describe the fanciful effects of the music, the results of the performance Li claims to see? Or are they a sort of free association in the poet's mind, the images that occur to him as he listens? Because Li He removes his physical presence from the poem (Li Ping's performance is more magical than real), the poet does not bother to specify whether we are meant to take these images as metaphors or as descriptive visions of the music's effects—effects that reach out to every imaginable kind of being, animate and inanimate.³¹ Li can accentuate this ambiguity by relying upon the theory of cosmic correlatives (*lei* 類): a certain kind of music would inspire certain mental images in a listener, but would also affect the natural world in a way analogous to the stimulation of the listener's mind. We can say that Li Ping's music sounds like crashing jade and phoenix cries and, moreover, that it would cause jade to crash and phoenixes to cry.

We have then a series of vivid images, some visual, some aural, that act in ambiguous and complex ways to bridge intuitively the gap between poet and musician/music. Further complexity is engendered by the absence of a coherent temporal scheme; there are few (if any) indications of causal links between lines and between scenes. Rather, Li He creates an organization based on space: as Li Ping plays "in the center of the land" (*zhongguo* 中國, also "capital"), he remains at the core while his music radiates outward toward the human world, the numinous world, the past and the present. In the end, this center of order coolly dissipates as we hear the fading notes reaching Wu Gang (where the fading is accentuated by the sudden stillness of the axe) and see dew soaking the lunar rabbit. The poem, and very likely the musical piece as well, ends in a chill silence. Yet we cannot tell if Li He writes here of a specific performance. Not only does the title of the poem lack a verb, but Li He's disintegration of temporal progression and his own personal absence from the scene suggest to us rather an ideal music, a general impression of Li Ping's talent and the poet's reaction to it.

Song: Retired Scholar Guo Strikes the Musical Bowls   郭處士擊甌歌

The gold serpent shudders awake
    in the ancient stone pool;   佶栗金虯石潭古
Shaopi Lake shakes with
    words from hidden bamboo.   勺陂瀲灩幽修語
Lady Xiang on her splendid steed
    ascends to divine clouds.   湘君寶馬上神雲
4 Sound of clashing pendants and harness bells
    fill the misty rain.   碎佩叢鈴滿烟雨

I have heard that the flowers grow thick by
    the thirty-six halls;   吾聞三十六宮花離離
And the soft wind blows in the spring
    while stars grow sparse.   軟風吹春星斗稀
In the Jade Dawn Palace, chill bell-stones
    break a murky dream,   玉晨冷磬破昏夢
8 And incense still clings to robes
    while dew remains undried.   天露未乾香著衣

A lock with orchid hairpin hangs
    down from a swaying ponytail;[32]   蘭釵委墜垂雲髮
Light echoes ring and chase
    the whirling snow.   小響丁當逐回雪
Mist in the clear-jade sky
    dampens the layered hills   晴碧烟滋重疊山
12 And the silk screen half-blocks
    the moon of peach blossoms.   羅屏半掩桃花月

The Son of Heaven in a Peaceful Age halts his cloud carriage;	太平天子駐雲車
The dragon burner puffs dense smoke, wisps that coil and clutch.	龍鑪勃鬱雙蟠拏
In the palace, eunuchs stand on duty, fans held to chests,	宮中近臣抱扇立
16　And serving girls lower their headdresses, dropping blue-green petals.	侍女低鬟落翠花
Pearls in disorder rattle about, jumping, rolling;	亂珠觸續正跳蕩
He lowers his head, unaware that the Gold Crow inclines.	傾頭不覺金烏斜
I heave a long sigh for your sake	我亦為君長歎息
20　And grieve that my letter's feelings, sent so far, seem colorless.	緘情遠寄愁無色
Let's not stain our fragrant dreams with willow silk—	莫霑香夢綠楊絲
A thousand miles of spring wind are powerless right now.	千里春風正無力

　　(*WFQ, j.* 1, pp. 5–6)

Title/ Guo Daoyuan 道源 was a noted musician of the musical bowls during the reign of the Tang emperor Wuzong; the instrument itself consisted of twelve stone bowls filled with varying amounts of water that were beaten with chopsticks.

1–2/ The roundness and depth of the bowls are compared to Lake Shaopi (in Anhui). *Jili* 佶栗 usually describes extreme cold or the shivering caused by the cold. Here a shudder (or shiver) seems to be meant, but the chillness of the water may also be implied. *Youxiu* 幽修 can mean "secluded bamboo," clumps of bamboo that are symbols for the reclusive gentleman. Here they very likely refer to Guo's chopsticks as well.

5/ Ban Gu's 班固 (32–92) "*Fu* on the Western Capital" 西京賦 mentions "thirty-six lodging halls" in the Han capital. Wen is probably imitating Li He's lines from "The Bronze Immortal Takes Leave of the Han" 金銅仙人辭漢歌: "Lichens are jade-green by the thirty-six halls" (*LHSJ*, p. 77). Because of this allusion, the *hua* 花 in this line would normally be read as "lichen"; but since in Li He's poem (and in similar poems) the image suggests a palace in ruins, and since Wen's palace obviously is not, "flowers" may be better here. However, if his stanza is meant to describe a completely different woman from the dancer in the next stanzas, the scene may be suggesting a context of "palace lament." In that case, the *hua* may indeed be lichen that point to the lonely condition of this particular part of the palace.

7/ I have read *yu chen* 玉晨 as one of the heavenly palaces of Taoist lore. It may be, however, that this phrase should be read literally, i.e., "in the jade-white dawn."

56   Words for the Singing

9/ The scene changes here to a dancing scene, although it is not entirely clear whether the woman who dances is the same one as in the previous stanza.
14/ Because the burner is shaped like a dragon, the sudden coils of smoke may be a cosmic empathic response to the arrival of the emperor himself.
16/ We could imagine the lowering of heads and the falling petals as signs that the girls are accompanying the dancer in her dance, but since they are "serving girls" and the line is paired with the eunuchs at attention, they are probably lowering their heads with respect before the imperial presence.
18/ "Gold Crow" is a kenning for the sun.
21/ Wen uses here the common pun on "silk" 思 and "[brooding] thoughts" 絲.

Wen, like Li He, makes no attempt to explain the circumstances of the performance; he begins with a description of the musical instrument as it is first struck (lines one and two), giving first its appearance, then its sound. He follows this with an evocative image of the music (lines three and four). Wen compares the bowls to pools and their trembling surface (stirred by the striking of the chopsticks) to the restless movement of the dragon within. The music is related to the action of cosmological forces; as the expansion of the waterbowl to the dimensions of Shaopi Lake occurs, melody becomes a mysterious speech rising from unfathomable depths. Perhaps the emphasis on water and tutelary water-spirits leads Wen to use the Xiang goddess. Already we have a more rational juxtaposition of images than we find in Li's poem, even if Wen has yet to establish a coherent poetic narrative.

There is no reference in the two Xiang poems of the *Chu ci* to any horses ridden by the goddess herself; in both poems, however, we have the shaman-narrator pursuing the goddess, perhaps on a magical mount of some kind. Although Wen has given the goddess a horse in his poem, the emotional significance is similar: the two Xiang songs deal with a sexual hunt, the shaman's attempt to find the goddess, and either the anticipation of her arrival or the frustration of her withdrawal. Guo's music lets Wen hear the sound of the goddess's jade bells and ornaments tinkling wildly as she passes; the misty rain that enshrouds her presence may suggest the disappearance of the Goddess of Mount Wu into clouds and rain after her sexual liaison with the king of Chu. As Wen listens, his associations have become erotically charged: his thoughts are moving (unlike Li He's) in a specific, traceable direction. A distinctive characteristic of Guo's instrument is its use of water; this is matched throughout the poem by constant reference to wetness and dampness—not only in this brief image of Lady Xiang, but also in the dew, clouds, snow, and mist of the later stanzas. All are atmospheric phenomena that may be expected to arise sympathetically from the playing of a "watery" instrument. This imagistic reinforcement helps give the poem a strong structural coherence.

An elaborate fantasy provoked by the music (lines five to eighteen) forms the center of the song and is almost independent of it; a poem within a poem. Here, Wen's fondness for the erotic "palace style" emerges. Although similar stylistic usages can be seen in Li He's corpus, Li was attracted more to the sensuous intensity of palace poetry than to its sexual implications. Wen, on the other hand, takes a subgenre (poems on musical performance) and eroticizes it further, first by allusion in stanza one and then explicitly in this middle section. The idea of sensuality may be expressed in the classical compound *shengse* 聲色: Wen breaks the phrase into its component parts and expresses them as a stimulus and response. Guo provides the *sheng* (sound), Wen responds with *se* (appearance).

Wen sets off this middle section from the rest of the poem with structural devices. It begins with the *yuefu* tag line "I have heard" (*wu wen* 吾聞). Like another common *yuefu* tag, "Haven't you seen" (*jun bu jian* 君不見), the phrase is usually employed to break up the regularity of the meter and thus to underscore the more casual, folk-song qualities of the poem; the "I" and "you" are formulaic and collective, not personal and individual. Here, however, it jars amid sophisticated diction and self-conscious artistry; although Wen's poem is in song form, its theme demands a less popular treatment. Perhaps the phrase is meant to draw attention to its literal meaning: The "I have heard" refers not only to the convention (Wen introducing a scene common in the poetic tradition) but also to the musical performance (Wen listening to Guo's music). At any rate, the phrase creates a frame that emphasizes artificiality: if the scene that follows is part of Wen's musical daydream, it is an interpolation of art that comes between poet and associative image. He is "daydreaming" a crafted poetic scene. This central section is structurally closed as well by the anomalous six-line stanza at the end (lines thirteen to eighteen). The perpetuation of a single rhyme through one more couplet gives the section a finality before the frame poem resumes in line nineteen.

This middle section is characterized, as in Li He's *yuefu*, by an erratic movement in the perceiving eye and in the sudden intense observation of compositional detail; one can, however, make narrative sense of it, and here once again Wen moves away from the stylistic quirks of Li He. In the second stanza (lines five to eight), Wen transforms Guo's music into the striking of bell-stones outside the Jade Dawn Palace. We can read the name either as a reference to one of the palaces of the Taoist heaven or as merely an elegant substitution for an imperial dwelling. The former would be in keeping with the supernatural overtones of the first stanza, while the latter would be more appropriate to palace poetry, where numerous poems begin with the description of the languid palace lady. Of course, this ambiguity emphasizes the stanza's special function as introduction to the "subpoem" and as transition from the frame poem. The attention paid to her articles of adornment and the luxurious palace furniture (orchid hairpin, silk screen, incense burner) and the replacement of an individual presence with metonyms are standard tropes of palace poetry.

Throughout this stanza, the scene is still imprecise. A woman is being described, but we cannot tell the circumstances; we merely have a close-up of her, and the language suggests her awakening to the sound of musical stones outside her room—an implicit analogy to the sound of Guo's bowls. By line nine, we find that she is dancing; Guo's music now becomes her accompaniment. In the fourth stanza, the emperor visits the lady/dancer; the music continues, and so enthralled is he by the performance that, like Wen listening to Guo, he becomes oblivious to the passing of time. It is this line, in which Wen's fictional scene creates a listener, that allows the poet to return to the real occasion (Guo's performance). Emperor and Wen merge, and Wen leaves his reverie.

Running through the subpoem is a restless movement from exteriors to interiors and back again, a dichotomy that underscores the split between Wen's erotic daydream and the musician's performance. Our direction of sight moves in and out; starting outside the palace, we see the lady startled awake by the music outside; later, when we reach the dancer, "Light echoes ring and chase the whirling snow. / Mist in the clear-jade sky dampens the layered hills." The whirling snow is the dancer's sleeves, outside weather brought inside as a metaphor. The next line is a description of the dancer's forehead, using the conventional description of hills as eyebrows (the mist is her perspiration). The dancer herself is an outside landscape displaced to the inside. In the next line, the reader's eyes look outside the screen to the moon (or, to the metaphorical moon of the dancer's forehead) and, immediately after, he perceives the arrival of the emperor.

The last stanza brings us back to the occasional music-performance poem, and it in turn embraces a new series of conventions and devices. Since the sentiments expressed are those appropriate to parted friends, we can go back and read the first four stanzas as Wen's recreation of a past performance. We can speculate that the poem was sent to Guo after he and the poet had parted. This is confirmed by the mention of a "letter" in line twenty. What elevates this stanza from an ordinary parting-poem conclusion is the playful confusion of eroticism and friendship. First, Wen's imagined scene implies that the audience/performer relation is the same between emperor and dancer as it is between himself and Guo. Second, since Guo's music has provoked a classic erotic poetry scene in Wen's imagination, Wen's stoic forbearance in the last couplet has a double meaning. He will suppress the loneliness caused by being deprived of Guo's company and will endeavor to forget the "fragrant dreams" stirred by his music.

Wen still owes a great deal to Li He in this poem, particularly the abrupt shifts of viewpoint, the intensity of his visual imagination, and the dense, paratactic diction. Wen also follows Li in his propensity for changing subject matter almost arbitrarily and in his tendency to experiment with subgenre conventions. Both poets may be using imagistic techniques to better describe the workings of the mind—associative images, synaesthetic juxtapositions of aural and visual phenomena, a certain tendency to express subjective emotions through an idiosyncratic selection of seemingly objective detail. But after this, Wen's imitation ends. Although Wen's imaginative eye may jump erratically, he never makes it completely impossible for a perceptive reader to follow his line of vision or his train of thought; he never pursues the vertiginous, almost supernatural point of view that made later readers dub Li a "demon talent" (*gui cai* 鬼才). Wen also never strains for originality as much as Li does; rather, he prefers to play with and manipulate the conventions of poetic genres, in particular, popular song, in order to restore a freshness to those conventions. Wen would rather tickle us than shock us; no matter how arbitrary his visual dislocations may seem at first, there is always a sophisticated but very human mind underneath them, logical, impulsive, emotional, rational.

Ci as Subordinate Genre

It is a singular misfortune that Wen is chiefly remembered as a *ci* poet; this reputation has to some extent interfered with a clear realization of his accomplishments as a master of the *shi* form. The general perception is that because of Wen's familiarity with the world of popular entertainment, his attention was drawn to the early, popular *ci* lyrics; he recognized their potential and consequently became the first major literati poet to exert a significant creative effort in their composition. Moreover, he recognized *ci* as a distinct genre and treated it as such. His *shi* are syntactically loose and imagistically clear; in contrast, his *ci* are dense, rich, and difficult in their language, employing an "objective" approach in which their subjects of description (invariably beautiful women) are depicted without any direct, explicit reference to their emotions.

It is also generally believed that Wen assembled two collections of his *ci*, the *Wolan ji* 握蘭集 (in three *juan* 卷 [chapters]) and the *Jinquan ji* 金荃集 (in ten *juan*), thus demonstrating his belief that *ci* were fundamentally different from *shi* in nature and worthy of preserving. Wen is also credited with introducing Late Tang *shi* diction and imagery into *ci* and with exploiting the aesthetic effect of the stanza break (*huan tou* 換頭) in two-stanza (*shuang diao* 雙調) *ci*. These important innovations made his works exemplary for later *ci* poets, and when the first major anthology of *ci*, the *Huajian ji* 花間集, was compiled around 940, by Zhao Chongzuo 趙崇祚, Wen's predominance was well established.[33]

Although this opinion of Wen's work is largely correct within the context of *ci* history, it must be revised if we allow for the complexities of Wen's style and the creative inclinations of the poet and his times. I will briefly re-evaluate these claims and suggest an alternative and more detailed picture.

First, we cannot be absolutely sure that Wen did indeed prepare collections of his own *ci*. All of Wen's poetry suffered in transmission throughout the Song, and his collection seems to have reached a more or less definitive form only late in that dynasty. Lists of his works in the bibliographies of the Tang and Song are contradictory, and several different versions of his *shi* collection were in circulation at the same time.[34] It is also significant that sixty-six of Wen's surviving seventy-one *ci* are known through the *Huajian ji*, which, by and large, reflects the tastes of a circle of *ci* connoisseurs from the area of Shu 蜀 (modern Sichuan). If Wen had produced thirteen *juan* of *ci* (as speculation would have it), surely more would have been preserved by his admirers, or at least we would have a substantial number of *ci* surviving from sources other than the *Huajian ji*. It seems more likely that these *ci* connoisseurs collected Wen's efforts in the genre only after the poet's death (perhaps by combing the entertainment quarters) and that this small body of poems finally came into the hands of Zhao Chongzuo. They therefore represent the preservation efforts of a small circle of cognoscenti. The *shi* collection, on the other hand, had a different provenance; it was preserved either by Wen or by his admirers, and by the end of the Song its length had stabilized at seven *juan* with a "supplement" of one *juan* of later finds. Odds and ends were added by Gu Sili to form a ninth *juan* to the early Qing edition.[35] While we will never know the exact content of the collections mentioned in the bibliographies, Chia-ying Yeh Chao has suggested that we discount the possibility that any of them were *ci* collections per se.[36] It is more likely that the different collection titles listed in early bibliographies are various editions of his *shi*; one may note that while the *shi ji* 詩集 is listed separately from the *Wolan ji* and the *Jinquan ji*, *shi ji* is merely a name describing the contents and not a title as such. This makes it more likely that some editions of the *shi* collection, which varied widely in content, *did* have names—including *Wolan ji* and *Jinquan ji*.[37]

Moreover, Wen's influence on the history of *ci* overall and his importance within the tradition as a *ci* poet have probably been exaggerated. Although a major influence on the *Huajian* poets, Wen ceases to be important in the work that succeeded them; there are few references other than biographical anecdotes in critical works on the *ci*. Later, in the late Qing, he was rediscovered by Zhang Huiyan 張惠言 (1761–1802) (who, incidentally, read Wen's *ci* as political allegories).[38] His present status as "cofounder" of the genre with Wei Zhuang 韋莊 (836–910) springs almost entirely from the near canonical status of the opinions of the early twentieth-century critics Wang Guowei 王國維 (in his *Renjian cihua* 人間詞話) and Yu Pingbo 俞平伯. Although a strictly analytical review of Wen's reputation would be difficult to carry out, it does not take much examination to discover that Wen is mentioned more often as a *shi* poet than as a *ci* poet—at least until the Qing and possibly throughout that dynasty.[39]

A further problem with the traditional evaluation of Wen's contribution to *ci* is that his tiny corpus of lyrics are rather heterogeneous in nature. On the one hand, most of the two-stanza lyrics and almost all of the single-stanza lyrics share the styles of other literati *ci* of the Mid- and Late Tang.[40] They have syntactically "open" phrases, are less imagistically dense, and make explicit reference to the emotions of their subjects. On the other hand, a dozen or so lyrics—almost all of them to the tune of "Pusa man" 菩薩蠻 or "Geng louzi" 更漏子—are constantly quoted and discussed by critics; this has created the idea of a distinctive Wen "*ci* style." Although the importance of these anthology pieces should not be underestimated (they seem to have been influential at least in the formation of a *Huajian* school), they are hardly characteristic of Wen's *ci* production.

Critics may argue that the songs close in style and content to earlier *ci* poetry may have been written early in his career, before he wrote the "innovative" *ci* of the two major cycles. But the style of these supposedly later *ci* is not unique at all. As we shall soon see, they share many characteristics with Wen's *shi* style, particularly that of his *yuefu*. Let us begin with a *yuefu* with many similarities to poems discussed above, particularly "Song of Wu Garden" in Chapter 1 and "Lotus Bank Song" in this chapter.

Lament for Spring 惜春詞

The hundred-tongue asks the flowers, 百舌問花花不語
  but the flowers won't answer;
They linger, as if they resent 低回似恨橫塘雨
  the rain of Hengtang.
Bees compete for powdered stamens, 蠶爭粉蕊蝶分香
  butterflies divide up scent—
4 Unlike the drooping willows, who 不似垂楊惜金縷
  begrudge their golden threads.

"I wish you could retain 　your gentle beauty forever, And not be swept away 　with the east wind." The King of Qin's daughter knits her brows, 　faces the misty moon. 8　But the grieving red, bearing dew, 　is wastefully carried off.	願君留得長妖韶 莫逐東風還蕩搖 秦女含嚬向烟月 愁紅帶露空迢迢

(*WFQ*, *j*. 2, pp. 47–48)

1/ The hundred-tongue (*bai she*) is a name for the shrike or butcher bird.
2/ Hengtang: an embankment southwest of Nanjing; frequently evoked in landscapes of the Jiangsu area.

This poem lies clearly within the tradition of the Tang erotic vignette, with its penchant for personification, especially of flowers. This evocation of spring mood implies a conscious mind reading personal emotions (*qing*) into what is seen. Such a personal view lets the flowers emerge in the first stanza as nature's victims. Unhappy and mute, they refuse to respond to the birds and resent the rain. Their wealth is exploited and wasted by birds and bees; and they cannot maintain their integrity, unlike the willows.

We cannot perceive the source of this personal view, however, until we hear the woman's voice in lines five and six. She fears the passing of the flowers' season, because (as we would suspect from the poetic tradition) she reads the flowers as symbols for herself; this provokes her personal address to them. The east (spring) wind has a reputation for this literal and symbolic deflowering; recall Li He's lines: "A shame that in the evening this bewitching fragrance falls; / Married to the spring wind, they have no need of matchmakers."[41] The woman's wish to see the flowers remain is futile; she knits her brows as she sees the wind carrying them off after all. Wen calls her, elegantly, the "King of Qin's daughter"—Nongyu, who was carried off herself by Xiao Shi on a phoenix. Wen is playing on a favorite trope, the association between the passing of spring and the arrival of sexual experience. His own favorite kind of "objectivity" is at play here; the emotional reading of the landscape in the first stanza and the emotional response in the second are the woman's, not his.

Wen's most popular *ci* today are his "Pusa man" lyrics. The tune is divided into two stanzas, with the rhyme scheme *aabb/ccdd* and with line lengths 7-7-5-5/5-5-5-5. Despite the rhyme scheme and the uneven lengths of the pattern, these *ci* traverse familiar ground.

Pusa man (twelfth of fourteen) 菩薩蠻

Bright moon of last eve,
  just at midnight; 夜來皓月纔當午
Double curtains were still,
  no one spoke. 重簾悄悄無人語
In a secluded place, a musk incense trailed; 深處麝烟長
4 Lying down, she left on a thin layer of powder. 臥時留薄妝
"I still cherish the year gone by, 當年還自惜
But can't bear to recall past affairs; 往事那堪憶
Dew on flowers, the moon's brightness fades; 花露月明殘
8 Under my brocade quilt I feel the dawn cold." 錦衾知曉寒
  (*QTWDC*, p. 203)

The second stanza here has no pronoun identifying direct address, as in "Lament for Spring"; yet this *ci* does closely resemble the form of erotic *shi* poems, in which an objective description of a court lady is followed by her personal response at the end. Granted this tradition, it is highly likely that the last four lines are the words of the woman. The first stanza is a slow camera zoom, culminating in the erotic fetishistic touch of the makeup in the fourth line.[42] There is not a single line of this poem that could not be inserted into a Wen Tingyun *yuefu*, although, perhaps generally speaking, the language is *less* imagistically dense than is customary for most of his *shi* on similar themes.

Another, more famous "Pusa man" is often cited to show the "difficulty" of Wen's style; but those accustomed to Wen's *yuefu* (especially the *yuefu* influenced by Li He) will hardly find this poem difficult at all.

Pusa man (second of fourteen) 菩薩蠻

Within a crystal curtain,
  a pillow of crystal; 水精簾裏頗黎枕
Warm incense stirs dreams
  in mandarin duck brocade. 暖香惹夢鴛鴦錦
Along the river, willows like mist. 江上柳如烟
4 Geese fly beneath a sky of waning moon. 雁飛殘月天

Her lotus threads are a light autumn tint, 藕絲秋色淺
Cloth-doll ribbons cut unevenly. 人勝參差剪

Side curls concealed by fragrant red,	雙鬢隔香紅
8 Jade hairpins—a breeze in her hair.	玉釵頭上風
(QTWDC, p. 195)	

6/ The "cloth-doll ribbons" are *ren sheng*, hair ribbons cut in the shape of the human form. They are worn on People Day, the seventh day of the first lunar month.

7/ She is wearing flowers at her temples.

Professor Kang-i Sun Chang has observed: "What is immediately noteworthy is that the connection between the two stanzas of the poem is not very clear. Each stanza seems to portray a separate poetic scene, so that readers are required to find possible relations between the two stanzas."[43] Indeed; and those who have read Wen's *yuefu* should hardly find this unusual or unexpected. We have seen already how Wen exploits quatrain form to break poems into units and emphasizes the poetic transition from one section to the next.

In fact, the poem is structured around a number of Wen's familiar techniques, many of which derive from erotic traditions we have observed and will observe again: a voyeuristic tendency in description that moves in on the woman, who is unaware of the reader's prying eyes; the insertion of dream or memory scenes (Zhang Huiyan considers lines three to six a description of the dream "stirred" by the incense);[44] and a subtle movement between inside and outside that we have already noted in "Retired Scholar Guo Strikes the Musical Bowls" and the "Song of Wu Garden." These elements produce a relatively coherent poem: if we agree with Zhang and imagine a dream scene, lines three and four are probably describing the surroundings of the sleeping woman (making her dream the transient "dawn dream" [*xiao meng* 曉夢] typical of erotic verse). The stanza break then divides reality from dream. Another possible reading would posit a waking and a morning toilette between stanzas: the woman goes out in the second stanza for a turn about her garden. As in a number of Wen's *yuefu*, the emotional response of the woman is absent here, although it still may be read in the objects around her.[45]

Chia-ying Yeh Chao has characterized *ci* like this as *keguan* 客觀, a phrase meant to be translated as "objective."[46] Yet her concept of "objectivity" is somewhat different from what I have described as "objectivity" in Wen's *shi* style. She sees Wen's *ci* as almost abstract aesthetic constructs, in which women are held up for observation and their persons placed at a distance (hence, "objective"). In contrast, I perceive "objectivity" in the *explicit* absence of the poet. Whereas Professor Yeh's distinction is helpful in arriving at sensitive readings within the *ci* tradition (particularly in analyzing the *Huajian* style), it disregards the essentially conventional *shi* roots of lyrics such as this. As we have seen, Wen knew well the sensual and emotional connotations of objects and the roles they played in sexual exchange. He also knew the essentially voyeuristic nature of Chinese erotic verse; both the fetishistic description of women and the manipulation of their voice were prominent elements in the content of such verse.[47] Although it is true that Wen enjoyed "abstract" and "objective" portrayal of things, he probably wrote his *ci* for women performers; a male audience would have been sensitive to the erotic and sensual connotations of these "abstract" lines. Far from being a poetry of refined and distanced appreciation, they played an important role in the entertainment quarters of the time. Their difficulty for us today lies in their exploitation of a poetics of mood, emotion, and sexuality that we must learn. For the Late Tang audience, the songs did not need to be explicit to be understood.[48]

As I have said, Wen's more famous *ci* are close to his *yuefu*, sharing their style on a smaller scale; his other *ci* share a style common to the song lyric in the early and mid-ninth century.[49] Occasionally, however, Wen does seem to be experimenting with the potential of the new genre; when he does, he combines the richness of his *shi* language with a certain colloquial fluency.

Geng louzi (sixth of six)　　　　　　　　　　　　更漏子

 Incense in the jade burner,　　　　　　　　　玉鑪香
 Tears on the red candle:　　　　　　　　　　紅蠟淚
 They stubbornly shine on autumn grief　　　　偏照畫堂秋思
  in painted halls.
4 Emerald mascara light,　　　　　　　　　　　眉翠薄
 Side-curl clouds thin:　　　　　　　　　　　　鬢雲殘
 The night is long, coverlet and pillow cold.　　夜長衾枕寒

 Wutong trees　　　　　　　　　　　　　　　梧桐樹
8 And midnight rain　　　　　　　　　　　　　三更雨
 Don't know the grief felt　　　　　　　　　　不道離情正苦
  right now at parting.

Leaf by leaf,	一葉葉
Sound by sound,	一聲聲
12 They drop on empty stairs til day.	空階滴到明
(*QTWDC*, p. 210)	

As in the second "Pusa man" lyric, no woman's voice is explicitly present in the poem; yet the imagery turns away from the subtlety of the "Pusa man" lyric and many of the *yuefu*, which use objects to indicate a woman's state of mind. Instead, Wen employs more colloquial, emotionally explicit words. The use of *pian* 偏, "stubborn," in line three turns the opening image into a personification and nicely summarizes the woman persona's disgust with the intransigence of inanimate objects that are *wu qing* 無情, "without feeling." Similarly, the rain is explicitly accused of disregarding her grief. Most striking, of course, is the exploitation of the tune pattern for effect in lines ten and eleven. Here Wen can suggest tedium through the simplest of poetic repetitions. This *ci* achieves a clarity and simplicity that the poet either would not or could not employ in his *yuefu* and the more famous of the poems in the "Pusa man" cycle.

These readings and our study of Wen's *yuefu* techniques allow us to make some general observations about his contribution to the development of *ci*. First, Wen's imagistically dense *ci* are not stylistically and thematically distinct from his *shi* poetry; even his regulated verse often employs such language (cf. the poems in Chapter 1), and his *yuefu* are basically indistinguishable from *ci* written in his vaunted "*ci* style." Other lyrics are written in a fairly straightforward style already part of "common style" in the ninth century.[50] Second, there is no hard evidence that Wen made a major effort to preserve his *ci*; at least one may assume that he did not lavish the same care on them as he did on his *shi*. He probably perceived the *ci* genre as a popular verse form metrically distinct from *shi* and with a different music tradition.[51] Third, whereas earlier *ci* had employed a simple eroticism or eschewed erotic themes altogether, Wen introduced an obsessive, voyeuristic eroticism into the genre, an eroticism developed in his *yuefu* and many of his regulated poems. This may be his only substantial contribution to the evolution of the genre. Those who still wish to grant Wen the credit for creating a new *ci* style may at this point argue that his *ci* style influenced his *shi* poetry, and not the other way around.

However, I find it extremely unlikely that Wen would work out a distinctive and radically new style in a still undeveloped genre and then decide to transfer it to the genre he knew better; moreover, we know that this *shi* style already existed for the most part in the poetry of Li He. Fourth, Wen's exploitation of stanza divisions in his two-stanza *ci* does not reflect an interest in the distinctive potential of the *ci* genre; rather, it is an adaptation of the aesthetics of musical quatrains. Such stanza breaks are employed in exactly the same way, whether they are used in *yuefu* or in *ci*. This is borne out further by the large number of two-stanza, eight-line *yuefu* written by Wen. This is not to say that Wen's use of stanza breaks in *ci* were unimportant, especially in the history of the genre. I am simply asserting that Wen would not be conscious of doing anything particularly innovative. Manipulation of the stanza break would in fact have been natural when writing two-stanza *ci*, granted the history of the earlier (*shi*) song form. Surely some other composers of *ci* would have exploited the break in the same way if Wen had not.

In retrospect, it may be said that Wen's contribution to *ci* history was an invention of later practitioners of the genre eager to create a distinctive *ci* aesthetic. Wen made little stylistic differentiation between *ci* and *shi* when he wrote, and his own distinctive style found a comfortable home in both genres. While he was experimenting with musical poetry in general (both *ci* and the "sung *shi*" that Ren Bantang has analyzed), he created only a *personal* style through the use of dense imagery and diction, "objectivity," and the reinvention of the erotic tradition. Meanwhile, his *ci* admirers seized upon the *ci* poems as models for a new *genre* style, and during the Five Dynasties his work was re-evaluated and reinterpreted by new aesthetic guidelines.[52] Whereas single lines of *shi* verses by poets such as Du Mu and Li Shangyin were inserted into *ci* and consequently achieved new meaning and significance, Wen's slender corpus of *ci* was relocated as a whole in a new system of poetic values that he himself would not have recognized. Wen's *ci* became important with the flourishing of a reading tradition that emerged only after the poet's death.

THREE

Watching the Voyeurs

Dense curtains with strings of pearl,	密帳真珠絡
Warm drapes adorned with kingfisher feathers.	溫幄翡翠裝
Her Chu waist once knew preference and favor,	楚腰知便寵
4 But palace brows now struggle for prominence.	宮眉正鬭強
From her knotted sash hang gardenia seeds,	結帶懸梔子
On her embroidered collar, mandarin ducks in needlework.	繡領刺鴛鴦
Light and chill the night in the wardrobe;	輕寒衣省夜
She smooths the aloes-scented robes with a golden iron.[1]	金斗熨沈香

In this, one of his lesser-known verses, Li Shangyin produced what he considered an "imitation" of the verse characteristic of the Liang dynasty court poet Xu Ling 徐陵 (507–83). Xu, of course, is principally known for a sophisticated and subtly erotic genre of verse usually termed "palace-style poetry"; he wrote at a time when such poetry had come to its fruition under the patronage of the imperial prince Xiao Gang 蕭剛 (503–51), later Emperor Jianwen 簡文 (r. 549–51). Such verse is now found primarily in the *New Verses from the Jade Terrace* anthology, compiled by Xu Ling himself around 537.[2] In the palace style, a characteristic vocabulary and imagery developed to describe the way women looked, what they wore, what they did, and how they felt. It died out gradually in the Early Tang, but, as Li's poem suggests, a renewal of interest in palace poetry themes and techniques arose among a number of poets in the early ninth century.

This does not mean that when these poets—notably Li He, Li Shangyin, and Wen Tingyun—turned to palace poetry for new poetic material, they were able to create (or even wanted to create) perfect imitations of a dead style. Although Li Shangyin calls the poem above an "imitation," his lines are clearly a product of the Tang, not the Liang. True, the poem is not a regulated verse (a form not fully developed in the sixth century, but the dominant meter of Li's poetry), but its understated use of erotic description to reveal the woman's emotions *is* characteristic of the Tang. This court lady seems to be in disgrace and has been relegated to a minor position in the imperial wardrobe. Although we leave her as she engages in a simple task (ironing clothes), we can read through the images and come to an understanding of her loneliness and isolation; this evocation of emotion without its direct expression is more characteristic of the High Tang "palace lament" (*gong yuan* 宮怨), which, although influenced strongly by palace poetry, had developed a distinctive style of its own.[3]

On the other hand, by openly claiming that he was basing his poem on the style of Xu Ling, Li was asserting a worthy artistic status for such erotic poetry. The later poetic tradition tolerated the palace lament because it was open to allegorical interpretation: the swooning court lady was a figure for the worthy official whose advice was ignored by the government. The original palace poets, however, aggressively asserted the value of erotic poetry for its own sake, and their works are impossible to allegorize. Li's composition, though stylistically a Tang product, suggests a positive reevaluation of the earlier age's poetic values.

Moreover, Late Tang poets could use palace poetry to *comment* on the genre itself or to point consciously to the historical circumstances that produced it (the cultivated court life in the south during the fifth and sixth centuries). Poems of this kind are still characteristic works of their own times, although they gain their full richness only through comparison to the genre that influenced them—as is true in Western culture with the "neo-classical" works of Stravinsky and Picasso.[4] Several *yuefu* by Wen Tingyun are particularly striking examples of this sort of creative commentary. The few I examine below show how his awareness of the historical and cultural surroundings of the original palace poems enabled him to write works with greater depth and interest. To understand these poems, however, we should first turn our attention to the motivations underlying palace poetry.

The Dynamics of the Palace Poem

Some of the later Chinese distaste for the palace poem must come from a suspicion of the genre's "insincerity." "Serious" poetry is seen as a personal art that speaks to many people as individuals. It is a communication to the *zhiji* 知己, "[the friend who] knows oneself," either in the poet's own age or in later ages; it becomes the medium through which the author may be known and understood. This holds true even for the most ordinary occasional poems; although the sentiment may not be particularly deep or the supposed recipient not particularly close to the author, the underlying moral seriousness is present nevertheless.

During the Six Dynasties period, however, a literary tradition developed that seemed to contradict these poetic assumptions. Although literary theorists still insisted on the primacy of the classical formula for poetry, they also emphasized the importance of style or ornament (*wen* 文) in literary writing.[5] Much later, literary historians saw this as a sign of decadent "formalism" in the writings of the age, but it seems more likely that Six Dynasties litterateurs believed that style itself was an essential element in the artistic communication of the self. By the time *New Verses from the Jade Terrace* was compiled, there were additional, historical reasons for insistence on correct style. The guardians of the Chinese artistic tradition were for the most part descendants of northern aristocrats who had fled south when Luoyang, the northern capital, fell to nomadic invaders in 317. Determined not to relinquish their claim to true Chinese culture (in spite of the loss of the Chinese heartland) and equally determined to maintain a clear distinction between themselves and the "uncultured parvenus" of the southern nobility, they placed considerable store on the maintenance of correct literary style and of the original northern dialect.[6] Moreover, the decline of political and military prestige in the southern courts throughout the period made *wen* one of the last bastions of the exiles' authority, and one of the few possessions they could claim as a sign of their own continuing superiority over the northern "barbarians." Nor was this assumption entirely idle: the northern, non-

Chinese governments would often detain cultivated emissaries from the south and force them to join their own courts, as the famous case of Yu Xin testifies. Thus, the full mastery of the ornamental style was a sign of cultural mastery—a sign of solidarity with the governing class and an affirmation of its continuing right to rule. Although writers might continue to pay lip service to the ideal that poetry was the powerful expression of spontaneous emotion, they were more concerned with avoiding faux pas, exercising their wit and knowledge of classical allusion, and exhibiting their poetic control of the language through elaborate and elegant descriptions of physical phenomena.

With these historical conditions in mind, we can come to a clear appreciation of the cultural forces that produced palace poetry. Previously, the Chinese had written in a fairly straightforward and honest manner about sexual attachments. A number of the Nineteen Old Poems (*Gushi shijiu shou* 古詩十九首) are love poems, and, as we saw in the last chapter, Liu Song *yuefu* quatrains that made extensive use of a female voice soon attracted an elite audience of imitators. In imitating this folk poetry, however, literati poets made changes in keeping with their own cultural interests. As Joseph Allen has noted, these poets turned narrative poems into more lyrical, descriptive verse by altering the original narrative or reducing it to the status of allusion. Allen also points out that Six Dynasties literati *yuefu* portray women as less independent and either as more passively virtuous (in keeping with Confucian mores) or as more coy and flirtatious (a characteristic of the Qi-Liang period). In turn, they give more space to erotic descriptions of the woman's desirability. The female characters, whether actors in a vestigial narrative or personae expressing their feelings in the first person, have for the most part moved upward in the social scale from peasant girl to court lady.[7] Moreover, in poems written in a female persona, the late Six Dynasties penchant for elaborate description (in this case, of an erotic nature) often undermines the coherence of a first-person narrator. The first several lines of a poem might describe the palace lady, whereas the ending, in keeping with *yuefu* conventions, is her personal, spoken lament for a lost lover. Due to the general absence of pronouns, however, it is often impossible to determine at what point objective description becomes direct speech. This tendency toward objective description in *yuefu* imitations is part of the "eroticization" of another poetic subgenre, the *yongwu* 詠物 or "poem on things." The southern court poets, concerned with finding the correct descriptive equivalent for every phenomenon, often competed to capture the nature and aspect of objects; these inclinations naturally extended to the description of women and the objects around them. One might argue that almost every sixth-century poem in *New Verses from the Jade Terrace* is a *yongwu* of sorts, for even the *yuefu* imitations have become so descriptive and objective in style that at times the tune title or stock situation alone identifies them as examples of the genre.

At this point we can detect a widening gap between earlier "love" poetry and the "erotic" poetry of the late southern courts. Although moralists may frown on the actual confession of desire in a love poem (for example, in the famous "Ziye ge" 子夜歌 quatrains of the fourth and fifth centuries), such a poem still embodies the canonical expectations of the *shi* genre; it expresses direct emotion in the form of direct speech from one person to another. The language is often simple, as befits a poetry that aspires at least to the *appearance* of spontaneity. But the late southern court poets have made an act of communication one of contemplation and connoisseurship. The author of a palace poem addresses and woos not a lover but instead his fellow poets in an extended commentary on an object they all observe and seek to capture in language; if such a poet writes in a female persona, it is still commentary both on the *yuefu* tradition he imitates and on the feminine psychology he believes he is capturing in a convincing and subtle manner.[8]

Consequently, palace poems that describe feminine beauty may be termed "erotic" poetry rather than love poetry. It is important to keep in mind, however, that a male poet describing a sexually attractive woman can never be wholly objective. As in late Six Dynasties poetry on other subjects, descriptions of women reveal the poet's ability not only to control and manipulate language but also to discipline the passions. By attempting to create an aesthetic distance between poet and (desirable) object, a palace poet can indulge in titillation of the erotic without committing himself to the loss of control inherent in passion—a loss of control both in life and in the use of language.[9] This objectifying trend is matched by a countermove that places the burden of passion and loss of control on woman; a prominent aspect in the description of women in palace poetry is their sexual restlessness and frustration. In this respect, an essential text for the palace poets is the second of the Nineteen Old Poems, "Green Green the Grass on the Riverbank" 青青河畔草.[10] The reader's eye traces a path from a garden to a woman's boudoir and learns that the woman's husband is a faithless wanderer. In the last line, the woman admits, "A bed is hard to keep empty" 空床難獨守. This confession suggests the availability of the abandoned woman in poetic convention; later the *Jade Terrace* poets would refer constantly to empty beds, empty bedrooms, and cold (unoccupied) coverlets. For the perhaps more demure and cultured heroines of these verses, the implications of these catalogues are never made quite so obvious; but the empty bed is often the last thing the reader sees or the last thing the lady mentions.

I send word to a far traveler:	寄言遠行者
In an empty bedroom, tears like sleet.[11]	空閨淚如霰
Moonbeams shine across my pillow,	月輝橫射枕
And in lamplight, a bed half in shadows.[12]	燈光半隱牀
In vain the moon crosses the high tower;	空度高樓月
Never will my youth return.	非復五三年
And why must it shine on this bed	何須照牀裏
When there's only a single sleeper?[13]	終是一人眠

"Green Green the Grass on the Riverbank" is also an important model for the quintessential rhetorical movement of these poems: penetration. The reader's eyes move through windows, behind screens, into bedrooms, through incense smoke, under coverlets chill from the absence of sleeping bodies. The form of women's arms and legs are noticed through their silk robes; skirts are blown open by the breeze. In palace poems of eight lines or longer, this basic movement helps explain the seamless passage from description to direct speech. Discovering what a woman thinks is the final act in a long, delicate process of unveiling, a final disclosure. For the male poets there is no qualitative difference between exposing a woman's bedroom, her body, and her mind. All are open to the manipulative control of poetic language.[14]

This act of visual collusion—the careful organization of surface description to make the male reader participate in a process of sexual titillation—may be better understood if placed against the full meaning of the term *se* 色. In a limited context *se* can mean sexual desire, but in a broader sense it refers to the sensuous appearance of things, the attractive summation of shifting colors and forms.[15] In the palace poem, it is the way things look that matters; actual possession may be implied by the woman's final invitation, but it is the voyeuristic gaze that grants the lines their interest and power. The appearance of the erotic gesture and the stimulation it produces are more important than the act of sexual union.[16]

We may observe the play of these elements in a poem by Xiao Gang.

Matching a Poem by the Prince of Xiangdong: 和湘東王
A Famed Scholar Takes Pleasure in a 名士悅傾城
City-Toppling Beauty

	We call this lovely lady incomparable;	美人稱絕世
	Her beauty is like a profusion of blossoms.	麗色譬花叢
	Although she lived north of Li's walls,	雖居李城北
4	She now resides east of the Songs'.	住在宋家東
	She taught song at the Princess's mansion,	教歌公主第
	And studied dance at Han's Cheng Palace.	學舞漢成宮
	She often roams by the banks of the Qi,	多遊淇水上
8	Frequents Phoenix Tower.	好在鳳樓中
	Her heels so high, she hesitates to climb stairs;	履高疑上砌
	When her skirt gapes, she especially fears the breeze.	裾開特畏風
	Her blouse is thin, revealing her bracelets;	衫輕見跳脫
12	Her gems spread out form a confusion of dragonflies.	珠概雜青蟲
	Dangling silk encircles her curtains,	垂絲遶帷幔
	The sinking sun crosses the chamber window-lattice.	落日度房櫳
	Her makeup window is blocked by willow's hue;	妝窗隔柳色
16	The well water reflects the red of peach.	井水照桃紅
	"It's not that I begrudge riverbank pendants—	非憐江浦珮
	I'm ashamed that I let my spring bedroom be empty."	羞使春閨空

(*YTXY*, pp. 291–92)

Title/ The Prince of Xiangdong was Xiao Gang's younger brother, Xiao Yi 繹, who later became Emperor Yuan 元 (r. 552–55).

4/ The poet Song Yu, in his "Master Dengtu the Lecher" 登徒子好色賦, boasts that he remained unmoved by the beauty of a woman who climbed the wall to his house and watched him from her own garden to the east of his.

5–6/ The Princess may be Princess Pingyang 平陽公主, Emperor Wu's sister, who was famed for her entertainers. The Cheng Palace was the residence of Han Emperor Cheng's famed dancer and favorite, Zhao Feiyan.

7–8/ The Qi River in Henan was a frequent place for trysts, as often described in the Wei 衛 section of the *Classic of Poetry*. Phoenix Tower may simply be a term for any splendid habitation, but it may also refer to the story of the famed flutist Xiao Shi, who eloped with Nongyu on the back of a phoenix.

12/ The gems (or pearls) probably refer to a hair ornament of some kind; perhaps here they are gold dragonflies encrusted with jewels.

15/ The lack of interior lighting made it necessary for women to locate their makeup mirrors near a window.

17/ A reference to the story of Zheng Jiaofu 鄭交夫, who met two fairy maids on the bank of the Han. After a sexual dalliance with them, they gave him a pair of jade pendants that later vanished.

The title refers to a phrase often applied to femmes fatales. By suggesting the danger inherent in such great beauty, Xiao emphasizes the act of will needed in portraying her in elegant and controlled language. We pass from a description of her talents and her society to her fine dress and luxurious ornaments. Then, presumably because we (a male audience) have been drawn to her private quarters, we follow her to her bedroom window and her inner courtyard; the invitation comes shortly after. Xiao's woman may be a court lady or a courtesan; regardless, a reversal of roles occurs. Rather than selecting the woman he finds attractive, the reader enjoys the experience of being selected himself. He in turn becomes the object of desire, and the passions aroused by erotic description are transferred in turn to emotions expressed by the original erotic object. Although not all palace poems move through such an elaborate scenario, the poet could focus on various aspects of a process that ranged from formal introduction to the bed game: the woman's dance or song, her toilette, her disrobing.

Men are occasionally described in these poems, but only as masters of wealth and political power. Almost always these are prerequisites for anyone who would court a beautiful courtesan or prospective wife; women, after all, can be expensive possessions. Men are even shown in a state of desire, but this is usually controlled by displays of wit and comic hyperbole and is meant to testify to the value of the desired object rather than to the authenticity of male passion. Shen Yue's 沈約 (441–513) "Written for a Newly Wedded Youth" 少年新婚為之詠, for example, combines typical erotic description with an unusual use of a male persona.[17] Written in the voice of a bridegroom gloating over the looks of his wife (once again, the poet speculates on the body under the clothes), the young man recovers from his mock astonishment over her exceptional qualities by considering his own good points.

27 I view myself—though I'm haggard and thin, 自顧雖悴薄
My cap and carriage brighten the city corner. 冠蓋曜城隅
My tall gates are lined with grooms and coachmen, 高門列騶駕
30 On broad streets follow my teams of black horses. 廣路從驪駒
What shame have I for my *lulu* blade? 何慚鹿盧劍
Why belittle my official gait? 詎減府中趨
When she visits her family, she'll ask in her village, 還家問鄉里
34 "Who else was worthy to be my husband?" 詎堪持作夫

31/ The *lulu* blade appears occasionally in *yuefu* as the dagger worn by young gallants.

Palace poems are, then, primarily poems of a male social world, written for aesthetic and erotic appreciation and meant to demonstrate mastery of language, of wealth and status, and of women. In the more confident political world of the Sui and Early Tang, the re-establishment of Confucian moral values brought the subgenre into question. Coterie poetry did continue to play an important role at court, although (with occasional exceptions) the voyeuristically erotic dropped from sight.[18] Court and capital poetry instead became more explicitly public in its celebration of the aristocratic world of imperial audiences, public outings, and dignified versification parties. Poetic wit and convention were still vital, of course, but a greater seriousness of subject matter was demanded. Even *yongwu* poems became increasingly allegorical, as the subgenre came to speak more expressively about the implications of social and political relationships.

Only hints of the erotic style reappear here and there, particularly in the popular quatrain style (of which the "palace lament" is an important part). Such poems were too short to play out the rhetorical games of penetration and control, and their status as serious poetry deserving to be read was maintained by habits of allegorical reading. However, popular quatrains ultimately relied on the knowledge of palace-poetry conventions to be fully understood—just as palace-poetry conventions relied on the reader's knowledge of older *yuefu* tropes.

The Erotic *Yuefu* of Wen Tingyun

Wen's love of surface, though deplored by later critics, allowed him to explore greater complexities, to demonstrate how surfaces indicate unguessed depths within. For this reason, the quintessentially superficial verse of the palace poets attracted him strongly. In many of his *yuefu*, we find a poet surprisingly susceptible to the witty, erotic games of pure palace poetry, even as he brings new aesthetic interests to them. Consider, for example, poems by Xiao Gang and Wen that manipulate similar conceits.

Xiao Gang: *On a Beauty Surveying a Painting* 詠美人觀花

Painted on the hall, a fairy maid;	殿上圖神女
Forth from the palace, a lovely lady.	宮裏出佳人
How charming—both are painted,	可憐俱是畫
4 So who can tell the real from the false?	誰能辨偽真
A glitter in the eye can be made out in both,	分明淨眉眼
And both have the same slim waist.	一種細腰身
One thing can be taken to show the difference—	所可持為異
8 One's always in a lively mood!	所有好精神

(*YTXY*, p. 301)

This verse is a particularly apt example of precious palace-poetry wit. Xiao looks on passively, playfully pretending to an inability to tell the painting from the living woman. *Yongwu* on paintings often compliment the realism of the artist by hyperbolically confusing the world and its representation; here, however, the poem is not about the painting but about the woman viewing the painting. By pointing out similarities, Xiao implies that the situation is analogous to a woman looking in a mirror—all beautiful women are interchangeable, their qualities are shared and generic. Although his observations are rational and analytical, full of verbs of discrimination (*bian* 辨 "tell," *fen ming* 分明 "make out," *chi* 持 "to hold [as]"), the woman's act of perception involves seeing herself as other. If the painting is a portrait of herself, perhaps she is noticing how beautiful she is to male eyes; if it is the portrait of another woman, she may be sizing up a rival, someone who could replace her. But the reader (if male) can view both woman and painting with the eye of a connoisseur.

By basing his primary conceit on the ambiguous meaning of *hua*

畫 ("painted"), the poet calls attention to the problem of fathoming surface. Determining the true or false means discovering which woman has depth under the paint. One reading of the last line suggests that the real woman has a spirit that betrays its presence in her manner. But perhaps the poet is rebuking what he sees as the moody peevishness of one of his court ladies; then the painting could represent the realization of a male fantasy—the woman who is always in a good mood, who is *all* surface.

Wen Tingyun: *The Reflection* 照影曲

As she finishes her toilette in Jingyang, 景陽妝罷瓊窗暖
   the jasper windows grow warm.
Wishing to catch a reflection in the clear brightness, 欲照澄明香步嬾
   her fragrant steps move languidly.
On the bridge, her clothes multiply 橋上衣多抱彩雲
   and embrace many-colored clouds;
4 The goldfish are motionless 金鮮不動春塘滿
   in the deep spring pool.

The yellow seal pattern in her brow 黃印額山輕為塵
   she despises as dust;
Turquoise scales and red water-grass 翠鱗紅稈俱含嚬
   contain her frown.
Peach blossom of a hundred charms, 桃花百媚如欲語
   she looks about to speak—
8 Once she was peerless, but now 曾為無雙今兩身
   there are two of her!
    (*WFQ, j.* 1, pp. 16–17)

1/ Emperor Wu 武 (r. 483–94) of the Qi dynasty kept his ladies in Jingyang Palace; a bell rung at set times would command them to apply their cosmetics.
2/ "Clear brightness" is the sunlit water of a courtyard pool.
5/ This is very likely the round yellow dot that fashionable women of the Tang painted on their foreheads. She "despises [it] as dust" either because she is dissatisfied with her own looks or because she shows contempt for her "rival," the reflection.

In Wen's poem, as in Xiao Gang's, the poet observes the witty complexities that occur when one woman looks at another. Wen's motives may differ somewhat from Xiao's; he de-emphasizes his own role as discriminating observer, and he does not overtly produce the scene for the delectation of male companions. He is just as fascinated as Xiao, however, with the implications of surface and depth. As the woman pauses to look in the pool, her appearance disseminates onto the reflecting surface. Line three describes the superimposition of her clothes on the clouds of the reflection; on a two-dimensional surface, the two images merge, and her gauze robes become real clouds. The reflection suggests her connection with the Goddess of Mount Wu, who fades into the weather when she departs from her lover. And yet the poem shows that the pool is not simply a mirror but a surface with a depth; the woman can see the fish under the water, juxtaposed against her own frown, which in itself may be an index to thoughts "under the surface." For Wen, the pool is the ideal mirror for the woman, because it presents a realistic metaphor for the complex relationship between appearance and psychological subtlety. True, the ending has the same touch of precious word play as Xiao Gang's, with the same hint at woman's reproducibility, but Wen's emphasis on the pool's depths allows for the woman's emotions as well as her superficial seductiveness. Wen's myth of the feminine is no longer the beautiful surface but the lovely pool that conceals unfathomable complexities.

Another contrast will highlight Wen's reliance on the atmospheric, seasonal associations of palace poetry.

Wang Yun (481–549): *Spring Month (first of two)* 王筠: 春月二首之一

```
  The sun shines on the mandarin duck palace;        日照鴛鴦殿
  Duckweed springs up from the waterbird pond.       萍生雁鶩池
  Drifting dust comes in, following the light beams; 遊塵隨影入
4 Tender willows droop, bearing the wind.            弱柳帶風垂
  The black hawk pursues the young sparrows;         青骹逐黃口
  The lonely crane mourns for its captive mate.      獨鶴慘羈雌
  The sharer of my quilt is off in distant pleasures; 同衾遠遊說
8 Our knotted love so long separated.                結愛久生離
  And now is the time for a swift death;             於今方溘死
  What need for a branch of daylilies?               寧須萱草枝
```
(*YTXY*, p. 328)

10/ The scent of the daylily (*xuancao*) could make people forget the pangs of love; see *Classic of Poetry*, Mao no. 62.[19]

As in many palace poems, the existence of a persona is unclear until the end; in fact, only the last four lines demand a female speaker. Most of the poem, however, is concerned with a modal evocation of spring. Many of the images hint at the presence of an abandoned woman, of course; the mandarin duck palace, the willows embraced by the wind, the hunting hawk (perhaps the libertine husband in search of new conquests), the bereft crane. At the end we have, as always, the woman's emotional reaction. The landscape has become so overdetermined with emotional signposts that the personal reaction at the end seems almost unnecessary. We know what she feels like already, before we even hear her voice.

Wen Tingyun: *Spring Dawn Song*   春曉曲

The house overlooks the road where
    people come and go from Changxin Palace;   家臨長信往來道
In pairs the fledgling sparrows
    brush the misty grass.   乳燕雙雙拂烟草
The paper-canopied carriages ride lightly,
    their gold oxen are fat.   油壁車輕金犢肥
4 Dawn on the tasseled curtains,
    the spring cock cries early.   流蘇帳曉春雞早
The delicate bird in its cage
    still sleeping in the warmth;   籠中嬌鳥暖猶睡
Outside the curtain, the fallen flowers
    lie idly, unswept.   簾外落花閒不掃
One tree of withered peach
    nears the front pool—   衰桃一樹近前池
8 As if pitying the face of youth
    growing old in the mirror.   似惜紅顏鏡中老
    (*WFQ*, *j*. 3, p. 53)

1/ Changxin Palace refers to the palace in Luoyang where Lady Ban lived in loneliness. Compare Cui Hao's "Seventh Night Song" in Chapter 2. Wen uses elegant Han substitutions here, although he probably means merely to evoke images associated with abandoned ladies.

The poetic content is almost identical to Wang Yun's: an evocative description of spring is followed by mention of a woman's unhappiness. Some major differences, however, suggest a greater sophistication in the handling of poetic materials. Wen does not end with the expression of emotion through direct speech; he stays solely within the "objective," descriptive mode. He never produces any overt signs of the woman's presence, but is content to organize sensations in such a way as to suggest her feelings and actions. Because these phenomena take place around her, we would be justified in taking the entire poem as her poem, spoken in her voice; but unlike Wang Yun's poem, this is not a requirement for understanding the basic meaning.

Wen turns palace poetry's obsession with penetration into a more abstract organizational principle of inside/outside, much as he had done with "Retired Scholar Guo Strikes the Musical Bowls." At the very beginning, we learn that the woman's habitation faces a main street and from the description of noblewomen riding the streets in carriages pulled by gold-colored oxen, that she is aware of others' freedom to move about. As in a palace poem, we are drawn into her room; but once there, we are compelled to spend our time looking (like her) out of the window. The bird, of course, echoes her own imprisonment in the house, although (ironically) it sleeps contentedly while she has probably been up through the night and can now hear the earliest cockcrow. The peach tree clinches the poetic argument: as it leans over the pool, it catches sight of its own withered state, just as the lady may do in her own boudoir mirror. Wen's portrayal of the abandoned woman is expressed subtly from her own perspective; she no longer becomes a perceptual object that merely stimulates pity and desire.

In the longer erotic *yuefu* of Wen's, he shows a penchant for sophisticated poetic development that far surpasses most of the palace poets. In most of these works, Wen is not content with a mere evocation of beautiful surfaces; rather, palace poetry techniques and imagery may be used to comment on the dynamics of sexual relations. At times, Wen even becomes conscious of the role erotic poetry plays in social occasions.

A Night Banquet   夜宴謠

The long hairpins, a pair of dragonflies
   in her dangling locks;   長釵墜髮雙蜻蜓
Where the green fields end and hills slant,
   painted screens open.   碧盡山斜開畫屏
The curly-whiskered duke's son
   and guests of the five marquis   虬須公子五侯客
4 In one round down a thousand cups,
   like rain from the roof tiles.   一飲千鍾如建瓴
Phoenix-throated, the beauties sing—
   seamlessly, with perfection.   鶯咽姹唱圓無節
Brows contract—Xiang river mist—
   sleeves are whirling snow.   眉斂湘烟袖回雪

"In this clear night, kind feelings are shared by one and all;	清夜恩情四座同
8 So don't let the canal waters part, east and west."	莫令溝水東西別
Set upright, the candles weep, their scented beads wane.	亭亭蠟淚香珠殘
Dark dew and morning wind, gauze curtains chill.	暗露曉風羅幕寒
Imposing halberd banners flutter in ranks;	飄飄戟帶儼相次
12 Their twenty-four poles are dragon-bedecked.	二十四枝龍畫竿
Shrill pipes, flurried strings— a piece in symphony.	裂管縈弦共繁曲
Tiny ripples in scented goblets— drinkers toss off the spring brew.	芳罇細浪傾春醁
In the high rooms, guests disperse mid so many apricot blossoms.	高樓客散杏花多
16 With yearning, the new frog-moon stares down with amorous eyes.	脈脈新蟾如瞪目

(*WFQ, j.* 1, p. 4)

4/ *Jianling* are tiles with shallow depressions used to carry rainwater off the roof; they were delicately balanced to tip over when full and spill their contents. They make an apt comparison to the guests' tippling.

16/ A frog is said to live in the moon; here, its stare is *momo*, a term that describes the aspect of the eyes when wide open as well as the intense gazes that pass between lovers (or the flirtatious).

The social context of erotic poetry had changed by the Late Tang; such verse had come to belong not so much to aristocratic coteries as to musicians and singers of the demimonde and to the young literati who visited them.[20] In the southern courts, poets imitated *yuefu* themes or wrote *yongwu* for their own pleasure; in the Tang, poets wrote and dedicated poems to singing girls and listened as singing girls performed their own song lyrics. Dancers too became prime poetic subjects—sometimes praised for their art, sometimes evoked for their sensuality.[21] The seductive world of entertainment itself became a subject for poetic description; here, Wen's *yuefu* uses the language and content of palace poetry to portray the sort of scene where a new kind of erotic poetry might be written.

This is immediately apparent from the beginning; Wen plunges into a description of a woman in the very first line. Not only that, he depends on our familiarity with palace poetry to indicate to us that he is portraying a woman. Literally, the line reads, "Long hairpin, falling hair, a pair of dragonflies." If we know the conventions we know we have a line of erotic description; we know that the dragonflies are not literal insects, but the shape of the hairpin; and (perhaps most important) we may associate the falling hair with the disorder caused by the wild gestures of a dancer. Once again, a beautiful woman out of control.

But the poem is "out of control" as well, at least by palace-poetry standards. We have no proper context in which to view the woman; no elaborate descriptions build up her desirability or locate her within a series of allusions to previous beauties. There is no rhetorical introduction to the enumeration of her charms, and no attention is paid to her skill in womanly arts. Line two generates further confusion: convention tells us that a woman's painted eyebrows may be equated with spring hills. Yet here the mention of opening screens leaves us in doubt. If the hills are brows, are we being invited within the screen? Or are the hills painted on the screen itself? Or is the sentence telling us that the real hills outside can be seen after the screens are opened? The obfuscation of poetic attention breaks down the boundary between objects and people; the result is not a world in which a woman is a desired thing, the predominant object, but one in which she is only one interesting item that Wen wished to describe in evoking the atmosphere of the banquet. Wen's attention is not drawn just to evoking desire in his readers; the description of the woman is no longer the poem's central interest. Rather, the core of the poem lies elsewhere, in the dynamics of the social occasion itself. It begins in the middle of the banquet and progresses to the departure of the guests. But (as in the poems we examined in the last chapter) the stanzaic form breaks the portrayal of this progress into flashes of close observation. If a palace poem is a slow camera zoom, Wen's is a wild montage of images. We must examine the significance of each moment of vision to discover the progress of time.

After the evocation of the dancer's presence, we observe the observers, the scions of the great houses gathered for the banquet.[22] It is their introduction into the poem (in explanatory rather than descriptive terms) that locate us. They hardly show the tasteful restraint of the palace poets as they drink and revel in the performances of the entertainer and as they listen to an invitation from the singer. The very words that stimulate them are the sort of stock phrases placed in the mouths of palace poetry personae: the canal waters allude to Zhuo Wenjun's 卓文君 song of grief when she was abandoned by her husband, the Han poet Sima Xiangru 司馬相如 (179–117 B.C.).[23] The singer, like the palace poet, manipulates the sexual attraction of abandonment. Erotic mechanisms similar to those of palace poems are now visible within Wen's descriptive frame.

The third stanza uses another palace-poetry convention: contrasting the beauty of the woman with the power and wealth of her lover. But what those poets boasted of openly is only suggested by Wen's selective eye; gauze curtains turn by juxtaposition into the halberd banners of the guests' guards, possibly stationed outside the hall, so that we may sense the guests' wealth and power. This detail suggests the exclusivity of the banquet, which gradually breaks up, perhaps with the guests following various entertainers into their bedroom. But unlike most palace poets, Wen does not let us linger in a state of sexual anticipation; he does not provide us with a girl and an empty bed. Rather, he leaves us in the early morning chill, facing the amorous stare of the moon-toad.

It is not that Wen is consciously satirizing the methods of palace poetry and the expectations they produce. Rather, he understands the way they work and is fascinated by their effects and motives; even if his own techniques emphasize lush description (seen in his extensive use of palace poetry language), he is more concerned with using these techniques to explore other themes. "A Night Banquet" is not a particularly profound poem, but it lightly incorporates a classic and "serious" Chinese theme, the transitory nature of pleasure. In this, Wen employs the grand theme of "flourishing and fading" (*xingshuai* 興衰). The tragic implications of passing time is a motif Wen has ably adopted from Li He; as we shall see in the next chapter, he imitates Li in his use of it in grand historical poems.

In another long *yuefu*, Wen takes up the palace-poetry subgenre of *yongwu*, but unlike the earlier poets, he focuses poetic attention on a piece of clothing as it passes from woman to woman.

A Dancer's Robe 舞衣曲

Slender threads from lotus-roots
  sprout in the light spring; 藕腸纖縷抽輕春
They billow on the misty loom,
  and the lovely brows knit. 烟機漠漠嬌蛾嚬
The golden shuttle clicks,
  passes through the airy film; 金梭淅瀝透空薄
4 Sliced, the cloth drops from the scissors,
  a blown wisp of cloud. 翦落交刀吹斷雲

The Zhang family scion
  hears rain in the night, 張家公子夜聞雨
And facing Orchid Hall
  he broods on the dances of Chu. 夜向蘭堂思楚舞
Cicada robe and unicorn sash,
  Overcoming-Sorrow incense; 蟬衫麟帶壓愁香
8 The oriole is stolen,
  locked in golden threads. 偷得鶯簧鎖金縷

The pipes fill with orchid breath,
  their charming words grieve; 管含蘭氣嬌語悲
Snowy wrists on Tartar frets,
  mandarin duck silk. 胡槽雪腕鴛鴦絲
Strength of hibiscus ebbs,
  cannot settle; 芙蓉力弱應難定
12 Much wind in the willows,
  they cannot be still. 楊柳風多不自持

Her brow eases, she laughs and chats
  with the west window guest. 回嚬笑語西窗客
The stars are lonely and quiet,
  while the two gaze silently. 星斗寥寥波脈脈
It goes not with the King of Qin,
  rolled up on the ivory bed; 不逐秦王卷象牀
16 Bright moon fills the tower,
  peach-blossom white. 滿樓明月梨花白

(*WFQ*, *j*. 1, pp. 11–12)

8/ Substituting variant *xiao* 銷 for *suo* 鎖 gives "The oriole is stolen, melted into golden threads." I assume the oriole's song is meant here, although the bird may be a metaphor for the singer; see following discussion.

Here, Wen traces the career of a dancer's robe from its creation to its discarding. The poem is erotic because the robe is constantly near beautiful women; in this, Wen imitates a *yongwu* tradition of the palace poets, who would describe the bliss of a beautiful woman's possession, privileged to be near her always. Wen differs from them in his cinematic restlessness and in his curious detailing of the stages in the robe's existence. In so doing, he plays on a different group of conventions at each stage.

First, Wen uses the modal associations of women weaving at night: either the soldier's wife preparing winter clothes or the celestial Weaver Girl, who is allowed to meet the Herd Boy once a year on the seventh day of the seventh month. The knitted brows suggest both concentration and sorrow, and the lotus roots suggest a cloth fancifully made of threads (*si* 絲) of longing (*si* 思), and the lotus-root (*ou* 藕) a pun on the desire to pair (*ou* 耦). The robe's heavenly origins and its preternatural lightness are evoked by "airy film" and by "blown wisp of cloud." In this, it resembles the clothes worn by the woman in "The Reflection." Such a robe is suitable for the Goddess of Mount Wu as well, and the next stanza introduces associations with the southland. The scene shifts to an "Orchid Hall,"[24] and the Chu dances may refer to Lady Qi 戚, who danced as Emperor Gaozu sang, after he was forced by the machinations of Empress Lü 呂 to abandon his plan to appoint Lady Qi's son heir apparent. These allusions seem to cause melancholy and brooding for the "Zhang family scion" (a general term for a wealthy and powerful aristocrat), who listens to the rain, perhaps caused by the departing goddess; post-coital depression is suggested. The dance performance is meant to relieve his sadness, as is the perfume that scents the robe.

The robe has now passed from weaver to dancer; again, no one woman is picked out for exclusive association with it. Instead, Wen describes both the dancer and the female musicians, whose orchid breath fill their flutes and whose hands play over "mandarin duck silk [strings]"—thus evoking a connection between the silk of the robe and the silk of the instruments. The entrapment of the oriole in line eight metaphorically suggests the naturalness and musicality of the dancer; she is the oriole wrapped in the robe. Although the bird's song is not mentioned explicitly, a strange synaesthesia is suggested that reinforces the musical aspects of the robe already hinted at in the previous line. Moreover, a bird's entrapment by art may allude to Xiao Gang's quatrain "New Swallows" 新燕.

The new birds return with the season; 新禽應節歸
All fly to the flute tower. 俱向吹樓飛
They enter the curtain—startled by jangling bracelets; 入簾驚釧響
As they come in the window, they're blocked by dancers' robes. 來窗礙舞衣
    (*YTXY*, p. 510)

Art confused with nature: the force of music resonates with the elements. "Hibiscus" and "willow" in lines eleven and twelve may be the names of dancing girls; even if they are not, the dancer's motions are related to plants tossed by the wind. We can recognize this as part of the erotics of weakness in palace poetry; the dance may snare and entrap, but it also displays the vulnerability of the female, subject to male whims.

The first stanza showed the robe's creation; the second and third showed the robe in use. Now, as the party ends, the dancer chooses her lover from among the guests. Her laughter is a significant gesture: it dispels the frown of the weaving woman in the first stanza and the brooding of Zhang in the second. The robe came into being and operated in a world of desire and longing; now, seemingly, it has brought about the fulfillment of those desires and is no longer needed. Here, the Weaver Girl and Herd Boy are reincarnated as the two lovers. They look longingly at each other as the stars fade, and their gaze (*bo* 波 literally, "wave") replaces the waves of the Milky Way that originally separated the mythical pair. In line fifteen, reference is made to a *yuefu* title, "The King of Qin Wraps a Robe" 秦王卷衣. The *Yuefu shi ji* tells us that the original song described the King of Qin "rolling up a robe to give to the one he loves" (*YFSJ*, p. 1042); this is in keeping with the sole palace-poetry example of the theme (*YTXY*, p. 233). Here, Wen reverses the process of giving, but the line is ambiguous. It could be read as a conditional sentence, suggesting that the robe will be abandoned without being presented—"If she goes not with the King of Qin, it will be rolled upon the bed"—that is, either the guest turns down the dancer's advances or she turns down his. I interpret it to mean that the dancer has gone to bed with her guest and the robe has been removed and left behind in her room. As is typical with Wen, mood and possibility are present but not clear-cut narrative detail. The erotic connotations of bed and discarded robe are evident, as is the possibility of a sexual denouement. But, as in "A Night Banquet," Wen does not pursue the culmination of the erotic adventure; instead of showing us the woman without her robe, he shows us the robe without the woman—thus keeping faith with *yongwu* expectations, and frustrating palace poetry ones. He leaves us alone in the cold moonlight: human presence vanishes, as the robe's shifting roles in human relations end.

Once again, we see that Wen is fascinated by the potential of conventions to create meaning. At first, "A Dancer's Robe" may seem a random assemblage of images, a stream-of-consciousness game triggered by an object. But by organizing these images in a way that traces the career of the robe itself, Wen shows how the robe takes on different meanings, how it becomes a token in the exchange of poetic emotions. Deprived of these associations, it is nothing. Although "A Dancer's Robe" employs the palace-poetry language of sensuous surface, it moves away from the tradition of *yongwu* as embodiment of thing in language. In this, Wen prefigures the *yongwu* of Song *ci* writers like Jiang Kui 姜夔 (ca. 1155–1221), who drew attention to the emotional connotations an object implies rather than to the object itself.[25]

In yet another *yuefu*, Wen uses the old palace style to bridge the gap between his own times and the times when such poetry flourished. The results produce a complex situation in which the reader can use one beautiful surface to see beneath another.

Zhang Jingwan Gathers Lotus 張靜婉采蓮曲

Preface: Jingwan was a performer in the employ of Yang Kan. Her beauty was extraordinary. Kan wrote two lotus-gathering songs for her, but these original versions have disappeared from the body of *yuefu* that have survived. Hereby I make a song to await the attention of the "poem selectors." All the circumstances are recorded in the *Liang History*.[26]

Drooping tresses scented with orchid oil, 　a spring of red jade.	蘭膏墜髮紅玉春
Swallow hairpin rubs her nape, 　falls from her cloud-dish coiffure.	燕釵拖頸抛盤雲
West of the city, the willows 　face the gentle eve;	城西楊柳向嬌晚
4　And before the gate, rippling waves 　in the water of the canal.	門前溝水波粼粼

The unicorn prince, now 麒麟公子朝天客
　　a retainer at court,
Crosses the spring lanes, 珂馬瑲瑲度春陌
　　saddle-jades tinkling.
She is limp in his palm, 掌中無力舞衣輕
　　her dancer's robe light.
8　A trimmed piece of merman silk, 翦斷鮫綃破春碧
　　a broken piece of jade green.
Fluttering mist embracing the moon: 抱月飄烟一尺腰
　　her waist, one foot around;
Scent of musk-navel and dragon-marrow— 麝臍龍髓憐嬌饒
　　he loves her sweet charms.
Autumn silk brushes the water, 秋羅拂水碎光遶
　　shattered light trembles.
12　Dew heavy on the many flowers, 露重花多香不銷
　　their aroma does not melt away.
"Ducks in pairs call out, 鸂鶒交交塘水滿
　　pool water deep.
Green duckweed, golden seeds; 綠萍金粟蓮莖短
　　lotus stems short.
One night of west wind 一夜西風送雨來
　　brings in the rain;
16　Trace of powder grows haggard, 粉痕零落愁紅淺
　　my grieving red fades.
"From the prow I break off roots, 船頭折藕絲暗牽
　　but the threads secretly cling.
Lotus roots, lotus seeds 藕根蓮子相留連
　　still long for one another.
Your heart is like the moon, 郎心似月月易缺
　　so easy to wane.
20　Though on the fifteenth or sixteenth 十五十六清光圓
　　its bright light is round."
　　(*WFQ, j.* 1, pp. 12–14)

Preface/ "Poetry selection" (*cai shi* 採詩) was one of the ways the *Classic of Poetry* was supposedly compiled. It also refers to the method of folk song collection carried out by the Music Bureau of Han times. Here, of course, Wen is hinting that he is rounding out the corpus of *yuefu* that will be passed on to later generations. This may be a standard claim for literati poets writing *yuefu*, regardless of the moral content or subject matter. Liu Yuxi 劉禹錫 (772–849), for example, makes a similar assertion in his preface to "Gathering Water Chestnuts" 採菱行 (*QTS, j.* 356, p. 4007).

17–18/ Here we again have extensive use of the puns surrounding lotus that became common in the popular song quatrains of the fifth century. *Lian*—lotus flower—is a pun on "cherishing"; *ou*—lotus root—is a pun on "pairing." The threads of the lotus root, like the blossoms on willow trees, are *si*, "longing."

19/ A variant text has *wei* 未 for *yi* 易: "Your heart, like the full moon, has not yet waned." The suggestion is that his passion will eventually cool.

Wen's ostensible motives for writing are made clear in the preface. He suggests that in his own age a full understanding of individuals from the past has become impossible because of the loss of the texts in which they expressed themselves. Just as Yang Kan 羊侃 and his concubine perished long ago, so the songs that he wrote to ornament her skills have been lost as well. And yet Wen is hardly content to reproduce Yang Kan's own verses. Yang wrote poems *for* Zhang Jingwan, or so Wen claimed, and the *Yuefu shi ji* contains a series of lotus-gathering poems, some exclusively third-person, some with a female persona.[27] We can guess what Yang's poems would have been like; Jingwan would have sung them back to Yang, would have told him how much she loved him, and how she thought of him when she was out in her boat gathering lotus. It is doubtful that we would have found anything distinctive or special in them. If Wen in turn kept his poem in Jingwan's voice, he would merely be repeating the sexual game most palace poems play, and the motives for their writing would have become alarmingly transparent. Instead, Wen writes a poem *about* Jingwan and thus attempts to visualize the woman that Yang desired and wrote songs for; this in turn reveals the relations between Yang and his dancer, who become in themselves the poetic subject of *Wen's* poem. As a consequence, Wen lets us understand the context for a subjective response on the part of one of his characters—a lotus-gathering song has become not just an ornament for a dancer's performance but a demonstration of spontaneous self-expression, trapped within Wen's supposedly distanced frame.

The poem itself exhibits all the traits of Wen's difficult style: the montage-like shifts of perspective, the subtle allusions, the juxtapositions of images whose relationships to each other are initially unclear. A close reading exposes the poetic depths beneath the dazzling surface. As in "A Night Banquet," Wen begins with a syntactically dense description of a woman's features and her disordered hair. He places this against a sketch of a spring evening, with drooping willows leaning over a canal. "A spring of red jade" refers to Jingwan's face (the light pink of her cheeks accentuating the translucent white of her complexion); it explicitly relates her own youth to the season. As in "A Night Banquet," Wen moves away from the woman rather than toward her; he wants to show that she is the object not of our desire but of someone else's. In the second stanza, he consequently turns to the arrival of Jingwan's lover, who can only be Yang Kan. He too is conventionally described as the young aristocratic bravo whose power and wealth deserve a woman of great beauty.

At this point, we may pause and wonder what Jingwan is doing when her lover arrives. An ordinary poetic treatment of the theme would place her in a boat, gathering lotus. However, women go lotus gathering on pools and streams, not on the canals of the city, and the initial line suggests that she is dancing. Wen breaks with conventional lotus-song expectations and gives us Jingwan performing; meanwhile, we look out on the spring day and notice Yang's sudden appearance. Wen is thus prefacing the lotus-gathering scene with another one, in which Yang and Jingwan play the important roles.

As Jingwan finishes her performance, she turns to embrace Yang; lines seven and eight suggest the end of the dance. Line seven is a reference to one of the few things we know about the historical Jingwan: she was so extraordinarily slender she could dance on the palm of a hand, like the great Han dancer Zhao Feiyan. Here, we may imagine her exhaustion after the dance, as she falls into Yang's arms. And yet the juxtaposition of images in line eight suggest the lotus-boat theme: merman's silk is a common term of praise for the cloth of fine dancer's robes, but the merman's association with the water, combined with the image of a blade parting smooth silk (*bi* 碧, "jade-green," is often a poetic substitution for spring water), hints at the prow of a boat cleaving the flow of a stream. Perhaps the poem's opening is Jingwan remembering past times with her lover, and the undulating water-surface as she gathers lotus adds metaphorical detail to her daydreams. In that case, the parting of the water has an erotic resonance.

In the third stanza, the split between boudoir scene and river scene continues. Line nine is syntactically dense and obscure; it suggests, subtly, that her dancer's robe embraces her as the mists do the moon—not unreasonable, considering the frequent comparison of beautiful women to the moon. Palace poetry emphasizes the erotic associations of items that come in contact with the body, a contact that can serve as a replacement for human touch. Here the future embraces of Zhang himself are suggested. At this moment—when dance begins to merge imperceptibly with implied sexual dalliance—the metaphorical fog begins to clear. Silk brushes the water: a clear reference to her trailing sleeves as she leans over the edge of the boat. Although light still remains, the dew indicates that it is getting late. The scent lingers on the lotus in spite of the hour, but its placement here links the flower scent with the perfumed woman two lines earlier.

With the stabilization of the poetic scene, the poem shifts drastically. Line thirteen sounds like the opening line for one of Wen's shorter *yuefu*[28] or, for that matter, of a short lotus-gathering poem of the Six Dynasties. From here, conventional images abound: the pairs of ducks (longed-for conjugal fidelity), a reflection in the water that reveals signs of grief and aging, the lotus itself with all its punning associations, and the direct plea to the lover at the end. Because the last two stanzas bear such a strong resemblance to short, simple lotus-gathering songs, I have chosen to interpret all eight lines as the actual words of Jingwan (although only the last two lines have to be). I think it not unlikely that we are meant to read them as Jingwan's actual song, the song Wen has written for her to replace her master's. Regardless of how we interpret them, however, they bear a particularly strong emotional weight, following as they do the erotic scene preceding them. They make it even more likely that the boudoir scene occurs in Jingwan's memory as she goes lotus gathering, and the memory becomes the secret cause for her song of lament. By providing a context, Wen thus tries to grant the conventions of palace poetry a greater authenticity: he creates a situation in which we can see the clear emotional motivation for Jingwan's song.

What possible motive may he have for this elaborate process? In the long run, his creation of context and song is not a more authentic portrayal of a woman's psychological condition than Yang Kan's would have been—it is still too thoroughly governed by the conventions of the genre. Moreover, Wen still usurps the woman's will and voice at the end, as a palace poet would do. I would suggest, however, that his motives are more complex than a palace poet's and are governed more by nostalgia than by passion. Yang and Wen desire different things; the former supposedly desired Jingwan, and in the palace poetry manner he would have transferred that desire to Jingwan by writing a lotus-gathering song similar to the one in Wen's final two verses. Wen, for his part, longs for an entire age, that of the Six Dynasties, and part of his romanticization of that age necessitates covering over the acts of power and desire that underlie the writing of palace poetry, which he understands only too well. Thus, he fictionally recreates an authentic affair between Yang and Jingwan, even though his sources do not suggest such a relationship; then he shows Jingwan's "authentic" emotional response (*qing*) to the affair and to the scene (*jing*) while he attempts to remain aesthetically distanced. However, his desire for a bygone age is as evident as the palace poet's desire for the lady he describes in connoisseur's terms.

If these long *yuefu* of Wen's have anything in common beyond their shared referential and linguistic heritage in the late Six Dynasties period, it is their intense self-consciousness as commentaries on erotic conventions. Wen no longer belonged to an unbroken tradition of palace-poetry writing; although he could use palace-poetry conventions to evoke associations of the erotic, he must have felt that the genre had lost its power to stimulate or interest. He *could*, however, use palace-poetry language as a tool for exploring erotic themes. In some poems, he is a philosophical observer of the erotic, as in "A Night Banquet" and "A Dancer's Robe"; in "Zhang Jingwan Gathers Lotus," however, the old sexual tropes regain their power to evoke desire when they become animated with nostalgia for a romanticized past. The romance of the past can drive other poems of Wen's as well, and they will serve as the subject for the next chapter.

FOUR

Patterns of History, Failures of History

MOST EDUCATED CHINESE men, products as they were of a Confucian educational system, saw themselves as public figures, concerned with the well-being of nation and empire. To them, history was an essential (perhaps *the* essential) tool for a public career. To make sense of history was to make sense of one's life—to discover where one was and where one was going, and what kind of decisions were morally correct and efficacious. This role of history emerges not only in philosophical writings but also in literary ones. Poets usually discussed history in two "classic" subgenres, both of them highly moral and self-expressive in intent: the personal response to the ancient site (*huaigu* 懷古) and the moral and political evaluation of events (*yongshi* 詠史).

A poet of the High Tang—and unlike later writers, poets of the High Tang still had confidence in history—if asked for a list of notable historical figures in his poetry, would add moral notations that indicated the traditional Chinese judgments of each figure. Such a list would include both political giants and writers; for a poet, his literary predecessors were not just authors of texts to be studied but significant models for his own life.

After noting the largely legendary figures from the Confucian classics, our poet would begin with protagonists of the Warring States period; in particular, he might pay attention to the struggles between the southeastern states of Wu 吳 and Yue 越. After Yue had lost a war to Wu, Gou Jian 句踐, the king of Yue, vowed to destroy his enemy forever. He accomplished his plan by obtaining a beautiful peasant girl, Xi Shi 西施; he taught her the graceful arts and then sent her as a gift to his enemy. The king of Wu was so taken with her looks that he neglected his duties; the destruction of his kingdom was the inevitable result. The significance of these events for the morally conscious poet was obvious: to indulge in fleshly pleasures at the expense of social obligations brings disaster.

Our poet would then move on to the Qin and Han Dynasties. The first Qin emperor, Qin Shihuang 秦始皇 (r. 221–209 B.C.) would be cited for his hubris and ambition. His military adventures and his vast public works projects in particular would be mentioned as examples of how he brought suffering to the common people, and of course such faults would be used to explain the rapid disintegration of his empire after his death. Next would be the battling heroes, Xiang Yu 項羽 (233–202 B.C.) and Liu Bang 劉邦 (247–195 B.C.), who contested the control of China after the Qin. The former's military skills and generosity would be used to counterbalance his hasty temperament and his cruelty; and the latter would be praised as worthy of founding the Han because of his savvy ability to use good men to govern his domain, in spite of his coarseness and thickheadedness.

Our poet's list would include many subsequent Han emperors: Emperor Wen 文 (r. 179–156 B.C.) would be praised mainly for his evenhandedness and laissez-faire attitudes toward governing. However, his most notable successor, Wu 武 (r. 140–86 B.C.), would attain particular notoriety in poetry for many of the same reasons that the first Qin emperor did: he was set on expanding the empire's borders and in the process squandered the empire's wealth. Nonetheless, his fascination with the supernatural and with the cult of immortality made him a center for many legends that would add color to historical poetry—he was a fascinating figure, in spite of his many flaws. On the literary level, many of Wu's unsavory traits could be transferred to the most significant poet of his reign, Sima Xiangru 司馬相如 (179–117 B.C.), the flamboyant romantic court writer who eloped with his future wife and who praised Wu's excesses in extravagant language. After Wu, Emperor Cheng 成 (r. 32–6 B.C.) would be remembered primarily for his luxurious excesses, particularly his patronage of one of the more famous Chinese femmes fatales, Zhao Feiyan 趙飛燕.

The next period to attract our poet's attention would be the event-filled third century A.D.; although bemoaning the decadence of the late Han rulers, he would pay attention in particular to two charismatic leaders of the subsequent Three Kingdoms period: the founder of the Wei 魏 Dynasty, Cao Cao 曹操 (155–220), and the great strategist of the kingdom of Shu 蜀, Zhuge Liang 諸隔亮 (184–234). Although Cao was not yet the stock villain he was to become in later dynasties, the attitudes of Tang poets toward him were highly ambivalent: they would point to his imperial hubris and see its consequences in the naval battle of Red Cliff 赤壁, when Cao failed disastrously in his attempt to conquer the Yangzi delta kingdom of Wu; yet they would admire his earnest desire to patronize great literary and intellectual figures of his time, in particular the circle of writers later known as the Seven Masters of the Jian'an Era (196–220) 建安七子. Zhuge, on the other hand, had yet to be canonized in the Confucian pantheon, but he was already an exemplar of the noble and upright minister who serves his lord even when he knows that his cause is doomed. After his first patron, Liu Bei 劉備 (162–223), had died, he did his best to aid Liu's incompetent successor and died during an attempt to defend Shu against the more powerful Wei.

Next, our poet would focus on the great Wei Dynasty intellectuals: first, the doomed prince-poet Cao Zhi 曹植 (199–232), who suffered from the jealousy of his brother Cao Pi 曹丕 (Emperor Wen 文, r. 220–26) and was driven to an untimely death a few years later; second, and, more important, the group of wild dilettantes generally known as the Seven Sages of the Bamboo Grove 竹林七賢. Our poet might criticize the Sages for their unconventional attitudes and their egotistical vices, but he would also see their behavior as an embodiment of a classic literati dilemma: what is the proper way to behave under a tyrannical and unjust government.

Our poet would perhaps have little positive to say about the major figures of the subsequent Six Dynasties period; he would decry the decadence of the imperial courts, the violence of their Machiavellian plotting, and the attenuation of Chinese literary values that culminated in the much-scorned palace style of the sixth century (even though stylistic developments during this time made Tang poetry possible). He would still create a hierarchy of praiseworthy figures from the period, however: the reclusive Tao Qian 陶潛 (365–427), who was largely unrecognized as a great poet during his life; the landscape poet Xie Lingyun 謝靈運 (385–443), although his reputation started to fall well behind Tao's during the eighth century; and Xiao Tong 蕭統 (501–31), the crown prince of the Liang, whose *Wen xuan* 文選 anthology served as a summation of all that was worthwhile in the previous literary tradition.

These notables were not just the main representatives of the Chinese past; they had the same power over a Tang poet as the Greek heroes did over the Athenian dramatists. To live with history and with famous men as intimately as the Chinese literatus did is not simply to understand their importance—it is to feel them deeply, to respond to them emotionally and at times irrationally. History held as strong a power to move him as religious or sexual themes do the Western writer. For this very reason, if history is a tool, a guide for the just life, it may also occasionally happen that its importance and meaning are questioned; its lessons may seem confusing, contradictory, maddeningly amoral, or simply useless. In such circumstances, the literatus (and the poet) will suffer a crisis of belief in history's significance—a crisis as potentially devastating as a Western failure to believe in God: he cannot turn away from history's all-pervasive presence, but he can no longer trust that its truths are self-evident.

A painful historical skepticism did in fact emerge in the ninth century, partially because the polity itself (the focus for history's significance) was increasingly beset by internal and external crises, and partially because the literate classes (those who knew how to use history as a tool for ruling) had become more and more anxious about the preservation of their beliefs and their very lives. Historical poetry from this period has a tone different from that of all other ages.

These changes in historical poetry can be evaluated in part by noting the gradual change in the use of allusion (*diangu* 點古). Our High Tang poet would not have expressed his attitudes toward past figures as coherently as I have done; rather, he would rely on readers' shared attitudes and make mere passing mention of these historical figures, knowing that they would understand the reference's significance. When Tang society was more confident of its traditions, the allusion was an index to moral meaning. Since every educated reader knew the story, the role of the allusion in the poetic argument, not its potential for telling a story or for creating an aesthetically pleasing scene or pattern, made it significant. However, when the ability of history to instruct and remind the reader of his place in the social and historical order came into question during the Mid- and Late Tang, the amoral, aesthetic qualities of historical anecdote often came to the fore. The beautiful gesture or grand scene attracted the poet, and the poem he wrote occasionally came close to a fictional recreation of the past. Moreover, the gradual undermining of the view that events had ethical meanings allowed the poet the freedom to play with causality, irony, and hypothetical situations: he attempted to rewrite not only the traditional judgments but the very sequence of events themselves. Yet another possibility existed as well: the private character of historical actors at times seduced the poet into a private, small-scale examination of psychological motives, divorced from bigger issues. As we will see, all these approaches emerged as Late Tang poets played out their increasing skepticism toward the world order, and these trends affected Wen's historical verse as well.

Developments in Historical Poetry: Fictionality and Skepticism

The breakdown in the moral reading of history may be observed in two literary events: the evolution of an "historical song" subgenre, practiced mostly by Li Bai, Li He, and Wen Tingyun, and the emergence of a *huaigu* poetry largely divorced from moral sincerity and belief and increasingly preoccupied with artistic manipulation. Both of these trends evolved out of the increasing "fictionality" of poetry during the eighth and ninth centuries.

Whereas the "creation" of imaginary worlds (in imitation of a divine creator) has been an essential paradigm for Western poets, the Chinese have tended to define poetry as lived experience.[1] I touched on the implications in the last chapter, when I suggested that later critics regarded the Liang dynasty transformation of *yuefu* from folk song to artifice as "inauthentic." Even in the obviously fictional *yuefu* of the High Tang, the assumption often remained that the fictional persona was a transparent "mask" for the poet's true feelings and concerns. Almost completely absent is the detailed imaginative creation of scene that we can see in Western lyrical and narrative verse.

To create order out of historical events, however, historians have had to develop a fictional imagination when writing history. One has only to survey the rich literature of historical narrative beginning with the *Zuo zhuan* 左傳 and the *Shi ji* 史記 to see that Chinese fiction has its roots in such works. In poetry, of course, with its emphasis on lyrical expression at the expense of factual description, narrative would be less likely to develop. Still, if we are to find any tendency in poetry to create imagined scenes, the use of historical themes is an important starting point.

Perhaps the beginning of fictional scenic tendencies in Tang poetry can be traced to the long seven-character songs popular during the reign of Empress Wu 武 (r. 690–705). The authors of these particular works, however, were interested less in evoking a unique sense of place than in creating a mood, often for moral purposes, that helped bring home the message of the poem. As an example, we may briefly look at Lu Zhaolin's 盧照鄰 (ca. 634–ca. 684) "Thoughts of Old on Chang'an" 長安古意, clearly part of the "capital poem" tradition of seven-character songs that Stephen Owen has described.[2] Much of the poem attempts to realize vividly the scenes of Han Dynasty Chang'an, and in several places the description surpasses anything written previously.

Chang'an's broad avenues link up with narrow lanes,	長安大道連狹斜
There black oxen and white horses, coaches of fragrant woods,	青牛白馬七香車
Jade-fit palanquins go left and right past the mansions of lords,	玉輦縱橫過主第
Gold riding whips in a long train move toward barons' homes.	金鞭絡繹向侯家
Dragons bite jeweled canopies, catching the morning sun,	龍銜寶蓋承朝日
The phoenix disgorges dazzling fringes, draped with evening's red clouds.	鳳吐流蘇帶晚霞
A hundred yards of gossamer strands strain to enwrap the trees. (ll. 1–7)	百丈游絲爭繞樹

Lu's poem, however, lacks the coherence of a poetic self creating narrative objectively; nor does it possess a unity based on the coherent use of characteristic symbols (the method employed by Li He and Wen Tingyun in their longer *yuefu*). Rather, it links units through the operation of associative conventions. For example, at the end of the lush opening section of natural description is the line:

| While a single graceful flock of birds join their cries among flowers. (l. 8) | 一羣嬌鳥共啼花 |

The next line, which commences a section describing the imperial palace, begins with the last two characters of the previous line:

| Cries among flowers, playful butterflies, by the palace's thousand gates. (l. 9) | 啼花戲蝶千門側 |

Techniques such as these allow Lu to shift directions in a long poem without destroying continuity. Such shifts can be enigmatic. In early *yuefu* and in the Nineteen Old Poems, such shifts may have resulted from formulaic composition, in which the use of a certain image led to the treatment of a certain theme.[3] In more artful poets, however, the shifts may be a deliberate "archaization," an attempt to capture the feel of the earlier, more "authentic" poetry. Basing structure on such shifts, however, undermines the possibility of creating coherent narrative; the images do not tell a story.

Also evident in Lu's poem is a tone of moral remonstrance he inherited from the *huaigu* tradition. After describing the bustle and splendor of Chang'an, for example, Lu comments on the loneliness and isolation that are corollaries of such magnificence.[4]

| But those you gaze on before great buildings are those you do not know, | 樓前相望不相知 |
| And those you meet upon the paths, no acquaintances of yours. (ll. 15–16) | 陌上相逢詎相識 |

And in the last six lines of the poem, in which he describes Yang Xiong 揚雄 (53 B.C.–A.D. 18), his ideal scholar, Lu's moral disapproval of Han Dynasty Chang'an becomes clearer.

Where once were the golden stairs, the halls of white marble,	昔時金階白玉堂
We now see only the green pines remaining.	即今唯見青松在
Silent there in the emptiness, the dwelling of Yang Xiong,	寂寂寥寥揚子居
Year after year, every year, his whole bed covered with books.	年年歲歲一牀書

Alone are the cassia flowers,   獨有南山桂花發
 blooming on South Mountain,
They fly back and forth,   飛來飛去襲人裾
 fly into his sleeves. (ll. 63–68)

Here the language achieves the transparency and simplicity characteristic of the High Tang: the fusion of Lu's emotions and the scene becomes explicit. Whereas the other inhabitants of the city are portrayed in a lush language of surface, Yang Xiong's main emblems are the bed covered with books (an image of intellectual depth, of a mind turned away from appearances and ordinary human needs) and the cassia and pine, hardy plants that endure the cold. Exterior obscurity is exchanged for the interior enigma of personality, and the poem ends on a tone often found in *ganhuai* 感懷, the subgenre used for the expression of lofty moral sentiment. However, even though Lu's introduction of Yang makes his ethical stance explicit, criticism of society had been present throughout the poem in the choice of *yuefu* conventions and implicit moral judgment; as a result, Han Chang'an becomes Tang Chang'an, and Lu speaks as the frustrated official whose good advice is not heeded. In short, Lu sacrifices narrative to personal self-expression. This use of the past to voice opinions on personal, present-day issues is typical of the Chinese tradition until the eighth and ninth centuries.

The most prominent early experiments with true fictionality occur in the works of Li Bai, especially in his songs that describe historical events or dream journeys.[5] His influences here often come from the allegorical intent of poems like the *Li sao* 離騷 and Ruan Ji's 阮籍 (210–63) *Yong huai* 詠懷, but Li Bai pays greater attention to evoking the scenery itself rather than to developing hints of a universally significant meaning beyond the text. Nonetheless, the poet's character and personality are still the dominating force in these poems, because he is very much interested in showing us the flamboyant artistic consciousness behind the lines. Our admiration is meant to shift from the fabulous scene to the poet who has created it. One typical historical poem (an interesting transition from *huaigu* to fictional recreation of history) is an apt example of imagination combined with self-expression; here his subjects (Xiang Yu and Liu Bang) are introduced for their "picturesqueness" as well as for their usefulness in allowing Li Bai to indulge in some typical posturing.

Meditation on the Past: Ascending the   登廣武古戰場懷古
Old Battlefield at Guangwu Mountain

    The deer of Qin fled through the country grass;   秦鹿奔野草
    Those who pursued it were like flying tumbleweeds.   逐之若飛蓬
    The might of Xiang Yu shadowed the world,   項王氣蓋世
4 Purplish lightning darted from his eyes.   紫電明雙瞳
    He called to him eight thousand men,   呼吸八千人
    Marched through Jiangdong, rousing it.   橫行起江東
    But the Red Essence had beheaded the White Emperor—   赤精斬白帝
8 So with a cry of rage Xiang entered the Pass.   叱咤入關中
    Paired dragons cannot leap forth together;   兩龍不並躍
    The five planets appeared together in the sky.   五緯與天同
    Chu was destroyed—for it had no fine schemes;   楚滅無英圖
12 Han flourished—for it had merit well earned.   漢興有成功
    Stroking his sword, Gaozu cleared out the world,   按劍清八極
    Then, returning, he drunkenly sang "Great Wind."   歸酣歌大風
    Earlier, when the two foes came to Guangwu Slope,   伊昔臨廣武
16 Their abutting armies were to decide loser and victor.   連兵決雌雄
    "Send me a cup of the stew—   分我一杯羹
    My Venerable Sire is your dad too—"   太皇乃汝翁
    Old ruins of the battle on the fields,   戰爭有古迹
20 The fallen breastworks now form uneven barrows.   壁壘頹層穹
    Fierce tigers roar in caves and ravines,   猛虎嘯洞壑
    Starving eagles cry in the autumn sky.   饑鷹鳴秋空
    Soaring clouds in ranks, like troops in dawn formation,   翔雲列曉陣
24 An aura of killing spreads to the rainbow in its rage.   殺氣赫長虹
    To uproot rebellion is the task of heroes and sages;   拔亂屬豪聖
    How could some crude pedant fathom it?   俗儒安可通
    Poet Ruan, deep in his cups, cried out "children!"   沈湎呼豎子
28 But his wild speeches were hardly fair.   狂言非至公
    I clap my hands here by a bend in the Yellow River—   撫掌黃河曲
    How foolish was that Ruan Ji!   嗤嗤阮嗣宗
        (*QTS*, *j*. 180, p. 1840)

    Title/ When Liu Bang (Han Gaozu) and Xiang Yu were struggling for control of the empire, both their armies camped near Guangwu Mountain. Although Li Bai calls this a "battlefield," no battle actually took place there. Xiang Yu challenged Liu Bang several times to individual combat, but each time Liu refused. Finally Xiang managed to wound Liu in the foot with an arrow, whereupon the latter's army withdrew. Most of Li Bai's allusions here come from the biographies of the two antagonists in the *Shi ji*.[6]

    1/ Kuai Tong 蒯通, an advisor to the early Han general Han Xin 韓信, explained to his master the scramble for power that followed the fall of the Qin

Dynasty: "The web of Qin's government had rotted away and the strands of rule had gone slack.... The empire slipped from the house of Qin like a fleeing deer and all the world joined in its pursuit. As it happened, he with the tallest stature and swiftest feet seized it first."[7] Li Bai uses the image here to describe the scramble for power among the rebels.

3/ An allusion to the song Xiang Yu composed when he realized defeat was inevitable:

> My strength plucked up the hills,
> My might shadowed the world;
> But the times were against me,
> And Dapple runs no more.[8]

7/ A famous account in the *Shi ji* biography of Liu Bang describes how early in his career he beheaded a large white snake that embodied the fortunes of the Qin dynasty. The Han dynasty's representative color was red.

8/ Although Liu Bang was technically subordinate to Xiang Yu, he managed to reach the Qin heartland ("the land within the pass") before him. Xiang was furious, and thereafter the two were enemies. The general gist of this passage is that although Xiang had raised a mighty army, Liu Bang's fortunes were already on the ascendant.

10/ It was believed that at the time Liu Bang entered the Pass, all the five planets (lit., the "Five Wefts") were located in the constellation of the Eastern Well (Gemini). This was an auspicious sign of Liu's rise to power.

11–12/ It was commonly argued that although Xiang Yu was a braver and better commander than Liu Bang, his arrogance and inability to treat his advisors well led to his downfall; Liu Bang, though coarse and often thick-witted, knew how to employ good ministers.

14/ A song composed by Han Gaozu, expressing his ambitions as emperor and telling of his desire to employ talented men at his court.

17–18/ At the time the two armies met at Guangwu, Xiang Yu was holding Liu Bang's father hostage. At one point, he let it be known that unless Liu surrendered, he would boil Liu's father alive. Liu Bang replied that since he and Xiang had sworn brotherhood, such an act would be tantamount to patricide—and asked Xiang Yu to share a cup of his father's broth with him. Though a monstrously unfilial act, Liu Bang's words have been seen as proof that his dedication to winning the empire was such that he would put public values above private ones; the daring and cleverness of his reply also convinced Xiang not to follow through with his threat.

27–28/ When Ruan Ji visited Guangwu, he is said to have claimed, "The age has no heroes [compared to that of Liu and Xiang]; it's left to children to earn fame."[9]

One of the most distinctive aspects of Li Bai's historical poetry is the way he uses allusions. Unlike previous Chinese poets, he does not make reference to past actions as a guideline for moral judgments. Rather, he is impressed by the pure anecdotal gesture—Liu Bang's beheading of the white snake or the bravado of his taunting of Xiang Yu despite the imminent threat to his father. Because of this love of gesture, Li seeks out ways to make past scenes more vivid. Although the "deer of Qin" is a common trope for the struggle for imperial power, by placing it at the beginning he brings a new energy to the image: the ambitious power-seekers scrambling in their wild pursuit. Lightning darts from Xiang Yu's eyes, and he rushes through the pass in a rage. The direct, two-line quotation of Liu Bang's challenge to Xiang Yu is vivid as well: by placing it within the poem without framing comment, Li underscores the drama of the moment.

This particular poem is still far from recreating the fictional scene of the confrontation, however. There is little chronological coherence from line to line, and Li actually backtracks, giving a general history of the struggle before focusing on the camp at Guangwu. After just a few lines on the confrontation of the two armies, he makes a standard *huaigu* gesture and describes the echoes of the ancient battle in present natural phenomena. At the end, we realize why Li Bai has written this poem: he does not intend to explore the meaning of history, nor does he intend the more radical act of evoking an imaginative scene out of the past. Rather, he identifies his own spirit and personality with those of Liu Bang and Xiang Yu; he asserts that Ruan Ji was a fool for believing that great men could no longer be produced. Li's ego once again takes center stage.

Nonetheless, Li Bai's ability to focus on a vivid detail was the seed from which the historical song would grow. He himself came very close to writing fully imagined scenes, although usually on a small scale, as one of his more famous *yuefu*, the "Song of Roosting Crows" 烏棲曲, proves.

On Gusu Terrace, 　　when crows come to roost,	姑蘇臺上烏棲時
Within the King of Wu's palace 　　a drunken Xi Shi.	吳王宮裏醉西施
Songs of Wu, dances of Chu— 　　before their pleasures cease,	吳歌楚舞歡未畢
4　The green mountains are about to swallow 　　a half-hidden sun.	青山欽銜半邊日

When the water clock's golden vase has filled with water,	銀箭金壺漏水多
They rise to watch the autumn moon sink on Yangtze's waves.	起看秋月墜江波
When it rises again, gradually, in the east where then will be their joy?	東方漸高奈樂何

(*QTS*, *j*. 162, p. 1682)

The subject is a potentially moral one; because of the King of Wu's love of the beauty Xi Shi (whom he feted at Gusu), he lost his kingdom to Yue. But in spite of the tragic, possibly moral inquiry at the end, Li Bai avoids making this a true *yongshi*. He fails to meditate on the deeper meanings of history; instead, he portrays vividly the King of Wu and Xi Shi at one point in time (a carousal that lasts all night). More significantly, he keeps his own persona out of sight.

"Song of Roosting Crows" marks the invention of a new subgenre of Chinese poetry, the "historical song." It did not make a major mark in the works of Li Bai's immediate successors, however, perhaps because the fictionalization of history was morally questionable in poetry or simply because few later poets possessed Li's imaginative gifts. In the ninth century, however, when fantasy and aesthetic manipulation were less disparaged, the historical song came into its own, mostly through the efforts of Li He and Wen Tingyun.

The dominating presence of the poetic self is less present in the historical songs of Li and Wen. In Late Tang authors, the hypersensitive emphasis on fragmented imagery and the actualization of a subjective vision paradoxically creates a more "depersonalized" poetic universe, one that depends entirely on the idiosyncratic thought processes of a poet but avoids directly introducing the poet, his outlook, and his opinions. We have already noted this to a certain extent in Wen's poem to the musician Guo (see Chapter 2); in historical themes, the associative universe created by such poems becomes instead an imaginative recreation of past events.

Some of Li He's most famous poems, such as "The King of Qin Drinks Wine" 秦王飲酒, "Lord, Don't Dance" 公莫舞歌, and "The Bronze Immortal Takes Leave of the Han" 金銅仙人辭漢歌, fall within the realm of historical song.[10] "The Terrace of Liang" (see Chapter 2) provides a stunningly clear portrayal of the carousals of the ancient prince—a portrayal that carries Li Bai's earlier imaginings one step closer to a fully fictional scene.

> He struck the bells, drank his wine,
>   shot his arrows at heaven.
> Gold tigers on his creased robe
>   were spitting bloody spots.
> Dawn after dawn, dusk after dusk,
>   he lamented the churning seas,
> So with a long robe he tied down the sun
>   and took pleasure in the year.

As I noted in Chapter 2, Li He was able to exploit the aesthetics of the popular quatrain to emphasize the passing of time and to fragment the scene and thus suppress an explicit "I" in the poem. The poet is still present in these songs, but he surfaces only through the selection of images; here the images are not simply *yuefu* tropes, as in Lu Zhaolin's poem on the capital, but a vivid focusing on unusual objects and gestures. Overall, Li He's musical style was ideal as a springboard for fictional recreation, in which moralistic judgments on historical events are either absent or subdued, and in which the beauty of visualization becomes the focus and purpose of the poem.

The development of the historical song subgenre is, however, only part of a major change in Tang poets' conception of history. This change is reflected most clearly in their use of the two generally acknowledged subgenres of *shi* that dealt with history, the *huaigu*, or "meditation on the past," and the *yongshi*, or "poem on history."

Although Chinese critics and poets have used these terms somewhat freely without articulating the precise difference between the subgenres, we may for the sake of clarification specify their general direction in earlier poetic practice. The *huaigu* required a description of a specific place as it appeared to the poet in his own age, most often an abandoned and decayed site; the poet was usually assumed to be present at the site at the time of composition. He often visualized the site in former times (especially if it was a palace or city) and contrasted the glory of that time with the ruins of the present. Moral judgment on historical actors was usually explicitly evident; in any event, the reader often saw such judgments in the poet's distinctive observations on events. The reader also expected the poet to be strongly moved by the ruins and to meditate on the merciless forces of time and on the tragedies of his own existence as a human actor in the universe. Although many Tang *huaigu* are written in "song" form (for examples, see Gao Shi's "Old Daliang" in Chapter 2 and Lu Zhaolin's poem on Chang'an above), the standard for the subgenre was a regulated verse in which the poet told of his arrival at the site in the first lines, contrasted past glory with present scene in the middle couplets, and expressed an emotional reaction in the last couplet.[11]

The *yongshi* does not require the fusion of scene and emotion characteristic of the *huaigu*. Rather, the poet makes an intellectual evaluation of historical events and characters that have impressed him as worthy of notice. Such poems are often strongly didactic, digressive, or even philosophical in content and may even resemble the biographical "judgments" found in the dynastic histories. Generally speaking, both historical subgenres demand that we take the forces of history seriously, that we see ourselves collectively as historical beings molded and influenced by past events and subject to the continuing process of flourish and decay.[12]

As several major Mid- and Late Tang poets became increasingly interested in history as subject matter for verse, new developments complicated the meaning of history in such verse; their work displays an increasing awareness that the vivid description of dramatic events can effectively intensify the artistic effect of the poet's statement. We have already noted the imaginative scenes in Li He's works; other poets, even in their regulated verse, might conjure up a brief scene from the past, if only for the length of a couplet.[13] For example, in Liu Yuxi's famous "Meditation on the Past: Western Pass Mountain" 西塞山懷古 (*QTS*, *j*. 359, p. 4058), he describes the Western Jin commander Wang Jun's 王濬 naval invasion of the state of Wu in 280. Wang sent ships to break the chains the Wu defense forces had flung across the Yangzi river; he then forced the surrender of Wu forces at Shitou, near the capital. The first four lines read:

When Wang Jun's galleys descended on Yizhou,	王濬樓船下益州
The kingly aura of Jinling withdrew in darkness.	金陵王氣黯然收

Patterns of History, Failures of History 109

> A thousand feet of iron chain
>   sunk to the river bed,
> As the flag of surrender
>   issued forth from Shitou.

千尋鐵鎖沈江底
一片降旛出石頭

Liu has substituted the typical *huaigu* perspective (i.e., the perspective of Liu himself as he visits the area) for an imagined vision. We may note as well how Du Mu's poems on Huaqing Palace (see Chapter 2) envisage the sudden arrival of a lychee-bearing horseman and the wild dances of An Lushan. Such visions tend to confuse the reader's sense of where the poet is during these poems—the poet's presence at the actual site is becoming less significant, although he may still mention the occasion for his musings in the title or in a preface.

Li Shangyin's poems best reflect this trend. Although some of the titles of Li's historical poems do include words that indicate context of composition, such as *guo* 過 or *jing* 經 ("[I] pass" or "visit"), most are simply names of places or historical phenomena devoid of verbs: "Northern Qi" 北齊, "Dragon Pool" 龍池, "Mawei" 馬嵬, "Sui Palace" 隋宮. Commentators usually employ such poems to reconstruct Li's movements and thus implicitly categorize them as *huaigu*. The validity of such biographical speculations does not affect the content of the poems themselves: by minimizing his own presence and introducing a certain amount of imaginative recreation, Li is really writing a kind of sensually vivid *yongshi*.[14] The following poem is an excellent example of how Li employs a limited fictionality to make the poem more vivid; here, he is condemning the dissipation of the second Sui emperor, Yang 煬 (r. 605–17) and comparing it with the behavior of the incompetent last ruler of the Chen, Chen Houzhu 陳後主 (r. 583–89), whose land had been destroyed by Yang's father.

The Sui Palace 隋宮

> The halls and palaces by the Purple Stream
>   are locked in smoke and mist;
> So he desires to take the weed-covered city
>   and make of it an imperial home.
> If the jade seal had not returned
>   to the one of royal countenance,

紫泉宮殿鎖烟霞
欲取蕪城作帝家
玉璽不緣歸日角

4   Brocade sails would have reached
      all the way to heaven's edge.
    Even today the rotting grass
      produces no fireflies,
    And the drooping willows for all time
      harbor evening crows.
    Down below, if he ever meets
      the Last Lord of Chen
8   How could he ever bear to ask again
      about "Rear-Court Flowers"?

錦帆應是到天涯
于今腐草無螢火
終古垂楊有暮鴉
地下若逢陳後主
豈宜重問後庭花

(*QTS, j.* 539, p. 6161)

1–2/ The "Purple Stream," according to Sima Xiangru, flowed through the imperial hunting domain. Here, it is an elegant name for Emperor Yang's palaces in Chang'an. Because it was earlier believed that Bao Zhao's 鮑照 (414–66) "*Fu* on the Weed Covered City" 蕪城賦 described Yangzhou 楊州, that city is referred to here. The lines refer to the boredom that Yang felt at his capital and his move to the more beautiful and comfortable Yangzhou, then the southern terminus of the Grand Canal.

3–4/ That is, if the Mandate of Heaven had not been predestined to pass to the first Tang emperor, then the Sui pleasure excursions would still continue today on the Grand Canal at Yangzhou.

7–8/ A legend tells of an encounter between Yang and the ghosts of Chen Houzhu and his concubine Zhang Lihua 張麗華 while the emperor was living in Yangzhou. When the emperor asked Lady Zhang to sing Chen Houzhu's lyrics to the composition "Rear-Court Flowers," the Chen ruler castigated Yang for his decadence.

In eight lines Li Shangyin has worked his way through several of the accepted deeds and facts associated with Emperor Yang: his journey to the site of Southern Dynasties luxury, his boating parties, his similarities to Chen Houzhu (including a love of seductive music), and his loss of the empire. This is still very much a *huaigu*; it juxtaposes images not to recreate a specific scene but to emphasize the "rise-fall" pattern in a schematic way in order to illustrate the forces of history at work and to contrast past glory with present desolation and failure. This owes much to the rhetoric of parallelism, which invites stark superimpositions of allusion and allusion, image and image. It is also fairly easy to discover a note of criticism here; Li is the lofty historian who makes a moral equation of Sui with Chen. In the end, one was no better than the other.

Yet Li's poem breaks away from certain hallmarks of the classic regulated *huaigu*. Like Li He's songs, it too betrays an interest in fictional recreation. Moreover, Li Shangyin suppresses his own presence: only the third couplet suggests his own reaction to a real scene. It is quite possible that the poet wrote this far from the ruins of the Sui empire: surely if he can imagine the glories of the past, he is equally capable of describing a plausible scene in the present that he has not actually seen with his own eyes.

A quatrain on the fall of the Southern Qi dynasty in 501 further illustrates Li's deliberate concealment of his presence.

Song: Qi Palace 齊宮詞

When the troops arrived at the Palace of Eternal Life, 永壽兵來夜不扃
  though night, the gates were unbarred.
No more will the golden lotuses 金蓮無復印中庭
  leave their prints on the central court.
The songs and piping at Liang Terrace 梁臺歌管三更罷
  ceased at midnight;
While still the wind alone shook 猶自風搖九子鈴
  the small jade bells.
  (*QTS, j.* 539, p. 6174)

1/ The Palace of Eternal Life was one of the buildings erected by the Emperor Fei 廢 (r. 499–501) of the Southern Qi (also known as the Marquis of Donghun 東昏侯) for one of his consorts, Lady Pan 潘. The troops are those of Emperor Wu of the Liang dynasty, who exterminated the Qi in 501. The palace gates were left open, and the emperor was enjoying himself with feasting and music when the enemy arrived.

2/ Emperor Fei supposedly had lotuses of gold spread on the ground in the central court of his palace. When Lady Pan walked upon them, he would say, "A lotus springs up at her every step."

3/ By referring to a Liang dynasty palace here, Li expands his discussion of the Qi to the Southern Dynasties as a whole.

4/ The bells mentioned here were made of jade or metal and were attached to the eaves or curtains of palaces and temples.

What is striking here is Li's synthesis of fictionally imagined desolation that occurs in the historical past with a possible real desolation in his own time. Silence descended on the Qi court as the army arrived to destroy it; the Qi emperor's one mark on the world, the footprints of his ladies, are destroyed as well. But the jade bells still rang, an ironic reference to the continuity of nature, signified by the wind that sets them in motion. Maybe Li visited the ruins and heard the bells, guessing what it had been like; maybe he never came near them. The recognition of some important cessation in the past (the music stopped) and the timeless indifference of the wind, past and present, abolishes the processes of time and the importance of Li's actual presence at the ruins.

Another development in later historical verse may be seen as a consequence of aestheticism. Artistic consciousness posits a need to create pattern out of experience or even to create experience to fit a pattern. To accomplish this, poets not only attempted to free themselves from a description of what they merely saw but also sought new rhetorical and structural devices to use within the narrow genres of regulated verse, which increasingly dominated ninth-century poetic output. Not only do historical poems provide the opportunity to create a movement from past to present as they move from couplet to couplet, but they make analytical assertions whose impact depends more on the rhetorical power of parallelism than on the balanced judgments of historical writing. Most obvious of these are conditional statements that suggest the implications if things had turned out differently (contrafactuals). As Li Shangyin wrote in "The Sui Palace":

> If the jade sail had not returned
>   to the one of royal countenance,
> Brocade sails would have reached
>   all the way to heaven's edge.

At times such statements are accompanied by metalepsis, or the attribution of an effect to a seemingly trivial and distant cause, as when Du Mu writes about the Battle of Red Cliff (*QTS, j.* 523, p. 5980). Zhou Yu 周瑜, commander of the Wu forces, defeated Cao Cao's fleet with the help of fire and a favorable wind; his victory not only spelled the doom of Cao's plans to annex Wu but also prevented him from obtaining the extraordinarily beautiful wives of Zhou Yu and the Wu emperor, the Qiao 喬 sisters. Cao had had a terrace built, within which he planned to confine his wives after his death. Du Mu depends on our knowledge of these facts to make a startling connection:

> Had the East wind not been　　　　東風不與周郎便
>   with Zhou Yu that day,
> Springs deep around Copperbird Terrace　　銅雀春深鎖二喬
>   would have caged the two Qiaos.

Another example: Wei Zhuang recalls that Li Si 李斯, the prominent Legalist minister who helped the first Qin emperor achieve power, gained insight into administration when he noticed that during a time of chaos rats were allowed to eat grain from the public granaries unmolested, although they were driven from the manure in the privies. To this Wei connects a seemingly unrelated incident: the Taoist magician Xu Fu 徐福's expedition during the Qin emperor's reign to seek the Isles of the Immortals:

Had Li Si not been enlightened as he faced the public granaries,	李斯不向倉中悟
Then Xu Fu would not have traveled beyond the realm of things.	徐福應無物外遊
(*QTS*, *j*. 700, p. 8048)	

In this case, the demands for originality in parallel structure have led to a rewriting of true historical causation. Two seemingly trivial events become causally linked; in between lies one of the most significant periods in Chinese history, the career of the first Qin emperor, now subsumed within an inevitable mechanism.

For the most part, these factors create a sense of unease and ambiguity in much of Late Tang historical poetry, because fictional imagination or rhetorical exaggeration tends to obscure the didactic value of historical events. One can see this development in a *huaigu* by Liu Yuxi on Gusu 姑蘇 Terrace, which was erected by the King of Wu to house Xi Shi (*QTS*, *j*. 358, p. 4042). The second couplet is a conventional *huaigu* observation:

Fine silk gauze vanishes with the generations;	綺羅隨世盡
Though deer, as in old times, are many.[15]	麋鹿古時多

A standard juxtaposition: human possessions and beauty are destroyed, but nature lives on. The next couplet, however, is a startling one:

The walls, erected by the force of steel mallets	築用金錘力
Crumble through the scampering of rats mid the stones.[16]	摧因石鼠窠

One wonders if the striving for novelty and interest in the rhetoric of causation have not resulted in a stronger statement on human vanity than Liu might have intended. To suggest that rats *caused* the walls' destruction grants nature a hyperbolic violence that borders on the nihilistic. Not only is the human world impermanent; the merest effort from a morally indifferent nature sends the greatest edifices crashing down. Liu has struggled to order language for the sake of novel effect and has in passing hinted at a universe that is increasingly unreasonable and indecipherable.[17]

If Liu, a Mid-Tang poet, used parallelism to accentuate historical ironies only intermittently, Du Mu manipulates it to produce a poem that consists entirely of ironies when he writes on the tomb of the first Qin emperor.

Visiting Mount Li 過驪山作

While the First Emperor traveled East 始皇東遊出周鼎
   to recover the Zhou tripods,
Liu Bang and Xiang Yu looked on freely, 劉項縱觀皆引頸
   both with necks craned.
To conquer and pacify the world 削平天下實辛勤
   is surely an exhausting task:
4 Instead he only impoverished 卻為道傍窮百姓
   the commoners by the roadside.
The black-haired people were not foolish; 黔首不愚爾益愚
   you rather were the foolish one,
Imprisoned, the solitary man 千里函關囚獨夫
   in the broad land within Hangu Pass.
When the shepherd boy's fire reached 牧童火入九泉底
   to the bottom of the underworld,
8 It turned you to ash before 燒作灰時猶未枯
   you'd had the time to rot.
   (*QTS*, *j*. 520, pp. 5945–46)

Title/ Mount Li, east of the capital and the site of a Tang spa, was erroneously believed to be the site of the Qin emperor's tomb.

1/ The Nine Tripods, supposedly cast during the legendary Xia 夏 dynasty, were lost with the fall of the Zhou. The Qin emperor believed that the recovery of these bronzes (long sunk in the Si 泗 River) would lend a cachet of authority to his own dynasty.

2/ The identification of the Han founder simply by his surname Liu is an ironic deflation.

5–6/ Basing his rule on the Legalist philosophy of Han Feizi 韓非子, the Qin believed that people could be controlled more successfully if kept foolish and ignorant.

6/ Historians attributed the fall of the Qin partially to the emperor's unwillingness to leave his power base within (west of) the Hangu Pass (present Shaanxi province) when eastern China began to rebel against him.

7-8/ Qin Shihuang's tomb was believed destroyed during the rebellion following his death by a fire started accidentally by a shepherd boy.

The first Qin emperor is not portrayed affectionately in Chinese literature, but he is usually treated with some awe and respect; the pride of emperors was deflated by poets but may also appear as a subject worthy of tragic representation. Here, however, the Qin ruler is rendered as foolish, ineffectual, and cowardly, ruined first by two opportunistic rebels, then by the shepherd boy's accident. Almost every line is rooted in an ironic reversal—his attempt to force peace and unity on the common people results in their own ruin, although in the end they prove wiser and more enduring. Yet this poem, for all the distinctive stringency of its attack, loses sight to some extent of the old moral goals of *huaigu* and *yongshi*. Though a study in hubris, it is more a self-conscious exercise in wit and irony. Du Mu practices his abilities at Qin's (and history's) expense.

A limited use of historical irony is not incompatible with moral criticism, but its emergence in such a virulent form implies widespread questioning of the shared attitudes of a culture. Du's poem reveals a fundamental discomfort with the moral equations of the historical process. Such discomfort is much more evident in the poems of Li Shangyin. The ending of "The Sui Palace" is a case in point: Li emphasizes the personal tragedy of Emperor Yang, portraying it with an odd combination of pity, irony, and contempt. Although we may acknowledge the presence of a proper moral lesson (namely, that the last Sui emperor had, through his own vices, repeated the feckless performance of Chen Houzhu on a larger scale), the former's sheepish embarrassment in the underworld has a touch of the comic that belies a strictly moral purpose. Moreover, when Li turns to the Southern Dynasties period, irony is more evident and moral seriousness is called even more into question.

On History

Northern lake, southern dike;
   the water stretches far.
A single flag of surrender
   from atop a hundred-foot pole.

詠史

北湖南埭水漫漫

一片降旗百尺竿

A span of three hundred years—
   all the same early morning dream:
In what way does Mount Zhong
   possess a dragon coiled?
     (*QTS*, *j*. 539, p. 6173)

三百年間同曉夢

鍾山何處有龍盤

  1/ "Northern lake" is Lake Xuanwu 玄武, north of Jinling 金陵, the Tang name for the Southern Dynasties' capital city of Jiankang 健康. The dike is probably Cockcrow Dike, christened by Emperor Wu 武 (r. 483–94) of the Southern Qi dynasty (see poem by Wen Tingyun below).

  2/ An image meant to signify the surrender of the Southern Dynasties to the Sui armies, though Li is clearly influenced by Liu Yuxi's famous couplet from "Meditation on the Past: Western Pass Mountain" (discussed above).

  4/ Mount Zhong near Jiankang was believed to possess the aspect of a coiling imperial dragon. Zhuge Liang, the third-century statesman, first used the term, describing Mount Zhong as "truly a dwelling for princes and emperors." The aspect Mount Zhong provided to the area is often termed "kingly aura" (*wang qi* 王氣).

Li is clearly attracted to the ephemeral beauty of the south, with its lovely lakes; yet, amid this scenery, he ironically notes the banner of surrender—a banner he visualizes in his mind, of course. The vague stretch of water merely accentuates the quality of dream Li imposes on history in line three; the rugged solidity of Mount Zhong is thus undermined. Wu Diaogong argues, with some justification, that Li is telling us that the phenomena of history depend on the actions of people, not on cosmological factors.[18] Although this message is present, I would suggest that Li's response to history here is considerably more problematic. The poem's third line, with its suggestion of inevitable transience, suggests that all political power may be doomed and that the cautionary value to later generations of history to advise and warn may be negligible. The traditional attack on Southern Dynasties pride and weakness has become a general skepticism.

  A different problem of interpretation is presented by another quatrain of Li's.

Southern Dynasties

Earth's escarpment stretches on,
   Heaven's escarpment is long.
The kingly aura of Jinling
   matches the Jasper Luminescence.

南朝

地險悠悠天險長

金陵王氣應瑤光

Yet do not boast that this place divides all under Heaven;	休誇此地分天下
Just look at Consort Xu's face, with cosmetics half-applied.	只得徐妃半面妝
(*QTS, j.* 540, p. 6183)	

2/ The Jasper Luminescence is one of the stars in Ursa Minor. Various parts of the world corresponded to, and were under the influence of, certain stars in this constellation, and the area of Wu was under the auspicious influence of this particular star. For "kingly aura" (*wang qi*), see note to line 4 of Li Shangyin's "On History."

4/ Consort Xu was Xu Zhaopei 昭佩, a concubine of Emperor Yuan 元 (r. 552–55) of the Liang noted for her surliness and lack of beauty. On the rare occasions that the emperor visited her, she emerged from her rooms only half made up; the emperor then departed in anger.

Jinling's natural surroundings supposedly make it impenetrable to attack, and Li Shangyin's description of the city in the opening lines places it clearly in such a historical, topographical, and cosmological context. He invites us to take the traditional view of Jinling's importance, to picture it to ourselves as we know it from our reading of other accounts and other poems, surrounded by forbidding cliffs. Jinling's favorable astrological siting is touched on as well. At this point, however, the poet uses a rhetorical counterproof to alter the way we look at the landscape. It was another convention to compare the landscape around Jinling to a beautiful woman, especially the renowned Xi Shi. Here, of course, Li chooses instead the boorish Xu Zhaopei for comparison. There is a particularly savage irony in the metaphor; certainly by Six Dynasties aristocratic standards, Lady Xu's behavior was particularly heinous in its violation of decorum and grace. By equating her unattractiveness and her shameful dishabille to the flimsy political power of the dynasty itself (makeup half applied = control of only half of China), Li mocks the imperial order of the period by making it both trivial and ornamental—and thus ludicrous even by the standards it set for itself. But how seriously are we to take a poem that compares a dynasty (no matter how incompetent) to a concubine? How seriously does Li take the forces of history? What does his attitude conceal?

Du Mu and Li Shangyin were attracted to the Southern Dynasties and turned to them often in their *huaigu* and *yongshi*; this attraction betrays complex attitudes. Both could savage the moral bankruptcy of the Southern courts, yet both could not help evoking the beauty of the southern landscape and the seductiveness and luxury of Southern court society. Surely both poets were also aware that their own poetic inclinations, their interest in the aesthetic and formal qualities of verse, connected them in some way to the late Six Dynasties poets. Most important, they undoubtedly knew that the Six Dynasties resembled their own age in its political decay and social chaos. They found it impossible to disregard their sense of kinship with this earlier age, nor would their sense of moral responsibility allow them to ignore the historical lessons that might be learned once that kinship was acknowledged. Yet complete and honest identification would be too painful, for it would imply the coming demise of their own age. Best to ease anxiety by the use of irony, wordplay, and rhetorical organization: the old *huaigu* and *yongshi* issues can still be discussed, but only if mediated by a self-conscious artificiality; emperors can be personalized, turned into buffoons or pathetic protagonists, deprived of their historical significance; the fall of a dynasty can be dismissed by a general, all-embracing pessimism that claims all political orders are ultimately destroyed, regardless of moral worth; and historical causality can be brought into question by artistic metalepsis and ironic juxtaposition.

Patterns of History: The Illusory Scene

When Wen Tingyun wrote historical scenes in *yuefu* form, his overwhelming interest in the poetry and culture of the Six Dynasties led him to focus on that period. The first poem in his collection, "Song: Cockcrow Dike," outlines the rise and fall of the Southern court through the superimposition of images. Wen alludes to the invasion of the Yangzi delta by the Sui armies and the last Chen ruler's cowardly response. According to the historian Sima Guang 司馬光 (1019–86):

The Lord of Chen, greatly agitated, intended to flee, but [his minister] Xian Zhengse said: "When the Northern troops arrive, you must do nothing to offend them. In a great matter such as this where could Your Majesty go? I beg that Your Majesty straighten his gown and cap and put his palace in order, just as Emperor Wu of the Liang did in his audience with Hou Jing [a rebel who eventually deposed him]." The Lord of Chen took no heed; leaving his couch he fled, saying: "I cannot face the spears and blades; besides, I have my own plans." Following a dozen or so palace women, he ran out of the rear hall of Jingyang Palace, intending to jump down a well. Xian would not allow him and remonstrated with him strongly, and the Marquis of Xia, Gong Yun, Keeper of the Rear Palace, blocked the well mouth with his own body. The Lord of Chen struggled with him for a time and finally managed to put himself inside.

Later, when the enemy troops were investigating the well, they called down it but heard no reply. Just as they were about to throw stones down, they heard a cry. As they pulled up [the Chen emperor], they were surprised to find him extremely heavy. When they had managed to extricate him, they discovered that the Favored Ladies Zhang and Kong had ridden up with him.[19]

Note how Wen here carries the quatrain stanza form to a more sophisticated level, exploiting continuity within stanzas and the disjunction between them.

Song: Cockcrow Dike 雞鳴埭歌

When the Southern Dynasty emperor 南朝天子射雉時
    went shooting pheasant,
The Silver River glittered, 銀河耿耿星參差
    stars littered the sky.
When the bronze water clock stopped, 銅壺漏斷夢初覺
    then he first woke from his dreams;
4 And as bejeweled steeds drove the dust high, 寶馬塵高人未知
    people knew nothing of it all.

Fish darted "east of the lotus," 魚濯蓮東蕩宮沼
    stirring the palace pool—
And nesting birds hung suspended 濛濛御柳懸棲鳥
    in royal willows' misty green.
Crimson blushes in myriad doors, 紅妝萬戶鏡中春
    the spring season in their mirrors.
8 From the jade tree, one cry— 碧樹一聲天下曉
    all the world turned morning.

Exhausted after three centuries 盤踞勢窮三百年
    is their coiling, crouching force.
From the crimson direction, the aura of destruction 朱方殺氣成愁烟
    turns to melancholy mist.
Comet tails sweep the earth, 彗星拂地浪連海
    waves cover the sea;

120   Patterns of History, Failures of History

12 Battle drums ford the river
　　and dust floods the sky.
　Embroidered dragon and painted quail
　　stuff the palace well.
　Wild fires, wind-driven,
　　burn the Nine Tripods to ash.
　Now the palace provides river swallows with nests,
　　weeds grow from the steps,
16 Hoarfrost glitters on the
　　twelve metal men.
　Level green, lush and thick,
　　stretches to Taicheng's foundations.
　The warm-colored spring is empty
　　mid ancient slopes overgrown.
　Who could have known that song tune—
　　"Jade Trees and Rear-Court Flowers"—
20 Would linger on, mid crab apple trees,
　　their branches white as snow?
　　　(*WFQ, j.* 1, pp. 1–3)

戰鼓渡江塵漲天
繡龍畫雉填宮井
野火風驅燒九鼎
殿巢江燕砌生蒿
十二金人霜炯炯
芊綿平綠臺城基
暖色春空荒古陌
寧知玉樹後庭曲
留待野棠如雪枝

2/ The Silver River: the Milky Way.

5/ This is an allusion to a line in the anonymous *yuefu* "South of the River" 江南辭: "Fish play east of the lotus leaves" (*YFSJ*, p. 384). Wen employs it here to evoke the Chinese literary feeling for the lush beauty of the south.

7/ The "crimson blushes" are the palace ladies as they emerge from their morning toilette. The phrase "myriad doors" is a standard kenning for an imperial palace. The spring season is a metaphor for their youth.

8/ Allusion to the morning-cock who dwells in the branches of a great tree in the distant east; its cry as the sun rises compels all worldly roosters to answer it.

9/ "Coiling and crouching" is a term often used to describe Mount Zhong near Jiankang; see note to line 4 of Li Shangyin's "On History."

10/ The "crimson direction" is the South. It was also the name of a city in the Warring States kingdom of Wu and may serve as an elegant substitution for Jiankang.

12/ A description of the Sui army approaching the Chen capital.

13/ "Embroidered dragon" and "painted quail" describe the clothing of the emperor and his consorts.

14/ For the Nine Tripods, see note to line 1 of Du Mu's "Visiting Mount Li."

16/ The Twelve Metal Men were cast by the first Qin emperor from the weapons he had confiscated throughout his empire; once again, a symbol of imperial power (and an ironic one, with its implied comparison between the powerful Qin Shihuang and the feckless Chen emperor).

19/ "Rear-Court Flowers" was a song tune to which Chen Houzhu wrote lyrics; he often ordered his palace attendants to sing it and other songs of his own composition.

The first eight lines portray the splendor of the Southern Dynasties, but Wen builds on other atmospheric portrayals of the south and on erotic palace-poetry diction to evoke a land in which the splendor consists not of military glory but of wealth and luxury. Already a mode of presentation different from that of Lu Zhaolin's emerges: Wen chooses a representative scene located in a specific place (Cockcrow Dike) and at a specific time (dawn). Although one may argue that the scene is a generic one and could have occurred at any time within a two-hundred-year period (for assuredly the "Southern Dynasty emperor" of the first line does not have to be Emperor Wu of the Qi, the putative christener of Cockcrow Dike), the details Wen relates here are placed in a careful narrative order and are not random. They are not Lu Zhaolin's *yuefu* tropes, nor are they Li He's erratic imagistic shifts. Right at the beginning Wen's use of the word *shi* 時 ("time") in the first line makes the entire phrase a dependent clause. We begin with a specific moment, when the emperor sets out on his hunt. The end of the descriptive sequence comes with another moment, in line eight: "From the jade tree, one cry—all the world turns morning." Between lines one and eight the reader's perceptions move first through scenes indicative of the waning night (stars' glitter, the drained water clock, the sleeping people's unawareness of the horses of the imperial hunting party); then, through scenes of dawn (the fish pond, now visible in first light, birds perched amid morning fog, the palace ladies emerging from the chambers to watch their lord depart). These observations are pictures, not single actions; they are occurring indefinitely in the past. Thus the single cockcrow acts as culmination, announcing day (the end of this sequence of dawn description) and the emperor's full glory as well (*tianxia* 天下, translated here as "world," can also mean "empire"). We can now see why Wen named this poem after the dike: on the one hand, the image encompasses both place and time and can be read as a symbol of the Southern Dynasties at their height; on the other hand, through its association with hunting parties and palace harems, it suggests the more complacent, luxury-loving world of the South. One might also note that a number of Wen's erotic poems begin with a dawn scene and the sensual portrayal of ladies awakening. Valiant hunters may be setting out, but they have risen from the beds of their women. Although Wen indulges in no moral judgments here—an earlier poet might have exploited any one of these lines for an immediate didactic comment—he portrays a world dangerously soft. For Wen, the Southern Dynasties world is doomed not because of its immorality but because of its fragility.

In the next section, lines nine to fourteen, he sets out to explicate the consequences of that fragility. Here, the images are not clearly tied to place or time and are ordered in a different way: combined with the first section they suggest a movement from foreboding to disaster and from external phenomena to private tragedy (from the sky and the area beyond the Yangzi to the well in which Chen Houzhu hides). The Chen's fall is not implicitly or explicitly connected to moral flaws or hubris; rather it is the result of a natural process, the exhaustion of force (shi 勢) and the dissipation of imperial power. In a similar way, the parallel structure of lines eleven and twelve suggests that the comet (a cosmic indication of social disaster) and the war drums (the approach of the Sui army) are analogous phenomena. We may go farther and say that another organizational technique of this section is the repetition of the same basic event (the fall of Chen) from different perspectives: the prophetic, the cosmological, the military, the personal, the political. Where the wild fires of the Sui consumed the vessels that symbolize the Chen's waning imperial authority, we find only the ruins of a destroyed state. Here, Wen manages to move from narrative to the consideration of broader historical issues. The language and style in the first and second sections are the same—both employ the visual images and fragments we have seen frequently in his other *yuefu*. In the first section, however, the fragments were pieces of a definite scene with a temporal and spatial coherence; in the second, they are symbolic emblems. The narrative detail becomes transformed into a rhetorical metonym; Wen can thus move from vivid scene to historical summation without once entering the poem personally.

In the ruined world of the Chen's fall (lines fifteen to twenty), Wen makes use of the conventional images that denote abandoned palaces, but the scene is made more chilling by the blurring of distances between the human and the non-human, the sentient and seemingly non-sentient. The palace still has its inhabitants: the twelve metal men, who, like Li He's bronze immortal, continue to live in a place from which real men have vanished; the swallows and crab apple trees that remain as reminders of better times. The song of Chen Houzhu still lingers here, as in Du Mu's famous "Mooring on the Qinhuai" 泊秦淮 (*QTS, j.* 523, p. 5980).

Mist engulfs the cold water, moon engulfs the sand.	煙籠寒水月籠沙
At night I moor on the Qinhuai, near a wineshop.	夜泊秦淮近酒家
The wineshop girl doesn't know the pain of fallen states;	商女不知亡國恨
Across the river she still sings "Rear-Court Flowers."	隔江猶唱後庭花

And yet, in Wen's poem the song is singerless and the hearer invisible. We have not the slightest suggestion here that the poet (like Du Mu) overheard the song as he strolled among the ruins of Jiankang. Du Mu's poem may be calming in its sadness, for it speaks of the continuity of human beauty in the midst of historical change; however, Du Mu may be suggesting the ominous recurrence of decadence in his own century. Either way, a certain judgment on events is implied on his part. Wen's poem gives us only the silence. It is as if Wen is negating the presence of the poet as rememberer: the poem paradoxically records that no one is left to record.

"Cockcrow Dike" is brilliantly fictional, but is still severely limited as a *narrative* of events; moreover, it sustains a limited point of view by centering on the fall of the Chen as an historical tragedy. The Sui soldiers appear as destroyers, not as the renewers of the imperial system; for Wen, the identity of Chinese culture is tied to the south. However, in another historical song, "Nights of Spring Rivers and Flowered Moons," Wen incorporates both the Chen and the Sui into his historical vision and creates a poem with greater narrative complexity; here, as in Li Shangyin's "The Sui Palace," the comparison between Chen Houzhu and the second and last Sui emperor becomes the guiding structural element.

Song: Nights of Spring Rivers and Flowered Moons 春江花月夜詞

As the "Jade Tree" song ended, the sea-clouds blackened;	玉樹歌闌海雲黑
The flowered courts turned at once to a green and weedy land.	花庭忽作青蕪國

> The Qinhuai still has its waters,
>   but they lack feeling:
> 4 Still in Jinling, they set
>   spring's colors rippling.
>
> Now the second emperor of the House of Yang
>   sits at peace upon his secluded throne;
> He drives no more his bright carriages,
>   has tired of his dragon team.
> Instead, a hundred brocade sails
>   fill with gusts of wind
> 8 And gold lotus spreads out
>   to Heaven's very edge.
>
> Pearls and kingfisher plumes glitter,
>   as their sparkle glints and fades.[20]
> Dragon-heads split the waves,
>   grieving fifes resound.
> For a thousand miles the river steeps the sky,
>   betrays the water-spirits;
> 12 A myriad branches strike the nose
>   with their piled and scented snow.
>
> As the water clock turns, clouds rise high
>   west of the infinite sea.
> From his glass pillow he hears
>   the Heaven-cock's crow.
> "Southern Strings" and "Dai Geese"
>   seem to speak,
> 16 And in one bout of tipsiness
>   all the world is lost.
>
> While the four directions convulse,
>   while smoke and dust rise up,
> His soul still travels in a dream
>   through the thick incense.
> From the Last Lord's overgrown palace,
>   the morning orioles
> 20 Come flying, cut off from here
>   by the Western River alone.
>   (*WFQ, j.* 2, pp. 49–51)

秦淮有水水無情
還向金陵漾春色
楊家二世安九重
不御華芝嫌六龍
百幅錦帆風力滿
連天展盡金芙蓉
珠翠丁星復明滅
龍頭劈浪哀笳發
千里涵空照水魂
萬枝破鼻團香雪
漏轉霞高滄海西
玻璃枕上聞天雞
蠻弦代雁曲如語
一醉昏昏天下迷
四方傾動烟塵起
猶在濃香夢魂裏
後主荒宮有曉鶯
飛來只隔西江水

3–4/ The Qinhuai flows past Jinling (as in Du Mu's poem quoted above).

5/ Yang was the family name of the Sui dynastic house; here of course Wen is speaking of Emperor Yang, but the phrase is meant to echo "Qin Ershi" 秦二世, the title of the equally unfortunate second emperor of the Qin.

8/ Gold lotus is a metaphor for the sails; here we have a description of the pleasure outings of Emperor Yang on the recently completed Grand Canal—more specifically at Jiangdu 江都 (Yangzhou), his southern capital.

9/ These are the court ladies who "manned" the boats in the pleasure excursions. Wen not only emphasizes the "effeminate" nature of these outings, but also plays on the lotus-gathering tropes of southern *yuefu*.

10/ Dragon-heads are prow ornaments. The fifes are grieving not because they are mourning a real catastrophe, but simply because they are playing the sort of sentimental popular music one would expect to hear at parties. See, e.g., "A Night Banquet" and "A Dancer's Robe," both translated in Chapter 3. However, it is tempting to read the quality of the music as a foreshadowing of dynastic fall.

11/ The first part of the line describes the vast expanse of water reflecting the night sky; the second part, the clarity of the moonlit water, in which sea creatures can be seen at play.

12/ Probably the blossoms of peach trees. We know that Emperor Yang did ornament the banks of the canal with willow trees; Wen may have turned them into peaches for poetic effect.

15/ "Southern Strings" originally indicated the instruments of southern aborigines. Both this and "Dai Geese" most likely refer to specific tunes or kinds of melodies.

19/ "Last Lord" is Chen Houzhu.

20/ "Western River" here indicates the stretch of the Yangzi from Jiangdu to Jinling, just a few miles upriver.

Wen's relation to his own poetic past becomes important here: whereas "Cockcrow Dike" was a *yuefu* of his own invention, "Spring Rivers" was a *yuefu* melody attributed to Chen Houzhu. Furthermore, although the Chen ruler's lyrics to the melody do not survive, a version by Emperor Yang does. Wen is linking both emperors by tune title, just as he links them by a framing device. The main body of the poem (lines five to eighteen) recounts an excursion of Yang's along the recently constructed Grand Canal. In mood this section resembles some of Li He's songs—notably, "The King of Qin Drinks Wine," which also portrays a ruler's ignorance of his own mortality; Wen, however, expands his perspective in lines one to four and nineteen to twenty by comparing Emperor Yang's glory to the oblivion brought to the Chen and suggests that the Sui will come to the same end. By using a tune title employed by both rulers, Wen tightens the screw one turn. Although irony in its classical Western sense does not exist as a defined rhetorical device in Chinese literature,[21] situational irony does occur often, especially in Chinese historical narratives. Here, without commenting directly on the similarities between the Sui and Chen courts, Wen can use such irony to create a greater depth by manipulating our historical memories to add to the poetic impact.

Wen, however, does not limit this association of the historical and poetic to his choice of tune titles; he also shows a sensitivity to convention and the modal demands of his genre. As would have been required of late Six Dynasties *yuefu*, Emperor Yang's version of "Spring Rivers" carefully touches on all the objects its title mentions—spring, river, flowers, moon; this is also a characteristic of the most famous example of the tune, Zhang Ruoxu's 張若虛 (ca. 660–ca. 720), which can serve as a catalogue of all the appropriate modal associations of this theme.[22] Wen introduces the right images as well but ties them into his depiction of Emperor Yang's world. The trees along the canal are in bloom; the moon shines in the newly channeled waters of the canal; and, most poignantly, the Western River, the symbol of passing time, flows ominously toward Yang out of Jiankang, the ruined southern capital.

Wen also makes use of musical associations throughout the poem. Chen Houzhu's "Rear-court Flowers" appears again, and, as in "Cockcrow Dike," its silence marks the end of the Chen. In line ten, "grieving fifes resound" at the emperor's party, perhaps playing the emperor's own version of "Spring Rivers"; even when Yang's empire is collapsing, he is engaged in music making (line fifteen). In each case, music is a sign of empire's dissolution, a reinforcement of the association of mournful music with chaotic times.

The vivid and meticulous recreation of scene that marked the first eight lines of "Cockcrow Dike" is present here also; the central excursion section is laid out carefully, even if a precise temporal and spatial arrangement is missing. Wen keeps this section tied to a specific historical past by mentioning in turn the well-known emblems of Emperor Yang's outings: the reader encounters familiar indicators at every turn (the sails, the palace ladies in their pleasure boats, the moonlit canal). In fact, all these elements together give an impression of the insularity of Yang's universe. Not only has he created all these things for his own pleasure; he cannot escape from them and is blinded by their attractions. This becomes clear in lines thirteen to sixteen: cosmic elements register the passage of time, but Emperor Yang remains unaware of their significance.

The cockcrow becomes menacing, demanding that the emperor wake from his dreams, but drugged from sensory excesses, he fails to notice his empire crumbling. The orioles who come to nest in the ruins of his palace at Yangzhou will be the final invaders of his realm. Wen ends with an image that echoes that of Liu Yuxi's famous quatrain on Jinling, "Black Robe Lane" 烏衣巷:

By the side of Crimson Sparrow Bridge, 　wild grass blooms;	朱雀橋邊野草花
At the mouth of Black Robe Lane 　the evening sun slants.	烏衣巷口夕陽斜
The swallows who once dwelt 　before the halls of Wangs and Xies	舊時王謝堂前燕
now fly into the ordinary 　houses of commoners.²³	飛入尋常百姓家

But, as in "Cockcrow Dike," Wen's image is more desolate; he points, not to the teeming return of humanity to the ruins but to ruins empty of all but nature.

"Spring Rivers" goes beyond "Cockcrow Dike" in sophistication; it violates readers' expectations by beginning with an ending, deepens the historical perspective by balancing the collapse of two kingdoms against each other, and ends before the final coup de grace on a quiet note of foreboding. It describes the expectant orioles rather than comets and destroyed imperial tripods.

Earlier I discussed the tendency in Li He's and Wen's work to avoid the introduction of the poetic self into the poem. In the Early and High Tang periods, poems with a moral dimension needed an explicit poetic presence to comment on the meaning of events—either the poet himself as he viewed, for example, the ruins of a fallen city, or the *yuefu* persona bemoaning various social ills. Many poems supposedly set in the Han, such as Lu Zhaolin's poem on Chang'an or dozens of frontier verses, satirize contemporary problems; such poems are warnings of moral decay and a vindication of the poet's own rectitude in an age of decline.

As we have seen, however, the moral uses of history in poetry were slowly disappearing, even in the *huaigu* subgenre. In Wen's songs, this lack of moral comment is even clearer. "Cockcrow Dike" has no explicit authorial comment. The moral comment of "Nights of Spring Rivers" may seem a bit clearer: Emperor Yang is blind to the troubles of his own empire, and the final image is a highly emblematic one, reflecting the consequences of misgovernment. Still, Wen's concerns seem more artistic than moral; by duplicating the Chen's fall in the Sui's, he hints at the inevitable repetition of the rise and fall of history, creating a beauty of symmetry along with the tragedy.

It is true that many of Li He's historical songs have been read as criticisms of his own age; "The King of Qin Drinks Wine," for instance, is seen as a critique of the Taoist obsessions of Emperor Dezong 德宗 (r. 779–805).[24] But even if we grant these readings validity (and many of us would not, I think), we must still account for the immense difference of mood between Li He's and Wen's poems. Wen, more fascinated by lush description and carefully controlled sequential structures, is cooler and more urbane; it is the tone of rage and madness in Li's work that has enabled later critics to see him as moral castigator. Li fits the Qu Yuan pattern more closely than Wen does.

This, of course, does not mean that Wen's social milieu would not have encouraged him to respond empathically to an age similar to his own, just as Li Shangyin and Du Mu often do. In fact, Wen's recognition of the decline of his age probably makes him more aesthetically aware of the symmetrical beauty of historical cycles and of the inevitable decline of political forces. Even if some lingering touch of the didactic may remain, it is less important than the pleasures of evocation, of becoming the poetic *creator* of the historical past. In a sense, Wen does not lament the loss of the past; he makes it up out of his own imagination. He is consequently less bitter than Li Shangyin or Du Mu and less haunted by the political failures of his times.

In the historical songs, the earlier the period, the smaller Wen's interest in moral criticism; correspondingly, his scenes become more fanciful and fantastic. Working backward chronologically from the Chen, we enter an increasingly imaginary world. First, there is his evocation of a famous anecdote concerning Xie An 謝安 (320–85), an important Eastern Jin statesman. After an early life spent in retirement, Xie held a number of posts; the climax of his career came with his military campaign against the invasion of the northern Toba ruler Fu Jian 符堅 and the victory of Jin forces in 383. Wen's poem can only be understood in the context of the following story, taken from Liu Yiqing's 劉義慶 book of anecdotes, the *Shishuo xinyu* 世說新語.

Xie An was playing encirclement chess [*wei qi* 圍棋] with someone, when suddenly a messenger arrived from Xie Xuan [Xie An's nephew, who was leading the defense against Fu Jian] at the Huai River. An read the letter to the end in silence and, without saying a word, calmly turned back to the playing board. When his guests asked whether the news from the Huai was good or bad, he replied, "My little boys [Xuan and his younger brother Shi] have inflicted a crushing defeat on the invader." As he spoke, his mood and expression and demeanor were no different from usual.[25]

Song: Duke Xie's Villa 謝公墅歌

South of the Crimson Sparrow Boat-Bridge
   a scented path twists its way 朱雀航南繞香陌
Toward Sir Xie's eastern villa,
   where spring green stretches far. 謝郎東墅連春碧
Doves sleep in tall willows
   as the world melts in sunlight; 鳩眠高柳日方融
4 Breezes waft through the ornamented kiosks
   among guests from the Purple Court. 綺樹飄颻紫庭客

By the striated catalpa chessboard,
   mid petals strewn about: 文楸方罫花參差
Before his mind's strategies are complete,
   stars fill the pool. 心陳未成星滿池
All the guests are speechless;
   wutong and bamboo are still. 四座無喧梧竹靜
8 By gold cicadas and jade staffs
   all chins rest in hands. 金蟬玉柄俱持頤

He knits his brow as he faces the board,
   sees a thousand miles; 對局含嚬見千里
The capital has already grasped
   the great serpent's tail. 都城已得長蛇尾
The cosmic energies of the Jiangnan kings
   are tied to his loosened gown; 江南王氣繫疎襟
12 He never permitted Fu Jian
   to cross the Huai waters. 未許苻堅過淮水
   (*WFQ*, *j*. 2, pp. 33–34)

  1/ Crimson Sparrow Boat-Bridge: a bridge in Jiankang near Black Robe Lane (see quatrain by Liu Yuxi above). It consisted of boats tied together.
  4/ Purple Court: elegant term for the imperial palace. Xie is being visited by high officials at his country estate.
  7/ Wutong and bamboo: i.e., musical instruments.
  8/ Officials wore gold ornaments in the shape of cicadas and carried jade staffs.
  10/ Troops from the capital have defeated the invaders.

Of all Wen's historical poems, this is the one that produces the most unified effect. Wen has basically put the *Shishuo xinyu* anecdote into verse; although we cannot fully understand the poem without the anecdote, we can see that Wen's interest in the event is close to that of Liu Yiqing. As Richard Mather points out, the *Shishuo xinyu* usually champions the values of sophistication and tolerance against the morally stricter virtues of government service and family loyalty.[26] Although Xie An was a wily and capable politician, this anecdote revels in his aristocratic, high-minded nonchalance and in his indifference to worldly success or failure; it occurs in a chapter entitled "Cultivated Tolerance" 雅量.

Obviously, Wen shares the *Shishuo xinyu* perspective; here he attempts to capture Xie's personality in his choice of poetic images. As the poem begins, we approach the villa from the city, and we see the contrast between city and country that emphasizes the loftiness of Xie's character. The villa is far from Jiankang, just as Xie is far from the court in spirit. Yet the court officials are forced to seek him out, for they are drawn to the power of his personality: in the first four lines, we follow the path they would take in visiting him.

And yet Xie An is hardly the Taoist recluse. He does not live among pines and isolated shepherds' huts, but on an estate of cultivated and domesticated order. Wen revels once again in spring descriptions, portraying a landscape of gentleness and warmth rather than grandeur. At the end of our path is Xie himself, engrossed in his chess game, surrounded by an almost effete array of artificial objects: ornamented kiosk, elegant chessboard, artificial pool, the staffs and cicada ornaments of the officials. Lines five and six give us the clue to the poem, however. Xie An is playing encirclement chess (better known as Go), an elegant game for the aristocracy and a model pastime for training in military strategy. Everywhere in Xie's garden an aesthetic pattern repeats Xie's game: the petals become pieces, the stars reflected in the pool become white stones on a black game board. Soon we know that Xie is engaged in more than a game; he is controlling the fate of the Jin army at the same time. "He sees a thousand miles"—not only farseeing in the strategies of the game, but well aware of developments on the distant battlefield. Xie's dress may be in disarray, but instead of the sash of a high official he binds himself with the aura of kings (the same *wang qi* mentioned in other poems set in Jiankang). He becomes the aesthete controlling events through sympathetic magic; as he surrounds and defeats his chess opponent Fu Jian's forces are routed.

History becomes pattern, and clashing armies become the stones on an elegant catalpa chessboard. As Wen portrays him, Xie is the great artificer of events, a man who can turn them into a tour de force that reflects his own skill and control. As in a magic act, significance lies not so much in what has been accomplished as in the panache with which it has been carried out.

There is more theatricality in another of Wen's poems, also set in the Jin. Here, he writes about the much less famous Emperor Ming 明 (r. 323–26), who was instrumental in bringing stability to southern China following the chaos of the early fourth century. In 324, he put down a rebellion by Wang Dun 王敦; Wen focuses on a particularly romantic incident from the time:

> Wang Dun was raising troops, intending an expedition [into Jin territory]; when the emperor secretly learned of this, he mounted a swift Bashen horse and went incognito to Yuhu in order to spy out Dun's camp and fortifications. Just as the emperor was leaving at dawn, Wang Dun dreamed that a sun turned about his city. Startled awake, he said, "It must be that that yellow-whiskered barbarian slave has arrived!" [Emperor Ming's mother, Lady Xun, was from Yan (present-day Hebei) and evidently had some non-Chinese ancestry.] He sent out horsemen to pursue him.
>
> The emperor espied an old woman selling rice by an inn. He gave her his seven-jeweled horsewhip and told her, "When those horsemen back there arrive, you can show them this."
>
> His pursuers arrived and inquired of the old woman. She replied, "He's gone by here already. He's far away by now." She then showed them the whip. Five of the horsemen dallied in bringing this information back, and they were all delayed a considerable time. In this way the emperor managed to escape.²⁷

Song of Huyin　　　　　　　　　　　　　　　　　　　　　　湖陰詞

Preface: Wang Dun raised a force and came to Huyin; Emperor Ming secretly went to spy out his camp and troops.²⁸ Because of this there is a *yuefu* tune entitled "Song of Huyin." Since the words are lost, I have made new ones to replace them.

Progenitor dragon with yellow beard　　　　　　　祖龍黃鬚珊瑚鞭
　　and coral whip;
Iron-dappled gold-faced steed　　　　　　　　　　鐵驄金面青連錢
　　patterned with black coin-patches.

Tiger-whiskers draws his sword, 虎髯拔劍欲成夢
　on the point of completing his dream—
4 But the sun hangs heavy on the rebel camp, 日壓賊營如血鮮
　bright as fresh blood.

Fierce breeze in the sea banners 海旗風急驚眠起
　startles him from sleep.
The distant glitter of heavy armor 甲重光搖照湖水
　reflects in the lake waters.
Flurried, the pursuing horsemen 蒼黃追騎塵外歸
　return from beyond the dust.
8 Dark and fading, their demon star 森索妖星陳前死
　dies before their ranks.

The sorrowing green on the five tombs 五陵愁碧春萋萋
　grows thick again in spring.
The jade horse of Ba Stream 灞川玉馬空中嘶
　whinnies in the open air.
Feathered dispatches like lightning 羽書如電入青瑣
　enter the chain-patterned palace;
12 Snowy ankles like hammers 雪腕如槌催畫鞞
　drive on the painted war-drums.

The White-Serpent Emperor, 白虹天子金鍠鋥
　with golden halberd's point,
Looks down on high from the Imperial Seat, 高臨帝座回龍章
　where dragon banners turn round.
Now the waves of Wu are still, 吳波不動楚山晚
　the peaks of Chu turn to evening;
16 Flowers press down on the balcony, 花壓闌干春晝長
　spring morning long.
　　(*WFQ, j.* 1, pp. 23–25)

　1/ "Progenitor dragon" is a term first applied to the first Qin emperor. Here it simply refers to any emperor. "Yellow beard": see the passage from the *Jin shu* above.

　3/ "Tiger-whiskers": Wang Dun; a typical epithet for a fierce barbarian or rebel.

　8/ "Demon star" is not a metaphor for Wang Dun but a reference to a comet that appeared at the time of the rebellion and was associated with him.[29]

　9/ The Han imperial tombs. Their returning green reflects the restoration of imperial order. Wang Dun was known to have rifled ancient tombs.

　10/ This is apparently an allusion to a Jin Dynasty general's discovery of a jade horse under the snow while camping with his men. He was busy putting down a revolt of the imperial princes at the time; his discovery of the horse was a prophecy of the recovery of imperial fortunes. The general was nowhere near Ba Stream at the time, however.[30]

11/ "Chain-patterned palace" (lit. "dark chains"): in the Han, palace walls were ornamented with a chain pattern and painted in dark colors. "Feathered dispatches": a cliché for the swift orders that pass back and forth between frontline troops and headquarters.

12/ "Snowy ankles": of the cavalry horses.

13/ White was the color of the Jin dynasty; the allusion to snakes as representatives of imperial houses stems from the famous anecdote of Han Gaozu's killing of a magical snake associated with the house of Qin (see note to line 8 of Li Bai's "Ascending the Battlefield at Guangwu Mountain"). The word translated as "halberd" (*huang* 鍠) is a type of three-pronged halberd blade associated with the royal house. By Tang times it was considered only a ceremonial weapon.

14/ The "Imperial Seat" is also the name of a star associated with imperial power.

Whereas "Duke Xie's Villa" is preoccupied with a movement toward Xie An and then away again as we recognize the import of his gestures, "Song of Huyin" begins with a movement back and forth between Emperor Ming and Wang Dun. The poem opens with a close-up of Ming, who is described with the lavish use of adjectives Wen customarily reserves for women; then we shift to Wang Dun's dream (yet another in a long list of dreams in the poet's works). Wang's vision here stands for the foolhardiness of his rebellion—just as his "dreams" are about to be realized, they are destroyed by his vision of the imperial sun. Then, in perhaps the most outstanding couplet in the poem, we follow Wang as he leaves his tent to look for his enemy: distracted by a flash of reflected light, he catches sight of Emperor Ming across the lake. One may easily speak of Wen's poetry in cinematic terms; here his techniques are at their most daring, from the description of the emperor to Wang Dun's dream (with the emperor perceived again in symbolic form) to a view of the emperor yet again, from a distance. Here the metaphorical sun becomes the distracting glint of armor; as it conceals itself in dust, the horsemen return from their futile search. We should not be surprised that Wang Dun's own avatar, the "demon star," declines at this point. The third stanza details (metaphorically and metonymically) the recovery of imperial power: the army is sent out to defeat the rebel.

The lights in the first two stanzas distract, dazzle, expose, and conceal; and the central rhetorical pole of both anecdote and poem is one of concealment and exposure. The emperor has come incognito, but his imperial presence manifests itself in Wang's dream; his light is exposed, then disappears behind dust. Next, the emperor goes "behind the scenes," so to speak, and changes into his full imperial regalia, no longer traveling in disguise but sitting on his throne—a star that becomes the final luminous avatar of his power. The gradual buildup of images in the third stanza has led up to this couplet of apotheosis (lines thirteen and fourteen).

Yet Wen ends with a couplet describing a peaceful natural scene. Since "Huyin" is about the suppression of an internal rebellion, a revolt that threatened the peace of China itself, Wen may be evoking the peace restored to the land by the defeat of Wang Dun. And yet a touch of sadness remains; at the time of Wang Dun's rebellion the Jin was in chaos, having just lost the north to nomadic invaders. Moreover, the last line with its balcony elicits comparison with "climbing tower" poems, which in turn have elements of the old *huaigu*, the meditation on historical sites. Could this be Wen's way of entering the poem at the end, unobtrusively suggesting that we are now viewing the transient past from the present?

However we read it, the ending is subtle and adds a further tone of theatricality. Emperor Ming has won after his grand costume change, and the play is over. History is swept from the stage again, and we see only the scenic backdrop.

A similar rhetorical move away from history and its consequences can be found in a poem on Emperor Wu of the Han; in his effort to conquer an aboriginal people in the Yunnan area, Wu discovered that their territory could only be reached by crossing Kunming 昆明 (also called Dian 滇) Lake. He subsequently built an artificial lake southwest of Chang'an, where a navy could practice maneuvers in preparation for the invasion, and named this body of water after its model. Here once again the possibility of irony arises, though probably without moral judgment.

Song: Naval Battle on Kunming Lake	昆明治水戰詞
The deep waters stretch far and wide, their glitter reaches to the sky.	汪汪積水光連空
Delicate patterns, piled up— joined ripples turn red.	重疊細紋交激紅
The Crimson Emperor, dragon-scion, fish-scale armored, rages:	赤帝龍孫鮮甲怒
4 One glance by current's edge and he glares once: a hidden wind is born.	臨流一眄生陰風

Lizard-skin drums thrice resound
    in reply to Heaven's Son; 鼉鼓三聲報天子
With pheasant banners, the beast-galleons
    rise as they cross the waves. 雕旗獸艦凌波起
Thunder roars as frothy waves startle,
    a white the size of hills; 雷吼濤驚白若山
8 Stone leviathan's eye is split,
    coiling sea serpents die. 石鯨眼裂蟠蛟死

By the shores of Dian Pool
    all is roar and clash, 滇池海浦俱喧豗
As Black Feather and Painted Albatross
    come out in their formations. 青翰畫鷁相次來
Arrow-feathers and spear-thongs—
    three million in number. 箭羽槍纓三百萬
12 Troops trample the Western Sea
    and cause the dust to rise. 蹋翻西海生塵埃

Now the Maoling immortal has left,
    as caltrop flowers age; 茂陵仙去菱花老
Blowing bubbles, the playful fish
    approach the misty isles. 喈喈游魚近烟島
Far away, in lingering sunlight
    a fishing skiff goes home; 渺莽殘陽釣艇歸
16 And green-headed river ducks
    sleep in the sandy grass. 綠頭江鴨眠沙草
        (*WFQ*, j. 2, pp. 32–33)

3/ The Crimson Emperor: red is the color associated with the Han.

8/ Emperor Wu had statues of jade leviathans erected along the banks of Kunming; during thunderstorms they reputedly roared and shook their tails.

10/ "Black Feather" and "Painted Albatross" are descriptions of boats—the first, from the boat's shape, the second, from the patterns painted on the hull. They became kennings for warships.

11/ "Western Sea" is another name for the wilderness of Qinghai 青海 in western China: a vast expanse of desert, compared visually to the sea.

As in "Duke Xie's Villa" and as in the first stanza of "Huyin," Wen comes close here to true narrative as he describes one specific military exercise in detail. In doing so, he explores the character of Emperor Wu, a historical personage much beloved of poets.

As we have noted, poems on rulers such as the first Qin emperor Shihuang and Emperor Wu reflect a fascination with strong character, pride, and the display of imperial might. Although such poems often contain an element of moral criticism, there is also pleasure in the exercise of power. Wen places Emperor Wu squarely in the middle of his poem; as we look over the waters of the lake, we see the emperor rising from the waters themselves. The red sunlight on the waves evokes his own imperial color; and as the descendant of dragons he displays his power over the watery element. The expansion of the Han empire springs forth through Wu's own colossal will: he summons the wind that drives his ships and then summons the ships themselves, which ply the waters like gigantic whales at his command. This is the power that can destroy the leviathan and the sea serpent: the eighth line may refer to Wu's battle with a dragon of the Yangzi, as related in the *Han shu*.[31]

But Emperor Wu's power is not limited to this artificial pool; just as the practice battle is a smaller version of the real battle to be fought, and this small Kunming Lake a model of Lake Dian in Yunnan, so his display here is merely a minor demonstration of the might of Han, just as Xie An's chessboard prefigured the battlefield near the Huai. By another act of sympathetic magic (carried out by a shift of perspective at the stanza break), the model lake becomes the real one, and actual war is waged. Furthermore, Wen suddenly broadens the perspective from one campaign in Yunnan to the entire policy of imperial expansion; as the troops fill vast Qinghai with their dust, we can read this desert as yet a larger field of enterprise: from artificial pond to gigantic lake to a metaphorical "sea" itself. From the empty waters of line one, Emperor Wu has conjured an entire world subject to his control.

We would suspect this rapidly expanding world held in place by Wu's will to be a fragile one at best; in the last stanza, Wen shows the world after the balloon bursts. These last four lines constitute a gentle quatrain of natural description, like the concluding couplet of "Huyin"; yet a sharp irony guides our reading. Maoling was Emperor Wu's tomb, and "Maoling immortal" is a pointed oxymoron, especially strong when applied to an emperor so obsessed with discovering the secret of immortality. Line fourteen line may have ironic dimensions as well. It suggests an anecdote in which the emperor helped a fish by pulling a hook from its mouth and was rewarded the following day by a gift of pearls; although he was able to preserve the fish's life, he is now gone, leaving indifferent fish behind him. Of course, the sudden shift from an ancient and glorious past to the calming landscape of the present is a *huaigu* technique, perhaps most brilliantly executed by Li Bai in his "Observing Antiquity at Yue" 越中覽古.

When the King of Yue, Gou Jian had returned from smashing Wu,	越王句踐破吳歸
His noble knights returned to their homes all dressed in brocade robes.	義士還家盡錦衣
The palace ladies, like blossoms, filled the spring palace	宮女如花滿春殿
Where today there is only the flight of partridges.[32]	只今惟有鷓鴣飛

In Wen's grander scenario, the poet argues not that humanity is unimportant compared to the eternity of natural process, but rather that humanity achieves its own preservation through the ideal of a life led naturally and unambitiously. Unlike "Cockcrow Dike," the poem produces a fisherman rather than a depopulated silence; but the fisherman is a natural creature, unconcerned with the vagaries of political power. Although this is not so obvious an attack as Du Mu's poem on Qin Shihuang, "Visiting Mount Li," the dismissal of Han's power is just as strong.

Wen's casual destruction of Wu's empire bears some resemblance to the couplet shifts in Late Tang regulated *huaigu*: there, too, ancient power is often contrasted with the omnipresent force of nature that sweeps it aside. As we have seen, the poets of the Mid- and Late Tang tended to observe antiquity's pride from a perspective that guaranteed its eventual triviality; history had lost its ability to make a significant mark for good or ill. A poet such as Wen may admire the glories of power with an artist's eyes, but in the end he too deflates the actions of rulers. Although at its extreme this attitude emerges most clearly in the Late Tang, it continues to lie at the heart of a Chinese worldview that sees human actions either as a part of nature or as a futile gesture rendered unimportant by that nature; Chinese historical tragedy is eminently more "organic" than Western.

Paul Valéry: *César*

    César, calme César, le pied sur toute chose,
    Les poings durs dans la barbe, et l'oeil sombre peuplé
    D'aigles et des combats du couchant contemplé,
    Ton coeur s'enfle, et se sent toute-puissante Cause.

> Le lac en vain palpite et lèche son lit rose;
> En vain d'or précieux brille le jeune blé;
> Tu durcis dans les noeuds de ton corps rassemblé
> L'ordre, qui doit enfin fendre ta bouche close.
>
> L'ample monde, au delà de l'immense horizon,
> L'Empire attend l'éclair, le décret, le tison
> Qui changeront le soir en furieuse aurore.
>
> Heureux là-bas sur l'onde, et bercé du hasard,
> Un pêcheur indolent qui flotte et chante, ignore
> Quelle foudre s'amasse au centre de César.[33]

(Caesar, serene Caesar, your foot on all affairs, your hard fists in your beard and your dark eyes inhabited by the eagles and the battles of a contemplated sunset: your heart swells, feeling omnipotent Purpose.

In vain the lake trembles and licks its rosy bed; in vain the young wheat trembles with its precious gold. You harden in the knots of your assembled form the command that must in the end split your shut mouth.

The ample world beyond the immense horizon—the Empire—awaits the torch, the decree, the lightning bolt that will change evening into furious dawn.

Happily, out on the waves, rocked by chance, a lazy fisherman floats and sings, unaware of what thunder masses in the core of Caesar.)

There is a startling similarity of images between Valéry's and Wen's poems. Valéry's Caesar stands like Emperor Wu over his personal lake, the Mediterranean, until a single command releases war throughout the world. From his center the poetic world radiates outward just as it did from Emperor Wu's, but the fisherman at the end of his sonnet is not the survivor of wars but a possible victim of the holocaust unleashed by ambition. Both East and West found great poetic potential in the evocation of raw power in ancient rulers, but the Late Tang poet found more pungent ironies in the futility of ambition than in the helpless peasants unaware of the unbridled forces of war about to descend on them. One may assume that the destruction caused by war in Tang China was considerably less than it was in late nineteenth-century Europe.

Xie An was an aesthete, Emperor Ming an actor, Emperor Wu a conjuror. In each of these poems, Wen turns historical events into a tenuous unreality. The ultimate development of these trends is the complete divorce of historical figures from their own times, as when Wen describes a fictional spring outing by a Han emperor. In such cases, a timeless world emerges not unlike that of the immortals; compare to Li He's "Dreaming of Heaven" and Wen's "Dawn Immortal Song" translated in Chapter 2.

Song: The Han Emperor Welcomes Spring 漢皇迎春詞

Spring grass lush and thick,
   a clear spell sweeps away mist. 春草芊芊晴掃烟
Palace walls hung with large-patterned brocades,
   their dark crimson fresh. 宮城大錦紅殷鮮

The sun from the sea as it shines
   seems to melt the immortals' palms; 海日如融照仙掌
4 The King of Huainan's small troop
   ring the bells tied to their caps. 淮王小隊纓鈴響
The east wind flutters about
   the blazing pennants, unfurling them; 獵獵東風展燄旗
And painted gods in golden armor
   crowd upon the emperor's screen. 畫神金甲蔥蘢網

The Great Lord in his palanquin
   welcomes Ju Mang; 鉅公步輦迎句芒
8 And roofed galleries are swept of dust
   by the length of simurgh brooms. 複道掃塵鸞彗長
Before the poles topped with leopard tails,
   Zhao the Flying Swallow 豹尾竿前趙飛燕
Has the yellow powder on her brow
   blown away by the willow breeze. 柳風吹盡眉間黃

Jade grass restrains its feelings,
   while apricot flowers rejoice. 碧草含情杏花喜
12 In Shanglin Park, orioles warble,
   and dancing silk threads rise. 上林鶯囀游絲起
Bejeweled horses shake harness rings,
   a myriad horsemen return; 寶馬搖環萬騎歸
The light of his favor secretly withdraws
   behind window curtain and lattice. 恩光暗入簾櫳裏

(*QTS*, *j*. 1, pp. 27–29)

Title/ The song describes a spring excursion, probably to carry out a sacrifice. See *Li ji*: "In the [first] month there takes place the inauguration of spring.... On the [first] day [the Son of Heaven] leads in person the three ducal ministers, his nine high ministers, the feudal princes (who are at court), and his great officers, to meet the spring in the eastern suburb; and on his return he rewards them all in court."[34]

3/ These are the statues of immortals built by Emperor Wu to collect dew for the manufacture of the elixir of immortality.

4/ The King of Huainan, Liu An 劉安 (d. 122 B.C.), was known for his interest in Taoism and to him is attributed the authorship of the *Huainan zi* 淮南子. I have taken this line to refer to a group of select Taoist adepts he is patronizing.

5/ The screen may refer either to the windows of the various palaces the procession passes or perhaps to the screens in the emperor's palanquin.

7/ Ju Mang was a minister of high antiquity who became the tutelary deity of Spring and of Wood, one of the five elements.

8/ In the Han, the lead carriage in an imperial procession was decorated with banners depicting mythical birds (*luan*, often translated as "simurgh") and ornaments with ranks of feathers tied to the curtains. Wen's line suggests the carriage's resemblance to a gigantic bird with feathers sweeping the palace galleries.

9–10/ Zhao the Flying Swallow is Zhao Feiyan, favorite of Emperor Cheng; her carriage was supposedly decorated with panther tails. We see here again a mention of palace ladies painting their foreheads with yellow powder.

12/ Shanglin: a large imperial hunting park near Chang'an, subject of a celebrated *fu* by Sima Xiangru. "Dancing silk threads" are willow catkins.

We may wonder which Han emperor is being discussed. Gu Sili, like any good late classical commentator, is concerned with this question, and he argues that the mention of Zhao Feiyan in lines nine and ten ties the poem to the reign of Emperor Cheng. Unless Wen wished to paint a sort of genre picture of Han glory, Gu is probably right: the seemingly anachronistic appearance of the bronze immortals and Huainan's wizards would be the intrusion of the supernatural into Emperor Cheng's world—not unusual, perhaps, for an emperor who, like Emperor Wu, was interested in spirits and magicians. Moreover, Emperor Cheng is quite probably on his way to a spring sacrifice, when he will renew his own ties to the numinous world.

And yet this introduction of the timeless and the supernatural toward the beginning of the poem makes Emperor Cheng himself a numinous figure. Wen's interest in the vivid description of detail, both natural and ornamental, situates Cheng in a glowing environment where everything is alive: bronze immortals, painted warriors, carriages transformed into magical birds, personified grass and flowers. We never see the emperor, only his possessions and his people: but he is the presence that creates the magic.

Wen comes close here to poems by himself and Li He that describe the realm of the immortals, and we can detect the narrow boundary line between historical descriptions and pure fantasy. He even manipulates the rhetorical convention of comparing the court to heaven: in describing a past glory, remote from us in time, he might as well be describing heaven itself. Furthermore, by ignoring the implications of Han glory and decline (Cheng's preoccupation with women like Zhao Feiyan is often cited as the cause of Wang Mang's usurpation a few years later), Wen revels in a pure fantasy of luxury and wealth.[35] We do not see Yang Xiong's book-filled room; we do not even have a sudden vision of a natural landscape free of historical actors. Instead, we have the emperor withdrawing into Zhao Feiyan's bedchambers, a return to the penetrations of old palace-poetry tropes! If the historian Sima Qian saw Han emperors' attempts to communicate with the spirits as one long account of gullibility, waste, and folly,[36] Wen sees instead a historical past in which the actors themselves have achieved the status of immortals—free of moral judgment and objects of beauty and wonder.

In retrospect, we can see more clearly the artistic accomplishments of Wen's historical *yuefu*. By adopting Li He's historical song form and imbuing it with his own tendencies toward elegant description and lush depiction of detail, Wen creates a series of poetic anecdotes. At their most detailed and precise, as in "Duke Xie's Villa" and "Naval Battle on Kunming Lake," Wen balances his own tendency toward descriptive fragmentation with a new attention to spatial and temporal order. He tells a story by implying relationships between one visual fragment and another. In poems on broader historical themes, he shifts back and forth from brief narrative to broader commentary, relying on an ambiguity that blurs the line between rhetorical metonymy and detail.

As I noted in Chapter 3, Wen's erotic songs rely on an implied poetic structure based on the received conventions of palace poetry: readers who had studied the palace poets would understand the implications of his images, although he himself left them unexplained. In these narrative songs, Wen uses anecdote and allusion, in a way startlingly new to Chinese poetry. Rather than serving as a reference point for judgment, allusion is a basis for detail: it allows Wen to utilize poetic space to guess at what the actual scene looked like and what aesthetic order it possessed. Moreover, instead of ruins and human figures left to wonder and wander among them, we discover a new ability to shape past events and use them for artistic purposes. The historical subgenres traditionally have often found the past a device for expressing truths about the present. Wen fashions instead an objet d'art.

Empathy Replaces Judgment: The Yang Guifei Poems

Wen Tingyun usually chose to discuss the Six Dynasties period in his historical songs, not in his regulated verse. Although the tone of irony that characterizes much of Li Shangyin's and Du Mu's poems on history does emerge in Wen's *yuefu* (especially in the Chen and Sui poems), he is more content to evoke the past as a magical fantasy, a display of pomp with masks and conjuring tricks. Wen stands on different ground from Li Shangyin and Du Mu, although his manipulation of history for aesthetic effect does spring from the same doubts about the capability of history to impart moral lessons.

Yet another aspect of Wen's use of history occurs in the *huaigu* poems that deal with the love affair between the Tang emperor Xuanzong 玄宗 (r. 712–56) and Yang Guifei 楊貴妃 (d. 756). We know from the works of Wen's contemporaries that by the ninth century Yang Guifei had already become a favorite subject of anecdote and legend; the most famous retelling, of course, is Bai Juyi's long narrative poem, "The Song of Lasting Pain" 長恨歌 and its complementary prose account by Chen Hong 陳鴻 (fl. 805). We may also note the existence of the ninth-century *Account of the An Lushan Affair* 安祿山事記, which alludes to various events in Yang's life. But most telling are the *huaigu* and *yongshi* by numerous Mid- and Late Tang poets that make passing references to names, events, and places; such poems presuppose a familiarity on the part of the reader with many details in Xuanzong's reign and bespeak the popularity of the theme only two or three generations after the rebellion. A brief synopsis of the popular conception of the events will serve to introduce Wen's poems on the subject.

The first few decades of Xuanzong's reign were marked by universal peace and prosperity, and the emperor proved an able administrator. As he grew older, however, he took less and less interest in matters of administration. One day he happened to see a consort of one of his sons, a woman from the Yang family, and immediately fell in love with her. He took her away from his son and set her up as his chief concubine (a status somewhat below that of the empress proper), giving her the title *guifei* or "prized consort"; because the emperor was a devout believer in Taoism and a patron of the Taoist religious establishments, he also made her a sort of Taoist lay-nun, giving her the title of Taizhen 太真 or Great Verity. From this time on, he abandoned governmental matters, spending much of his time at the Huaqing Palace, a mansion located on Mount Li, a hot springs resort east of the capital. There he and Yang engaged in wild and unbridled pleasure, usually marked (at least from the stern Confucianist's point of view) by luxurious waste and lascivious self-indulgence. There Yang Guifei would dance her famous dance, "Coats of Feathers, Rainbow Skirts," supposedly inspired by a dance performance on the moon seen by one of the emperor's musicians in his dreams. Xuanzong's chief minister, the hated Li Linfu 李林甫, was then replaced by Yang's cousin, Yang Guozhong 楊國忠, who soon proved himself far more incompetent and greedy than his predecessor.

Meanwhile, an unknown half-barbarian general, An Lushan 安祿山, ingratiated himself with the emperor by flattering Yang Guifei and by playing the buffoon at court. The emperor, led into trusting him, appointed him commander of the crucial border area of Yuyang 漁陽 to the northeast, in the vicinity of present-day Beijing. In 755, An Lushan rebelled and marched with his army on the eastern capital of Luoyang, which quickly fell. He then turned west and marched on Chang'an. The imperial troops, poorly led and torn by political dissension, were easily routed, and An Lushan soon captured the Tong 潼 Pass, on the only open road to the capital. The emperor was forced to flee south to Sichuan (then known as Shu) with Yang Guifei and her hated cousin; before he left, however, he consigned imperial authority to his son, who was ordered to the northwest to rally the imperial armies and to recruit allies among the nomadic tribes of central Asia.

On his way to Shu, the emperor's bodyguard mutinied at the post station at Mawei 馬嵬 Slope and refused to proceed unless both Yang Guozhong and Yang Guifei were executed. The emperor reluctantly agreed, and his chief eunuch strangled Yang Guifei and buried her by the roadside. Shortly afterward, Xuanzong officially abdicated and made his son emperor; his successor is known to history as Emperor Suzong 肅宗 (r. 756–62). Although it was over ten years before the rebellion was completely suppressed, Suzong soon brought most of China back under imperial authority, and the now-retired Xuanzong returned to the capital. He ordered his eunuchs to find Guifei's grave and to reinter her corpse in the capital; by the time they found it, however, her remains had already long decayed.[37]

Presumably Late Tang poets would handle a Tang theme with more caution than they would a Six Dynasties subject. The Tang, after all, was a far greater dynasty than the ephemeral Southern courts, and poets would feel pressure to treat the actions of their own polity with greater seriousness. The events were also much closer to them in time; in his childhood Wen could have known people who had seen the end of Xuanzong's reign. Bai Juyi, while treating Xuanzong romantically, did not neglect to condemn his behavior; even the ironists Li Shangyin and Du Mu, though attracted by the opportunities of its aesthetic representation, for the most part treated the rebellion as a great public tragedy.[38] How Wen treats the subject, then, is an interesting litmus test of his place in the Late Tang poetic and intellectual world.

His most ambitious attempts to address the theme are three long *pailü* that technically fall into the *huaigu* subgenre: "Visiting Huaqing Palace: Twenty-two Rhymes," "Huaqing Palace: Matching Secretary Du [Mu]" (both discussed below), and a poem in eighty lines on the Court for Reception of Foreigners (*Honglu si* 鴻臚寺), which housed a banqueting hall frequented by Xuanzong (*WFQ*, *j*. 9, pp. 190–95). The second of these is modeled on Du Mu's "Huaqing Palace: Thirty Rhymes" 華清宮三十韻 (*QTS*, *j*. 521, p. 5950). All of them attempt to trace the entire scope of Yang's relationship with the emperor.

Long *pailü* are among the most difficult Tang poems to appreciate today. They were often written as virtuoso showpieces—the form demands that a poet maintain tonal regulation and a single rhyme over dozens of lines. The *pailü* was also the *shi* genre in which a poet was expected to demonstrate his mastery of the classics and of obscure and erudite vocabulary. These qualities contribute to making the *pailü* a conservative form in the context of poetic developments in the Mid- and Late Tang. Moreover, *pailü* are also structurally loose, despite their rigid metrical requirements: couplets often form a chain of vaguely connected units extending indefinitely through the poet's ability to sustain a rhyme.

It should hardly come as a surprise, then, that Wen's *pailü* on Xuanzong and Yang Guifei lack the originality of his historical songs. One may note even here, however, the existence of certain characteristic elements: the avoidance of moral comment (only the vaguest implicit criticism can be read in them); a stronger interest in describing the wealth and luxury of the Huaqing outings, as opposed to the political catastrophe of the rebellion; and an imagistic vividness that, although generally unexploited, again reveals Wen's interest in detail. For example, "Huaqing Palace: Matching Secretary Du [Mu]" 華清宮和杜舍人, a more interesting poem artistically than its model, has moments of vivid beauty and witty irony.[39]

The moon locks in the silence of a thousand gates;	月鎖千門靜
The sky is lofty—a single flute is chill. (ll. 25–26)	天高一笛涼

and:

Blood buries the consort's face;[40]	血埋妃子貌
Blades smash the guts of "lucky boy." (ll. 35–36)	刀斷祿兒腸

This last couplet evokes Yang's and An Lushan's death in one graphic pairing; behind it lie Yang's comic adoption of An Lushan as a son and his christening as "lucky boy" (a pun on his name). The violent death of the "mother" is placed against the end of the rebellious "son." Also powerful is Wen's final description of the palace ruins; here we can see the Late Tang sensitivity to couplet art:

49	Sparrow eggs are left under carved eaves;	雀卵遺雕栱
	A spider-silk net hangs from painted rafters.	蟲絲冒畫梁
	Purple moss glistens where it invades the walls;	紫苔侵壁潤
52	Red-blossomed trees are fragrant where they block the gates.	紅樹閉門芳
	Watchmen on guard piece together the mandarin duck tiles,	守吏齊鴛瓦
	Peasants plowing find turquoise earplugs.	耕民得翠璫
	Where they took pleasure in the delights of bygone times,	歡康昔時樂

56 Where former troops trained on parade grounds, 講武舊兵場
   Now the dusky grass lies deep in the haze on the cliffs 暮草深巖靄
   And unseen flowers fall scented on the paths. 幽花墜逐香
   I cannot bear how an old man, white hair hanging, 不堪垂白叟
60 Strolls here, snapping branches off the imperial canal willows. 行折御溝楊

The best of Wen's *pailü*, however, is his "Visiting Huaqing Palace: Twenty-two Rhymes" 過華清宮二十二韻 (*WFQ, j.* 6, pp. 139–43). It repeats the same "story" as the others, but to greater effect, mostly because of its reduced length, tighter structure, and interest in specific detail.

   I recall in those bygone days of Kaiyuan: 憶昔開元日
   In an era of peace they engaged in marvelous excursions. 承平事勝遊
   The Precious Consort shared imperial favor with none, 貴妃專寵幸
 4 While the Son of Heaven enjoyed a wealth of seasons. 天子富春秋
   The moon lit the Rainbow Skirt Palace, 月白霓裳殿
   The wind dried the Jie Drum Mansions. 風乾羯鼓樓
   The guardian of the cockfights had his flowered apron, 鬥雞花蔽膝
 8 All the horsemen, their jade scratchers. 騎馬玉搔頭
   Filigree wheel-hubs: the palace entertainers; 繡轂千門伎
   Gold saddles: the viscounts of ten thousand households. 金鞍萬戶侯
   The clouds soaked their swallowtail fans; 薄雲欺雀扇
12 Light snow invaded their sable robes. 輕雪犯貂裘
   Passing travelers heard the music of Shao and Hu, 過客聞韶濩
   Those who dwelt there knew the imperial crown's fringes. 居人識冕旒
   The air so pleasant, spring came unrecognized; 氣和春不覺
16 Mists were warm, scarcely melting on the clear days. 烟暖霽難收
   Fine ripples soaked the jasper tiles of the bathing pools; 澀浪和瓊甃
   Bright sunlight glittered on the rainbow pendants. 晴陽上彩斿
   Wispy-tressed ladies rolled up their robes lazily; 卷衣輕鬢嬾
20 Their pale brows shyly peeked in their mirrors. 窺鏡澹蛾羞
   Screens closed off the hibiscus awnings; 屏掩芙蓉帳
   Drapes were pulled aside on tortoise-shell hooks. 簾褰玳瑁鉤
   Double pupils distinguished a bend in the Wei River, 重瞳分渭曲
24 A slender hand pointed to the imperial heartland. 纖手指神州
   By imperial benches they lost themselves in the daylilies, 御案迷萱草
   Their divine robes made the pomegranates jealous. 天袍妒石榴
   Deep ravines concealed the bathing phoenix, 深巖藏浴鳳
28 While splendid fields were made lovely by a sunken dragon. 鮮隰媚潛虬

They did not know that the vermin of Handan 不料邯鄲蝨
Would suddenly turn into the cattle of Jimo. 俄成即墨牛
The points of swords waved in Taihao, 劍鋒揮太皥
32 Flames on banners, sweeping Chi You flags. 旗燄拂蚩尤
The court favorite went along with the retinue, 內嬖陪行在
While a lone minister prepared a secret plan. 孤臣預坐籌
The precious hairpin left its kingfisher feathers behind, 瑤簪遺翡翠
36 And frosty spears halted the Emperor's coursers. 霜仗駐驊騮
Their lovely smiles and paired flights were broken; 豔笑雙飛斷
The fragrant soul ceased with a single cry. 香魂一哭休
Early plums lament the road to Shu, 早梅悲蜀道
40 Lofty trees block the view of Zhaoyang Hill. 高樹隔昭邱
Now imperial chambers are close to thick clouds of sunset, 朱閣重霄近
And green cliffs grieve through all of time. 蒼厓萬古愁
From then to now, water from the palace of hot springs 至今湯殿水
44 Is choked as it flows before the district office. 嗚咽縣前流

1/ The Kaiyuan era (713–42) became a term for Xuanzong's reign in general, although Xuanzong's relation with Yang did not begin until the following Tianbao 天寶 period (742–56). Since the Kaiyuan period was the height of Tang prosperity and power, it later became synonymous with the Golden Age preceding the rebellion.

6/ "Jie Drum" was a kind of martial, "barbarian" music greatly prized by Xuanzong. It serves here (and elsewhere) to demonstrate the Emperor's preference for the wilder, more popular, and more sensuous music of Central Asia.

13/ *Shao* was the court music of the sage-emperor Shun 舜 (trad. 23rd century B.C.); *hu*, of the Shang dynasty (trad. 1766–1123 B.C.).

15/ The air was made warm by the hot springs; hence the use of Huaqing as a winter residence.

23–24/ Shun was said to possess double pupils. Xuanzong is meant here, of course, and the "slender hand" belongs to Yang Guifei.

25/ Daylily: the cure for sorrow and lovesickness.

27–28/ The "bathing phoenix" is Yang herself (Xuanzong first caught a glimpse of her while she was taking a bath); the "sunken dragon" is an emblem for Xuanzong as well as a description of a river flowing by the resort.

29–30/ Handan, in northeast China, was the origin of An's revolt. "Jimo cattle" refers to Tian Dan's 田單 defense of Jimo, a city in his home state of Qi during the late Warring States period. When a general from the state of Yan 燕 besieged the city, Tian gathered a herd of cattle, tied daggers to their horns, attached burning torches to their tails, and hung cloth patterned with dragons on their backs. He then drove them before the Yan army and sent his forces out behind them. Enraged, the cattle stampeded and demoralized the enemy, leaving them easy prey for the troops that followed.[41] Wen is being self-consciously clever here by finding two animal images for the rebels; the Jimo cattle may be specifically appropriate because they were seemingly docile animals who proved to be deadly.

31/ Taihao, another name for the sage emperor Fuxi 伏犧, was also the deity of the East; this line is an elegant description of An's forces moving west on the capital.

32/ Chi You was the rebellious minister who warred with the Yellow Emperor. A "Chi You flag" is a nickname for a comet or simply a flag meant to resemble a comet. A comet, of course, is often an omen of disaster.

33–36/ In four allusive lines Wen portrays the flight of the emperor and Yang from the capital and the death of Yang's cousin (the minister Yang Guozhong) and of Yang herself. Line thirty-three mentions her presence in the emperor's retinue; line thirty-four alludes to Chen Xuanli 陳玄禮, commander of Xuanzong's guard, who plotted with the heir apparent to murder Guozhong. "The frosty spears" are metonyms for the rebellious imperial guard who demanded Yang Guifei's execution.

40/ Zhaoyang Hill: The Tang emperor Taizong 太宗 (r. 626–49) was deeply attached to his consort, Lady Sun 孫, who was buried at Zhaoyang. He built a tower nearby from which he could see her grave. The general import here is Xuanzong's enforced separation from Yang's own place of burial; even after he returned to the capital in retirement, he found it difficult to obtain permission for Yang's reburial.

41–44/ Wen finally concludes in the *huaigu* manner (the palace in its current condition of decline). The district office may have been a nearby government headquarters where Wen composed the poem.

The token description of Xuanzong's able rule and the prosperity of the empire is gone; Wen immediately launches on a twenty-four-line description of the excursions themselves (lines five to twenty-eight). The poem does not make Xuanzong out as a man blinded by his own wealth and luxury and lulled into false security by the peace inherited from his predecessors; rather, it claims that prosperity manifests itself in banquets, music, and pleasure. The second couplet (lines three and four) allies the emperor's favors to Yang with the prosperity he enjoys in the world at large; Wen also compares Xuanzong's banquet music with the music of the sage-emperors and mentions the presence of ministers of state at the palace (lines thirteen and fourteen). When An Lushan rebels in line twenty-nine, we are struck only by his ingratitude and by the pathos of the disaster; the poem regrets not the fall of the empire but the end of the feast. The scale is thus more modest and personal, and Wen's favorite poetic device of "close-ups" (or, technically, metonymic and synecdochal substitutions) come easily into full play, reinforcing the personal aspect of life at Huaqing and making it more concrete. In the procession to the palace (lines seven to ten), each group in the entourage is identified by some distinctive possession, and, by once again using palace-poetry images, Wen evokes court ladies by articles of clothing and items in their boudoir (lines eleven and twelve, nineteen to twenty-two). Wen also uses images to evoke the Huaqing Palace specifically, as opposed to any site of imperial splendor; not only does he make musical allusions to Xuanzong's court (lines five and six), but he also touches on Yang's luxuriant baths in the hot springs (line seventeen) and the emperor's strolls with his favorite on the palace grounds (lines twenty-three to twenty-six). When the rebellion has destroyed this pleasure, Wen dwells not on the national disaster, but on Xuanzong's personal unhappiness and deprivation (lines thirty-seven to forty); at the end, Wen succeeds in moving the emperor's sorrow from the personal realm only by introducing a pathetic fallacy (lines forty-one to forty-four), which he can now distinguish as he visits the ancient site. Xuanzong's grief can still be seen in the clouds and the cliffs.

In several shorter poems on the Yang Guifei–Xuanzong theme, the relatively concise genres of quatrain and *lüshi* allow Wen to make sharp, pithy observations and to juxtapose images (real and imagined) without going beyond the aphoristic. Read in a sequence based on Xuanzong's own career, they give us, not a long narrative, like Bai Juyi's "Song of Lasting Pain," but a series of shifting perspectives from various stages in Xuanzong's story. In many of these poems, two temporal movements are important: first, the standard *huaigu* movement from subject's past to poet's present, and, second, the relationship of what occurred at any specific site (Mawei Station, for example) and what had happened before and would happen after. Wen, with his penchant for fragments, is intensely aware that a specific site represents only part of a long and complex biography; it can stimulate the memory not only of the poet, but of the poet's subject also.

First, two quatrains on a familiar topic.

Huaqing Palace: Two Poems 華清宮二首

I

Windy trees in clear rows, 風樹離離月稍明
   the moon slightly bright;
The Nine-Heaven dragon aura 九天龍氣在華清
   resides at Huaqing.

Palace gates locked deep, 宮門深鎖無人覺
no one aware—
4 But at midnight, within the clouds, 半夜雲中羯鼓聲
the sound of a Jie drum.

II

The imperial chambers lie deep within, 天閣沈沈夜未央
the night is not yet done;
In jade clouds, a faerie music; 碧雲仙曲舞霓裳
she dances the Rainbow Skirt.
A single note from a jade flute 一聲玉笛向空盡
dissipates in midair;
8 The moonlight fills Mount Li, 月滿驪山宮漏長
the palace water clock drips long.
(*WFQ, j.* 9, p. 199)[42]

The Jie drums are matched with the Rainbow Skirt dance just as in the third couplet of Wen's longer poem on Huaqing; here, he splits the couplet and writes a quatrain on each line. Like Du Mu in his quatrain series on the same subject, Wen visualizes an outsider looking toward the palace; but unlike Du (and unlike his own usual practice), he chooses not to visualize any specific images of Xuanzong's extravagance. Rather, he emphasizes the isolation and silence and suggests that the palace may well be empty; then remotely, almost beyond hearing, perceived as though floating from the clouds, the imperial music reaches the ear. The effect is unearthly, almost haunting; and we experience once again a frustration of *huaigu* expectations. Do the poems take place in Xuanzong's own day, or in Wen's? If the latter case, is Wen imagining the music, or is he suggesting a supernatural continuation of the emperor's feasts?

The supernatural suggestion—as well as the music's connection with the clouds and the identification of the Rainbow Skirt with the world of "faerie" (the Taoist immortals)—links the emperor and Yang with an implied immortality. The emperor was a devoted disciple of religious Taoism, and Yang herself was enrolled as a Taoist nun. Wen's poems here move beyond the polite identification of the imperial palace with the Taoist heaven and bring Xuanzong's story into the supernatural realm, a tendency already exploited by Bai Juyi. The music is ethereal and transient at the same time, blocking our ability to determine if Xuanzong falls victim to history or transcends it altogether. As one might expect, these quatrains have no element of moral criticism and irony, unlike Du Mu's.[43]

The next poem in the series is ostensibly a *huaigu* on Mawei Post Station; the main metaphor here is the comparison between Xuanzong's flight to Shu and King Mu's (trad. r. 1001–946 B.C.) legendary visit to the Queen Mother of the West 西王母, a divinity who lived by the Jasper Pool 瑤池 at the far western edge of the habitable world.

Mawei Station 　　　　　　　　　　　　馬嵬驛

King Mu once traveled
　beyond the ordinary world; 　　穆滿曾為物外遊
His six dragons passed here
　and tarried for a time. 　　　　六龍經此暫淹留
No sign of the returning soul
　in the dark mist that melts; 　　返魂無驗青烟滅
4 Sunken blood vainly turns
　to grief in green grass. 　　　　埋血空成碧草愁
The fragrant palanquin returned
　to the Palace of Lasting Joy, 　香輦卻歸長樂殿
And morning bells descended again
　from the Jingyang mansions; 　曉鐘還下景陽樓
But he's not able to see her again
　at Sweet Springs; 　　　　　　甘泉不得重相見
8 Who says the General of Peaceful Accomplishments
　was indeed a lord of old? 　　誰道文成是故侯
　　(*WFQ*, *j*. 4, p. 90)

2/ "Six dragons" is a conventional kenning for the emperor's team of horses.

5/ This refers to Xuanzong's eventual return to Chang'an. The Palace of Lasting Joy was an imperial palace in both Han and Tang times and came to have particular associations with Xuanzong and Yang Guifei.

6/ Jingyang: the consorts' quarters.

7–8/ A reference to the death of and mourning for Lady Li 李, one of the Han Emperor Wu's favorites. After her death, the emperor hung her portrait in Sweet Springs Palace and remained inconsolable. A wizard from Qi, Shao Weng 少翁, promised to summon her spirit and in fact made her appear before the emperor. As a reward, the emperor granted him the title General of Peaceful Accomplishments. Shortly thereafter, Shao Wang's magical powers waned, and he was eventually executed.[44]

Wen's comparison of Mu's journey and Xuanzong's flight to Shu is appropriate because Xuanzong had to travel west for some distance before he could head south through the passes to Sichuan and because King Mu lost a favorite concubine, Lady Sheng 盛, during the course of his journey and was forced to bury her at a roadside shrine; Lady Sheng's death is thus a symbol for the death of Yang. The modern reader may find the equation of Mu's glorious adventure and Xuanzong's ignoble flight absurd (both may be designated by the euphemistic verb *xing* 幸, used for an emperor's travels), but the poem projects no ironic dimension. Rather, it identifies Xuanzong with a figure of legend and associates him with the Taoist pantheon (the Queen Mother of the West had become a Taoist divinity by Tang times and Mu's own journey, ostensibly undertaken as a search for personal immortality, came to have strong significance in Taoist writings). Xuanzong will live on after his consort dies; the poem seems to suggest that the cortege stops because a woman perishes and not because her death has become necessary. Once again, Wen is concerned not with history but with the emperor's personal loss.

Because of this emphasis, the second couplet is probably not the scene as it appears before Wen's eyes but a description of the conditions that make it impossible for Xuanzong to recover Yang: not only has her soul fled, but her body has decayed as well, as the eunuchs who attempted to disinter her discovered. Next, Wen imposes a *huaigu* context on the emperor himself, as he imagines him returning to his old palace, where every room must have some association with the Guifei. The last couplet then becomes not Wen's emotional response to the site of Mawei Station, but Xuanzong's to his loss of Yang. Here the emperor's predicament is compared to that of Emperor Wu; he despairs that he can find no one to summon Yang's soul for him and is given to doubt whether Shao Weng had really been capable of calling Lady Li's spirit, or perhaps even wonders whether the historical account is reliable. The "Who says..." is not one of Li Shangyin's ironic retorts but rather the frustration of a deprived lover.

Interestingly enough, Li comes closest to Wen's aesthetic approach in a poem on this very subject.

Li Shangyin: *Mawei (second of two)*　　　　　　　　馬嵬二首之二

He knows, uselessly, that beyond the sea　　　海外徒聞更九州
　　yet another nine provinces exist;

Yet before he can divine a life to come this present life ceases.	他生未卜此生休
In vain he hears his Tiger Guard transmit the evening watch;	空聞虎旅傳宵柝
4 Never again will the Rooster-man report the morning levee.	無復雞人報曉籌
On this day the Six Armies together halted their steeds;	此日六軍同駐馬
While in the past, on Seventh Night, they laughed the Herd Boy to scorn.	當時七夕笑牽牛
What profit to be the Son of Heaven for a stretch of forty years	如何四紀為天子
8 When you're worse off than the Lu clan, who managed to get their Mochou?	不及盧家有莫愁

(QTS, j. 539, p. 6177)

1/ The Warring States philosopher Zou Yan 騶衍 held that the "nine provinces" of China were merely one land area among nine that made up the world. Xuanzong envisages a land of refuge for himself and the Guifei, either in this life or the next.

3/ The Tiger Guard are the troops who accompanied Xuanzong on the trip to Shu.

4/ The Rooster-man acted as timekeeper and watchman in the imperial palace.

5/ The "Six Armies" was a standard term for the emperor's troops in the capital. This refers to their mutiny at Mawei.

6/ Xuanzong and Yang Guifei, happily united in the palace, mock the Herd Boy's frustration at only meeting with the Weaver Girl once a year.

8/ Allusion to a *yuefu* tradition that describes a beautiful girl, Mochou (whose name means "Don't Worry"), who marries into the wealthy Lu family.

As in a traditional *huaigu*, Li constructs his poem around a central opposition of past and present, but as in Wen's poem, the past and present are Xuanzong's, not the poet's. Xuanzong's act of remembrance is simulated perfectly by the construction of the parallel couplets, lines three to six: the first line of each couplet describes the "present" (that is, Xuanzong after the death of Yang); the second line of each couplet describes the happy past. Li pictures Xuanzong himself looking around him and then comparing his surroundings (guards, mutinous troops) to his memories (palace watchmen, the Seventh Night festival). This creates a doubling within the *huaigu* format: Li remembers someone remembering. The emperor's final response, the comparison with the fortunate husband of Mochou, shows once again Li's portrayal of Xuanzong's *personal* grief and the recognition that it is his public role that has interfered with his private happiness. Some later traditional Chinese readers read the last couplet as ironic criticism (and indeed this note of criticism does occur in Li's poetry, as we have seen), but a juxtaposition with Wen's very similar verses suggests instead an empathic link with the deprived emperor.

Wen wrote another *huaigu* on Mawei, this one set at the site of Yang's strangulation.

The Buddhist Temple at Mawei 馬嵬佛寺

The wild pheasants cried in the night; 荒雞夜唱戰塵深
  the dust of battle was thick.
At dawn the elegant carriages 五鼓雕輿過上林
  passed by Shanglin Park.
Only then did he know that "city-toppling beauty" 才信傾城是真語
  was an apt phrase indeed;
4 Only by crushing her into the earth 直教塗地始甘心
  were the soldiers satisfied at last.
The paths through gardens of Qin 兩重秦苑成千里
  had turned to a thousand miles;
One stick of Tartar incense 一炷胡香抵萬金
  was worth a thousand in gold.
Since Dongfang Shuo died, 曼倩死來無絕藝
  his extraordinary art has vanished;
8 No one in later times was willing 後人誰肯惜青禽
  to cherish the magic Blue Bird.
  (*WFQ, j.* 9, p. 186)

5/ Two of the emperor's gardens in Chang'an, Hibiscus and Apricot, were collectively called the Qin Gardens. The allusion here is to the numerous roofed paths that Xuanzong had constructed to connect his various palaces and parks.

6/ Emperor Wu of the Han was once given a kind of incense by the ruler of Yuezhi, a northern barbarian tribe; its scent could resurrect the dead.

7–8/ Dongfang Shuo 東方朔, a palace advisor under Emperor Wu, knew that when a magic blue bird arrived, the emperor would soon be visited by the Queen Mother of the West.

Again, Xuanzong's memory is evoked as an organizing principle: the poem opens with the emperor's recollections rather than the poet's analysis. First, Xuanzong recalls his hurried departure from the capital. On the way west, he passed Shanglin Park, the royal hunting preserve, where he and his retinue had previously taken their pleasure. As he fled, he recognized that his obsession with Yang was to blame for the disaster; he ironically noticed that the cliché for a beautiful woman, "someone who can topple a city," has a more literal meaning as well. Then, at Mawei, the soldiers recognized the truth of this also; the parallel line describes these very soldiers causing Yang's own ignoble downfall. She is reduced to dust, like the city she "brought to ruins."

Returning to the present, after her execution, Xuanzong thinks without enthusiasm of the dangers of the approaching journey to Shu; he compares this flight to the pleasure excursions with Yang in the gardens of the capital (his ornamented carriages must now accomplish a much more arduous trip). Recalling again that he has lost her, he dreams of ways of bringing her back to life: obtaining a stick of incense that might resurrect her or seeking the advice of Dongfang Shuo, who was well-versed in Taoist lore. Once again, the poet is discreetly absent.

After Xuanzong departs Mawei Station, he proceeds to the next stop, Gazing Garden.

Written on Gazing Garden Post Station 題望苑驛

Author's[?] note: Mawei Station lies to the east, the Duanzheng Tree to the west.

A thousand twigs of pliant willow, a single branch of apricot.	弱柳千條杏一枝
Mist half-caused by spring rain within, and half, by willow floss hanging.	半含春雨半垂絲
Hard for a man to reach the chill well at Jingyang;	景陽寒井人難到
4 Only the dawn now recognizes the morning bells at the Palace of Lasting Joy.	長樂晨鐘曉自知
How many years have flower shadows reached to Broadview Court?	花影幾年通博望
In what age did a tree receive the sobriquet of "longing"?	樹名何世號相思
Till today the moon that shines upon a dozen mansions	至今十二樓前月
8 Does not shine on Lady Sheng, buried in a western mound.	不向西陵照盛姬

    (*WFQ, j.* 4, p. 92)

156   Patterns of History, Failures of History

Title and note/ Gazing Garden Post Station was another name for the Broadview Garden, the site of Tongling Pavilion, built by Emperor Wu of the Han for his son Li. The Duanzheng tree was a cypress that Xuanzong supposedly encountered by the road as he continued on his way to Shu. Impressed by its beauty, he named it after Duanzheng Mansion at the Huaqing Palace.[45]

3-4/ Though in other places "Jingyang" represents the consorts' quarters, here the allusion is probably to the well within which Chen Houzhu concealed himself when fleeing from the Sui troops.

6/ Commentators quote an anecdote from the *Sou shen ji* of a tree growing from the tomb of a mourned wife that received the nickname "longing" 相思. Although Wen is alluding to this story, his main intent is to indicate the Duanzheng Tree growing nearby.

8/ Western mound: where King Mu buried Lady Sheng. See discussion of "Mawei Station" above.

Although this poem is harder to judge, I think it still likely that we are seeing events from Xuanzong's point of view and not Wen's. Perhaps we are experiencing Xuanzong's visit to Gazing Garden on his return from Shu. The second couplet suggests that the emperor longs to rejoin Yang (he thinks of Chen Houzhu and his favorites, who at least met disaster together); the envisioned emptiness of the Chang'an Palace is repeated from "Mawei Station." The third couplet is most complex of all, because it adds yet another layer of historical distance: Gazing Garden itself is a relic of a bygone time, since it was the site of a terrace erected during the height of the Western Han. In the fifth line, Wen may be wondering at the span of time that has passed since the Han or since Xuanzong's tragedy; if he thinks through Xuanzong's mind as the latter returns to this place, he may be implying that it seems like years to the aging emperor since he lost his beloved. Likewise, the sixth line may be Xuanzong's own emotional attempt to replace the legendary "longing" tree with his own Duanzheng cypress—meaning it was he who created the nickname, not some legendary figure in the past. However, any sense of chronological precision is undermined by the ambiguities of the imagery and the language. The end is clearer: Xuanzong's thoughts in Chang'an as he watches the moon and imagines that Yang (Lady Sheng) is below the earth and shut out from the moonlight.

Another quatrain describes Xuanzong's naming of the Duanzheng tree.

Written on the Duanzheng Tree   題端正樹

By the roadside, a cassia tree—   路傍佳樹碧雲愁
   its jade-green clouds grieve;
Once she followed his golden carriage   曾侍金輿幸驛樓
   when he journeyed to the post station.
Grass and trees flourish and fade   草木榮枯似人事
   like the affairs of men;
Green shade, lonely and still—   綠陰寂寞漢陵秋
   autumn at the Han tombs.
   (*WFQ*, *j*. 5, pp. 113–14)

  1/ I take "cloud" to be a metaphor for the tree's foliage. Wen has turned the cypress into a cassia, perhaps for this very reason. Cypress trees express solidity and unchanging rectitude, inappropriate for Wen's more sentimental purposes.
  4/ Since the tombs of the Han emperors are frequently emblematic in poetry of the passing of earthly and imperial glory, their use here (though they are nowhere near the scene of the poem) evokes the passing of Xuanzong and his age.

By linking the vegetative cycle and human life, Wen writes an effective but not distinctive *huaigu* of a more traditional nature. Wen, however, has no interest in convincing us that he really is standing before the tree: he turns a cypress into a cassia and shifts in the last line to a different scene altogether.

Wen makes an identification in many of these poems between Yang Guifei and two other famous consorts, Lady Sheng and Lady Li. Bai Juyi (for one) had already made these links: in a poem on Lady Li, for example, he mentions Lady Sheng (*QTS*, *j*. 427, pp. 4705–6):

Didn't you see how King Mu wept for three days,   君不見穆王三日哭
How with paired jades before the terrace   重璧臺前傷盛姬
   he wept for Lady Sheng?

Bai's "Song of Lasting Pain," of course, linked Li with Yang Guifei by repeating the story of a Taoist adept recalling the spirit of the dead consort back to earth. Wen's poems on the Yang theme exploit these identifications so frequently because he is preoccupied with the theme of personal loss. Whereas Du Mu and Li Shangyin often experiment with historical causation and question history's meaning, Wen is, for the most part, singularly uninterested in historical issues. Like them, however, he attempts to bridge the gap of time by reimagining the past and by avoiding a personal response to sites laden with moral connotations. Most of these poems show Wen's fictional creation of Xuanzong's own response to his experiences; unlike the traditional *huaigu*, they block or obscure the passage of time from the rebellion to Wen's own age and emphasize the past and future of Xuanzong's life as seen from the perspective of stages in his affair with Yang. Moreover, by linking Xuanzong's story with Taoist legends surrounding King Mu and Emperor Wu, he places the weight of poetic interest on the personal separation of living and dead, not on the greater themes of political responsibility and decline. Wen's final reduction of the public to the personal is summed up in a *yongshi* quatrain.

Painting of a Woman Seen at Longwei Station 龍尾驛婦人圖

We may scoff at the Kaiyuan with its sycophantic ministers	慢笑開元有倖臣
Who drove the Son of Heaven to a dust-covered exile.	直教天子到蒙塵
And yet now, when we see this painting, we can feel the same as he did:	今來看畫猶如此
How much more if we met in person such an unrivaled beauty?	何況親逢絕世人

(*WFQ*, *j*. 9, p. 204)

Title/ Longwei Station was a town in modern Shaanxi east of Mount Qi 岐. The poem suggests that the painting was indeed a portrait of Yang Guifei.

Xuanzong's poor judgment in ministers (Yang Guozhong is meant) can be forgiven, because none of us could have withstood Yang's charms. The quaint palace-poetry theme of real woman–painted woman re-emerges, with a heinous blasphemy against history's significance and indeed against the dynasty itself. I suggested earlier that Tang poets would have had to handle the Xuanzong–Yang Guifei story carefully and discreetly: they could criticize and sympathize, but respect for the empire should come first. Wen's poems display an attitude indifferent to empire; indeed, empire can be easily exchanged for beauty and luxury.

Other *Huaigu*: Empathy and Example

Both the historical songs and the poems on Xuanzong allowed Wen to indulge in a penchant for developing situations and character fictionally; although his own attitudes and perspectives on events may emerge occasionally, no single one of these poems manages to use history as stimulus (*xing* 興), as a source for personal emotion and contemplation.

Since self-expression was indeed the chief mechanism propelling traditional Chinese poetics, poets could utilize historical events not just for their moral significance but also for the examples they provided for their own lives and personal crises. Almost inevitably, the careers of noted men of the past would be compared to the poet's career, and actions and decisions of those distant figures could be imitated or eschewed. Although the most distinctive of Wen's historical poems avoided this use, he did turn occasionally to a more personal contemplation of past lives. Not surprisingly, the picture we form of the poet's ambitions and desires from such poetry is vague and contradictory. On the one hand, there is a lingering desire to serve the state and achieve fame; on the other hand, there is an admiration for recluses and hermits from the past. These poems achieve their interest not because they tell us more about Wen as a person, but because they embody so perfectly the conflicting attitudes of the Late Tang literatus—attitudes that became increasingly cynical or frustrated as the political fortunes of the Tang continued to decline.

The empathy that characterized the Xuanzong poems is of importance here as well. As scholars in Wen's generation discovered the shrinking significance of their own public acts, they might turn increasingly to the satisfactions of domestic life and to a consideration of what contributes to personal happiness. This questioning goes beyond the age-old debate of service versus reclusion; it cuts across all actions, public and private. When Wen describes one of the great success stories of Chinese history (Liu Bang, later Gaozu, the first emperor of the Han) he imparts to us Liu's nostalgia and homesickness, not his triumph. One legend recounts that after he became emperor, his wife, Empress Lü, longed to visit their own home town of Feng 豐 in Pei 沛 County (in modern Jiangsu). The emperor rebuilt the town of Liyi 驪邑 near the capital to resemble Feng and moved all the inhabitants of that town to this new location (Xinfeng, "New Feng"). Characteristically, Wen attributes the homesickness to the emperor himself.

Visiting New Feng   過新豐

    With a single sword, he took his chance—   一劍乘時帝業成
       the royal labors were accomplished.
    And this village from Pei County   沛中鄉里到咸京
       was brought to the capital.
    He had already made all the world   寰區已作皇居貴
       a noble imperial dwelling,
4 But wind and moon still filled him   風月猶含白社情
       with longings for a plain altar.
    In an old pavilion by the River Si   泗水舊亭秋草變
       the autumn grass turns;
    Tiles in ruin by a thousand gates,   千門遺瓦古苔生
       old moss grows.
    Until now, there still remains   至今留得離家恨
       the anguish of leaving home:
8 Chickens and dogs can be heard   雞犬相聞落照明
       while the sinking light is bright.
       (*WFQ*, *j*. 8, p. 169)

    5/ The River Si runs past Feng in Jiangsu. Either Wen is describing New Feng, which may have fallen to ruins after the Han (in which case the Si is a poetic substitution for the Wei), or he is envisioning the ruins of the old Feng after everyone has been moved.

The Han fell long ago, but New Feng is still a peasant village, perhaps not too different from the kind Liu Bang grew up in (though the signs of imperial patronage have fallen to decay). As in several of Li Shangyin's *huaigu*, Wen's poem moves from pompous splendor to the local and small, but his purpose, unlike Li's, is not ironic. Village life is timeless and unchanging, a Taoist paradise: the dogs and chickens in the last line remind the reader of the modest utopia evoked in the *Laozi* (section eighty), where the animals of neighboring villages can be heard by the peasants, but no one desires to leave his home and visit them. Yet this unchanging routine and its implied rejection of ambition and historical achievement were not always ideals embraced in Wen's poetry. We might contrast Han Gaozu's melancholy success to the melancholy failure of another Han dynasty figure, Su Wu 蘇武.

    Su Wu was an official during the reign of Emperor Wu sent as an envoy to the nomadic Xiongnu. The Khan refused to let him return to China, and he was forced to herd sheep for nineteen years. Eventually, Han officials tracked him down and, during a period of relative peace with the Xiongnu, convinced the Khan to release him. By the time he returned in 81 B.C., he was a broken old man, and Emperor Wu was dead; though rewarded moderately, he was not enfeoffed for his service until after Emperor Xuan 宣 was enthroned in 73 B.C. He was later deified, and Wen's poem was probably inspired by a visit to a shrine dedicated to him.

Su Wu's Temple	蘇武廟
Su Wu's soul melts away before the emissary from Han;	蘇武魂銷漢使前
His old temple and lofty trees are lost in a blur.	古祠高樹兩茫然
At cloud's edge, the geese break across a Tartar moon;	雲邊雁斷胡天月
4 At Longshou, sheep return mid the mist of border grass.	隴上羊歸寒草烟
The buildings and terraces on the day he returned were not First Order tents;	回日樓臺非甲帳
Although, when he left, with cap and sword, he was indeed in his prime.	去時冠劍是丁年
From Maoling, no seal of enfeoffment appears;	茂陵不見封侯印
8 In vain he faces the autumn waves and weeps over the swift stream.	空向秋波哭逝川

(*WFQ*, *j.* 8, pp. 171–72)

1/ "Soul melts away"—a standard term for extreme emotion. The Han emissary has arrived to seek out Su and bring him back after his nineteen years of exile.

3/ Longshou was a town on the northwest frontier, in present-day Gansu.

5/ When Emperor Wu went hunting in Shanglin park, he would erect First Order tents, which would be reserved for the housing of precious gems dedicated to the gods; the emperor himself dwelt in Second Order tents. Here, the disappearance of the First Order tents could emphasize an end to the splendor of Wu's reign and may prophesy Su Wu's failure to be recognized at court.

7/ Maoling was Emperor Wu's tomb.

Once again, Wen imaginatively blurs the distinction between past and present; in the first couplet, he compares Su's own emotion ("soul melts") to the indistinct scenery Wen sees before the temple. The second couplet, a standard parallel-couplet description of the Chinese frontier, may be Wen's description of the scene or his vision of Su's life as a shepherd; both are surely possible, since Wen would want to exploit the *huaigu* trope of unchanging nature (the sheep have not changed since Su's day) set against the mortality of a single life.

Like the Taoist village in "New Feng," Xiongnu life is unchanging (from the Chinese perspective, of course): it does not possess a history, and its activities are meaningless from the point of view of a society that demands a certain kind of ambition and effort from its elite, defined by a complex network of social relations. This has tragic ramifications for a talented Confucian official. Much as in folk tales where the man who visits the world of the gods for the briefest time discovers that years have gone by when he returns, Su returns to China to find that his world has changed. The greater poignancy here, of course, is that Su has aged with his own world, although he could not participate in its activities. It is this opposition that makes the third couplet powerful; for by reversing chronological order here (line five is Su Wu old, in his own "present," line six is Su Wu young), Wen simulates the act of recollection in Su Wu's own mind—it shows him returning to the capital, where the first thing he notices is an absence he did not expect. He then thinks back on his youth. With so simple an act, the poem imparts not a straightforward (and possibly ironic) objectivity, but rather a psychological sensitivity.[46] At the end, Su (like Confucius) weeps over the moving waters that are the inevitable reminder of passing time. The tragedy is not that he has aged like all men but that he has so little to show for his age. Once again Wen concludes with the emotional response of his subject. Although the absence of pronouns does not rule out the possibility that Wen weeps both for Su and for his own frustrated ambitions, the description of Su is not a mere emblem for the poet but a sensitive portrait of failure.

If Wen's depictions of Liu Bang and Su Wu are typical of Late Tang sensibilities, it is clear that such a sensibility sees a life of public service ending in (at best) disappointment and (at worst) failure and death. It is probably no coincidence either that more and more of the Late Tang poets wrote *huaigu* on the subject of Zhuge Liang, the strategic genius who abandoned his life of retirement in order to assist Liu Bei, emperor of Shu during the Three Kingdoms period. The statesman continued to serve Liu Bei's incompetent son, in spite of his awareness that Wei would eventually conquer Shu. In this particular poem, Wen writes at the site of Zhuge's death; in 234, Zhuge was encamped with his army at Wuzhang, in modern Shaanxi, south of the Wei River, during a last-ditch invasion of Wei. Camped opposite him was the Wei army under the command of Sima Yi 司馬懿. Before the two sides could come to battle, however, a strange star appeared over the Shu camp three times; Zhuge died shortly thereafter, sealing the failure of the Shu offensive.

Zhuge exemplified most perfectly the noble failure, the man who serves out of duty and loyalty, although he realizes that his actions are doomed.[47] Wen added one of the finest contributions to the poetic image of the hero.

Visiting Wuzhang Plain   經五丈原

Armored steed and cloudy hawk have passed beyond the dust;	鐵馬雲雕共絕塵
Willow shade lowers from above; spring in the Han camp.	柳陰高壓漢營春
In the clear sky, the aura of killing masses to the west of the pass;	天清殺氣屯關右
4 But at midnight, an ominous star shines on the banks of the Wei.	夜半妖星照渭濱
In this feudal state, the Sleeping Dragon tried to wake his lord in vain;	下國臥龍空寤主
In the central plain, capture of the deer lies not in human ability.	中原得鹿不由人
Near ivory couch and jeweled curtains no one spoke forth;	象牀寶帳無言語
8 From now on, Qiao Zhou would be senior minister.	從此譙周是老臣

(*WFQ*, *j*. 4, p. 104)

1/ Out of context, this line would seem to be describing some martial enterprise, perhaps a hawking expedition on the frontier. In context, the meaning is more emblematic of the character of Zhuge and of the troops under his command. "Pass beyond the dust" could refer to their lofty natures, but since "dust" has connotations of the world of ordinary or public affairs, which Zhuge chose to re-enter of his own free will, the line prefigures his death as well.

2/ The Shu kingdom chose Han for its imperial name, since it claimed to have inherited its mandate directly from the Han; but the willows also allude to Xiliu 細柳 (Fine Willows), the site where the Han general Zhou Yafu 周亞夫 encamped with his troops.

3/ "West of the pass": i.e., Shaanxi.

5/ "Sleeping (lit., 'recumbent') Dragon" was a nickname of Zhuge's when he still lived in seclusion; it referred to his latent abilities.
6/ "Capture of the deer": see note to line 1 of Li Bai's "Meditation on the Past: Ascending the Old Battlefield at Guangwu Mountain" translated above.
7/ I.e., no advisor close to the emperor dare speak his mind.
8/ Qiao Zhou became a powerful minister of Shu after the death of Zhuge. He ultimately urged the Shu emperor's surrender to the Wei.

Wen's Zhuge poem does not betray a strong empathic link between poet and subject; instead it seems content to employ brilliant poetic imagery and wit and indulges in the wry perspective of Li Shangyin's *huaigu*. The luxuriant willows in line two, which serve to link the Shu forces with the military might of the Han, are paralleled with the star that predicts the death of Zhuge and the fall of Shu. Wittiest of all is the use of Zhuge's nickname in line five: the "sleeping dragon" tries to wake his ruler; his failure to do so shows that it is not fated for him to capture the "deer" of the imperial mandate. The ending, of course, gives full play to Late Tang irony.

If public service is doomed to failure, then what of its classic alternative, reclusion? Wen generally views it more positively, although here too his praise is not unadulterated. Take, for example, his poem on a famous High Tang figure He Zhizhang 賀知章 (fl. 720). This poet and calligrapher was appointed to an office in the imperial library by the minister Zhang Yue 張說. After a series of posts, he attained the rank of secretary; but when he later fell ill and resigned his position, he returned to his hometown, where he lived in cultivated retirement until his death.[48]

The Imperial Secretariat Possessed a Poem of   祕書省有賀監
Secretary He's Written in His Own Grass Style;   知章草題詩，筆力
the Force of His Brush Was Strong and Powerful,   遒健，風尚高遠，拂塵
Its Style Lofty and Distant. I Swept the Dust   尋玩，因此有作。
Away and Enjoyed It Reflectively. I Then
Composed the Following.

A fisherman from Yue Creek,   越溪漁客賀知章
   He Zhizhang
Was unrestrained, loved the talented,   任達憐才愛酒狂
   and mad in his love of wine.
Past Mandarin ducks and reed blossoms   鸂鶒葦花隨釣艇
   he followed the fishing boats;

4 Among clams and *gu* leaves he dreamed in Hengtang.	蛤蜊菰葉夢橫塘
After several years of chill moonlight he was restrained by high office;	幾年涼月拘華省
But after one night of autumn wind he recalled his native land.	一宿秋風憶故鄉
He shed the ways to fame, and in the end, found his peace;	榮路脫身終自得
8 Turning back toward an auspicious land, he forgot it no more.	福庭回首莫相忘
Leaving the crowd, a simurgh, a crane, he returned to the sea of Liaodong;	出羣鸞鶴辭遼海
As he lowered his pen, dragons and snakes covered the broken walls.	落筆龍蛇滿壞牆
Since the death of Li Bai, there have been no distinguished drunkards;	李白死來無醉客
12 Worthy of pity, his divine brilliance— I mourn in the fading light.	可憐神彩弔殘陽

(*WFQ*, *j*. 4, pp. 106–7)

1/ He Zhizhang was from Kuaiji 會稽, in the old state of Yue. It was here that the great beauty Xi Shi was found washing silk at Ruoye 若邪 Creek (here called Yue Stream). Wen may also be associating He with Yue's minister Fan Li 范蠡, who later abandoned office to become a recluse.

4/ *Gu* is a kind of water grass; its grains, the *gumi* 菰米, are an important food grain. Hengtang was near Suzhou, in He's home district; it is often evoked as a symbol for the beauty and warmth of south China.

9/ The Han Taoist Dingling Wei 丁令微 studied the arcane arts until he was able to transform himself into a crane. When he returned to his home town in Liaodong (eastern Liaoning), he found that everything was in ruins. Wen uses the story here to indicate the long period He spent in government service.

11/ Li Bai became a friend of He's, although the former was a much younger man. Both were exceptional drinkers. Zhizhang is given credit for first calling Li "the banished immortal."

He Zhizhang may have been an exemplary figure for Wen because he passed through the stress of public service yet recovered his original nature. That he maintained his freedom even as an official is suggested by Wen's discovery of He's calligraphy in a government office: this profound production of an untrammeled spirit is discovered amid government documents and bureaucratic hustle and bustle.[49] But, like Dingling Wei, He found that time had passed and that his home was in decay; so he sat among the ruins and wrote, leading a timeless existence among the ravages of time. Yet this melancholy image sets the stage for the mourning of He's and Li Bai's passing at the end: even reclusion may become useless if the hermit loses his circle of "understanding friends" (*zhi yin* 知音) during his life or even after his death.

The place of art in Wen's paean to He Zhizhang suggests yet another solution for the educated Late Tang male: fame through literature. A number of Wen's other *huaigu* show an attraction for the great writers of the past; these poems debate the worth of literary accomplishment in the face of public failure. The following poem is on Chen Lin 陳林 (d. 217), one of the Seven Masters of the Jian'an Era. Originally in the service of another warlord, he earned Cao Cao's respect after his own master was defeated, in spite of his early hostility to the Cao family.

Visiting Chen Lin's Grave   過陳林墓

I've seen the writings you left us,
   found in the Histories;   曾於青史見遺文
And now, like wind-blown artemisia,
   I pass this tomb of yours.   今日飄蓬過此墳
If you, a man of letters, still possess a soul,
   you should come out and meet me;   詞客有靈應識我
4 One with a talent for domination first took pity
   on you, who lacked a lord.   霸才無主始憐君
But now stone unicorns lie sunken and buried,
   concealed in spring grass;   石麟埋沒藏春草
Copperbird Terrace is overgrown,
   it faces the evening clouds.   銅雀荒涼對暮雲
No wonder you faced the wind,
   with sorrow doubly great: 莫怪臨風倍惆悵
8 You were ready, with both pen and sword,
   to imitate "Going with the Army."   欲將書劍學從軍
   (*WFQ*, *j*. 4, p. 97)

5/ "Stone unicorns"—commentators take this as a reference to one of the terraces, Gold Tiger Terrace, that Cao Cao built after an important victory. Their reasons lie in a poem by Wen entitled "Gold Tiger Terrace" 金虎臺, in which he writes:

   Jade grass stretches to Gold Tiger,
   Green moss covers stone unicorns.   (*WFQ*, *j*. 3, p. 63)

Stone unicorns often marked Han Dynasty graves, however. If the unicorns do indeed indicate the ruins of Gold Tiger Terrace, then the line's meaning is repeated in line six, which refers to the decay of another of Cao Cao's edifices; both lines are then solely imagined by Wen. If the unicorns mark Chen's grave, then Wen is comparing the disrepair of the tomb to the transient power of Chen's patron, Cao.

8/ A complicated play of wit. Another talented member of Cao Cao's retinue, Wang Can 王粲 (177–217), was author of a ballad called "Going with the Army"; hence, Chen resolves to be both soldier and poet, to join Cao's forces, and to continue writing poems like Wang.

Wen's attitude toward Chen, though admiring, is still ambiguous. He acknowledges that Chen has won a degree of immortality through his works, and their preservation compares favorably with the aging tombs of the poet and of his patron, Cao (evoked in lines five and six). Yet Wen also suggests that Chen's deeper ambitions (to serve the state) were not successful, and this is the reason Wen gives for Chen's grief in line seven. By contributing his talents, Chen hoped to preserve Cao's political order, and that proved very fragile indeed. In the end, Chen is famous "only" because of his writings. Yet we cannot be sure what lesson the poem seeks to impart. Is art (as with He Zhizhang) the only immortality worth striving for? Or is a public life most noble but doomed to failure (as with Su Wu and Zhuge Liang)?

When Wen writes of the tomb of another Han writer, Cai Yong 蔡邕 (133–92), a possible attitude becomes clearer.

The Grave of Secretary Cai 蔡中郎墳

The ancient tomb is deserted, 古墳零落野花春
   a spring season of wild flowers.
I've heard it said that the secretary 聞說中郎有後身
   will have a new incarnation.
But the present age does not cherish talent 今人愛才非昔日
   in the way of days of old;
So don't throw away mind and effort 莫拋心力作詞人
   to become a man of letters.
   (*WFQ, j.* 5, pp. 110–11)

Cai's biography states that his talent and general bearing was so similar to the great *fu* writer Zhang Heng 張衡 (78–139) that he must have been the reincarnation of the late poet. Wen supposes this to be a continuing process and ironically suggests that Cai needn't bother returning to the human realm. Behind this poem is exasperated literary ambition: Wen sees himself as a talent similar to Cai (perhaps even his embodiment in a later age) and blames the times for his present failure.

It is often difficult to tell how much these poems represent Wen's honest sentiment and how much they present rhetorical plays on expected conventions. It is, however, notable that so many of them concern the careers of "men of letters" (*ciren* 詞人), people whose reputations resulted from their writings rather than from their deeds. Moreover, other poems suggest a real concern with issues of fame and eremitism. When Wen seems to speak for himself, without using a former writer or literary style as an intermediary, we have a possible glimpse of the frustrated artiste and a possible reason for his empathic identifications with the aesthetes of the past.

Rain on a Spring Day	春日雨
The fine rain drizzles, enters the red silk drapes.	細雨濛濛入絳紗
A lake pavilion; Cold Food Day; Meng Zhu's house.	湖亭寒食孟珠家
In the Southern courts, they rashly declared it a mark of exceptional talent:	南朝漫自稱流品
But when did a palace poem ever win you Apricot Garden?	宮體何曾為杏花

(*WFQ*, j. 9, p. 179)

2/ The Cold Food Festival was a holiday in late spring when cooking fires were extinguished. In poetry, it usually is a rainy day that produces melancholy in the poet. Meng Zhu was a singer to whom was attributed authorship of a romantic folksong. Here, Meng Zhu's house is a euphemism for a brothel.

4/ Apricot Garden: located in Chang'an, it was the site for feasts given by men who had successfully passed the government examinations.

Wen admits to his own dissipated habits, even as he acknowledges that the skills developed by such habits (the writing of "palace poetry") will do him little good. Is he being bitter or insouciant? Perhaps both; and we may see Wen here as he knew he appeared in Tang society.

The uses of history in Wen's poetry mark him as a poet unique within his own age, though still a product of his age's concerns. Whereas the historical songs reflect the literary artist's love of fictional creation, many of the *huaigu* and *yongshi* suggest an interest in the portrayal of character and an empathic desire to view historical events from the perspective of the participants. Occasionally, the portrayals come close to psychological realism. Although Wen no doubt shared the skepticism over the uses and import of history that Li Shangyin and Du Mu often manifested in their poems and at times exploded historical meaning with games of irony and wit, he evidently preferred to avoid irony and judgment and turned instead to the personal portrayal of others. Such a quality may be unique in historical poetry, it is true, but it is still in keeping with his age. Wen was manifesting the anxieties of the Late Tang literatus, who was becoming unsure of the benefits of public service, of old-fashioned reclusion, and even of literary craftsmanship. The result, for many, was a sensibility that focused increasingly not only on aesthetic cultivation but also on the private and the small-scale at the expense of the larger issues of society and polity. It is this anxiety—and this sensibility—that will concern us in the next and final chapter.

FIVE

Small Ambitions

IN THE PREVIOUS chapters I examined Wen Tingyun's verse against a background of cultural and literary developments that stand somewhat outside the mainstream of Chinese verse. Although his *yuefu* can be positioned in the context of musical song lyric evolution and of stylistic innovations characteristic of his time, his own transformation of the genre was unique; and even though his use of historical themes may be easily located within the general use of such themes in Tang poetry, here too his distinctiveness is easily discoverable. However, we have yet to investigate the rest of Wen's poetry, the regulated verse written on occasional themes. Part of the difficulty, as we shall see, lies in the "typicality" of such poetry.

Literary history inevitably creates a dilemma when it attempts to define "distinctiveness" and "typicality." Of course, no author's works can be understood without some knowledge of the characteristic trends of the literature within which the act of writing occurs. The "typical" literature of any period, however, is usually not prized because of its typicality: rather, some underlying distinctiveness in the style and content of certain authors leads us to canonize them as the "best" of a particular era. They are great because they are exceptions.[1] It is often harder to assess the value of writers who are seen as "typical," particularly because tastes change as quickly as ways of reading do, but we learn to appreciate the typical if we focus on the historically changing aesthetic criteria that make a text worth reading. I propose here to combine a hypothetical recreation of Tang modes of reading (instead of late traditional modes) with Western critical techniques. I do not plan to judge whether Wen's occasional regulated poetry is "good" or not; rather, I wish to discover a way of appreciating his poetry that explains his contemporaries' estimation of it.

Defining a superior "typical" literary performance, as opposed to a "distinctive" one, is not easy when reading Late Tang poetry. Beginning with the late eighth century, both the number of surviving poems by each poet and the number of poets whose work survives increases; meanwhile, the homogeneity of poetic genres (in this case, occasional regulated verse) grows dramatically. Although the proliferation of texts is not as severe as it would be in the Song, Ming, and Qing dynasties, the knowledgeable critic must arrive at judgments on individual poets' styles and interests based on reading hundreds of metrically and thematically indistinguishable poems. Occasional, regulated poetry is the background murmur against which "distinctive" poetic achievements and experiments are made. Critics, daunted by the subtlety required in reading this much verse, have been content to pay attention to exceptions; only a serious examination of the general tenor of Late Tang verse reveals how odd and unusual the two "canonical" poets of the Late Tang, Du Mu and Li Shangyin, often are.

It has been said that Wen Tingyun was a "typical" poet of his generation, largely because of his ability to compose regulated occasional verse. Couplets are often removed from his poems for the purpose of specific comment, and emphasis is placed on his craftsmanship rather than on the "profundity" of his expression. Although such craftsmanship is worth valuing for its own sake, it was the dislike of craftsmanship in late traditional China that turned Wen into a minor poet, even if there was occasionally a grudging appreciation of his talents.[2] Paradoxically—or perhaps because of this very judgment—the elements of his poetry that declare his independence and "distinction" (in the *yuefu* especially) have gone largely unrecognized. It is for this reason that I have been concerned to show him as a poet who produced verse distinctive in style and beauty. Our task now is to understand him as a poet "typical" of his time.

Couplet Craft and the "Safe Space"

In examining the glories of High Tang poetry, it is easy to forget that the poetics of the age argued not for great genius, self-expressive depth, or profundity but for a seamless craftsmanship that could conceivably be mastered by anyone with proper time and effort. If the texts excerpted by Kūkai 空海 in the late eighth-century *Bunkyō hifuron* 文鏡祕府論 are any indication, theorists contemporary with Wang Wei, Li Bai, and Du Fu were most concerned with defining a set of injunctions against errors in parallelism and tonality.[3] Until the ninth century, Li Bai was noted for his use of the marvelous, but he was not yet a subject for a cult of personality; Du Fu was virtually ignored. Only in the Mid-Tang did both the view of China's two master poets and poetics overall change in a way that anticipated late traditional literary theory. The moral aspirations of Han Yu, Bai Juyi, and their circles encouraged them not only to embrace self-expression as the new goal in poetry but also to create a new canon whose fountainhead was Li and Du. Largely for this reason the Mid-Tang period has no discernable style overall: the need for a personal style and the occasional contempt for the special skills of an artistic discipline led to a series of poets (Han Yu, Meng Jiao 孟郊 [751–814], Lu Tong 盧仝 [d. 835], Li He, Bai Juyi, Yuan Zhen 元稹 [779–831]) who rarely sounded like anyone else but themselves.

The preoccupation with literary skill and with self-conscious effort continued to run deep in the tradition, however, and with the passing of the Mid-Tang it rose to the surface once again. Despite some stylistic changes, the reigning conception of poetry remained consistent among most practitioners. Writers continued to hone their technical ability, and the few surviving poetic texts of the Late Tang, Five Dynasties, and early Song continue to prescribe the rules for correct writing.[4] Even though the Late Tang theoretical text most admired by later ages, Sikong Tu's 司空圖 (837–908) *Twenty-four Categories of Poetry* 二十四詩品, emphasizes expressivity, it still seems to posit a poet who can control expressive modes for his own affective devices.

Sikong Tu's poems on poetry are indicative of typical Tang poetics in that they describe an art that is forthrightly unambitious. The imagery used to clarify concepts is almost exclusively natural, and natural on a small scale. Despite a certain amount of metaphysical speculation on the nature of inspiration, it is clear that Sikong Tu sees supreme poetic achievement in the mastery of juxtaposed details and well-observed scenes.

In plainness dwell, and in silence:	素處以默
Nature's subtle motives are indeed faint.	妙機其微
Infuse them with perfected harmony,	飲之太和
And you may join the lonely crane in flight.	獨鶴與飛
It is like the warm breeze of spring,	猶之惠風
Which slowly turns within one's robes.	苒苒在衣
Jade-green peach leaves fill the trees,	碧桃滿樹
Wind and sun on water's bank.	風日水濱
Willow shade on a curving lane,	柳陰路曲
Gliding orioles form companions.	流鶯比鄰
In a lingering fog the mountains turn green;	露餘山青
Red apricot blossoms in the woods.	紅杏在林
The moon shines bright on decorated rooms,	月明華屋
A painted bridge in jade-green shade.	畫橋碧陰
Golden goblets fill with wine,	金尊酒滿
A companion-guest strums his lute.[5]	共客彈琴

These descriptions, used to illustrate certain "modes" of composition, suggest a modest aesthetics of effect. Although the fineness of observation and the effort of writing should not be underestimated, the result is a sociable poetry of pretty images, not a grand, moral poetry of earnest self-expression.

Occasional regulated verse was the essential genre for the poetry of craft; it provided the standardized themes and conventionalized emotions against which the achievements of such craft could be measured. Verse epistles, parting poems, poems composed at specific places or upon meeting friends—these did not change in their general import. The result for the critic is an emotional and thematic sameness that makes evaluation difficult. Although traditional Chinese poetics might demand sincerity, conventions demanded a propriety that regulated emotional response. The quality of sameness has never become obvious in High Tang poetry, partly because the surviving number of poems by poets like Wang Wei and Meng Haoran has never been great enough to betray the underlying conventionalities. In the case of the Late Tang writers, however, where we may have hundreds of occasional regulated poems by the same poet, we may wonder at the honesty of so many tears shed over partings and so much melancholy occasioned by travel. Anyone reading several hundred regulated verses might understandably conclude that such poetry is a mere phatic communion.

If we turn from surface meaning, however, and examine the poets in the context of their social and political world, more interesting and compelling motivations emerge that may revivify our reading of Late Tang verse. After the brief "renaissance" under Dezong, the Tang dynasty entered the long twilight world of fragmentation and danger that produced much of the cynical historical poetry examined in the last chapter. While the central authority in Chang'an wielded less and less power and officials at the capital braved purges by political cliques and eunuchs, the outer provinces became semiautonomous under regional military governors. The concurrent rise of strong non-Han governments on the frontiers formerly controlled by the Tang created dangers for those who lived on the edge of the empire. This fragmentation (an anticipation of the chaos of the Five Dynasties period) contributed to a growing regionalism in Chinese literature; whereas previously there had been only Chang'an and the (supposedly inferior) provinces, writers now became increasingly loyal to their own home areas, at times living out an entire writing career away from the capital. This trend first made itself felt with the poets of the Yangzi delta region; but soon other areas (the central Yangzi, for example, and Sichuan) achieved a certain prominence as literary centers as military governors patronized literary men. Writers and aspiring bureaucrats were often less anxious to make names for themselves in the politically dangerous capital when they could find jobs in other places.

One might even suggest that the fragmentation of the regulated verse poem into discrete parallel couplets was a manifestation of the fragmentation of the political and social order. However, a more obvious result of Late Tang political conditions may be seen in the turning away in part from big themes and the increasing attention to artistry and to detail. Whether attention to "couplet craft" was a result of a subconscious crisis of belief or simply a decadent avoidance of realistic description, such attention was an inevitable outcome of ninth-century social and political crises.

The emergence of couplet craft in Chinese poetic writing begins in the Mid-Tang, concurrently (and paradoxically) with the great experimenters; the guiding spirits, most probably, were Jia Dao and his circle.[6] Jia himself was a close friend of Han Yu and Meng Jiao, but the goals of his poetry differed radically from theirs. On the one hand, he was a seemingly casual and sociable poet; unlike his more famous contemporaries, who were becoming increasingly conscious of poetry as a legacy to posterity, Jia was content to keep verse writing as a form of intimate communication. On the other hand, Jia was a compulsive craftsman, obsessed with the need to fashion language in aesthetically satisfying ways.[7] For him, the production of poetry was no longer a natural process but a mechanical one, in which natural resources were tapped through an almost physical struggle.

Playfully Sent to a Friend 戲贈友人

Each day that I don't write a poem 一日不作詩
The sources of my mind become an abandoned well. 心源如廢井
Brush and inkstone are the well pulley, 筆硯為轆轤
4 Chanting verses is like the well rope. 吟詠作縻綆
In the morning I come to draw again— 朝來重汲引
And, as always, obtain clarity and coolness. 依舊得清冷
I write this to someone who shares my feelings— 書贈同懷人
8 In my words, so much effort and toil. 詞中多苦辛
    (*QTS, j.* 571, pp. 6626–27)

The manipulation of language was one way of seeking approbation from his peers when his official life was essentially unsuccessful; whereas morally earnest poets could use poetry to proclaim their uniqueness or their uprightness in the presence of social and political corruption, Jia could use it as an alternative path to public success. Through him, Chinese poetry became both less and more important—no longer part of the moral and cosmological world, but a complex and difficult *profession*. A social occasion was for him not a way of cementing solidarity between members of the literati class, but an opportunity to impress others with his talents.

Seeing off Tang Huan on His Return to 送唐環歸敷水莊
Fu River Village

Maonü Peak faces your door; 毛女峯當戶
The sun is high, but you have yet to comb your hair. 日高頭未梳
The earth is encroached by the sweep of mountain's shadow, 地侵山影掃
4 Leaves bear the writing of the dew-tracks. 葉帶露痕書

On a piney path a monk seeks herbs; 松徑僧尋藥
In a sandy stream a crane looks for fish. 沙泉鶴見魚
On this single stream, fine scenery— 一川風景好
8 I resent that I have no dwelling there. 恨不有吾廬
　(QTS, j. 572, p. 6641)

Jia, who was a monk for many years before he abandoned the calling to take the government examinations, seemed to have found the reclusive life the most satisfying subject for poetry; the polite parting poem to the hermit or monk is a staple of his output. What is particularly noticeable here is the subordination of personal expression to the non-literary purpose of polite social exchange. The images are not necessarily ones that Jia Dao sees himself; rather, they are the ones he imagines will surround Tang Huan. Once he has created this vision, his conclusion is a polite note of envy, an admission that Tang has it much better than himself. We cannot know for sure if Jia Dao really "felt" this longing for a piece of real estate, because so many poems end on just this note. Despite the intimate tone, this is extroverted poetry; it is interested in producing an effect, in impressing its addressee.

　Jia Dao's poetry produces its effects by exploiting the surprise of the ordinary. Because he generally uses simple and basic poetic language, clear syntax, and common imagery, the exceptional quality of a poem must result from a novel arrangement of these elements. The lines of poetry (especially the central couplets) must be immediately comprehensible, so that their magic and surprise rise to the surface of consciousness only afterwards. They must create a sort of "double-take." Lines three to six of "Sending off Tang Huan" are commonplace in their imagery, but they expose, on a second reading, a heightened perception in the poet's mind that skews vision in a uniquely subjective way. The shadow of the mountain "sweeps," a human gesture that civilizes the landscape even as it provides a powerful and original metaphor for the scene. The hermit is placed in a "literary" nature that writes intelligible marks on its woodland pages. He seeks immortality in his herbs, a natural part of his way of being, just as the crane seeks fish for its own sustenance. Jia's poetic world grows out of a sort of "hyperreality" caused by staring at an everyday object so long and intensely that it loses its ordinary qualities; the detail achieves both a magical *esse* independent of conventional signification and a new relatedness with other things and forces to which it had previously seemed unconnected. This is the closest Chinese poetry came to the sort of epiphany modern Western readers expect in William Carlos Williams.

However, the profound gaze cannot be sustained for the length of the poem. Such intensity would exhaust the reader: wonders on top of wonders can only pall (a social poetry, after all, cannot be "difficult"). Instead, the epiphany may be best observed as a contrast, like a jewel that stands out when placed in a commonplace setting. Furthermore, the brilliance of Jia's couplets betrays a self-conscious fashioning rather than "spontaneous" self-expression; heinous though such a suggestion seems, he may have composed his couplets in advance of the poetic occasion. Where a previous poet might use the social occasion itself as the "inspiring moment" for a convincing verse, Jia cannot rely on a social moment to produce beauty but must separate the act of writing from the social occasion. Although no proof of this possibility exists, a reading of his poems suggests it is highly likely.[8]

Although his poem to Tang Huan translated above maintains some level of inspiration through its first six lines, other examples demonstrate the technique of setting off a couplet much better.

Passing the Night at a Mountain Temple 宿山寺

	The numerous peaks thrust up in chill color,	衆岫聳寒色
	The temple building from here can be made out.	精廬向此分
	Meteors show through the sparse trees,	流星透疏木
4	A running moon cuts back against the scudding clouds.	走月逆行雲
	On the highest peak few people come;	絕頂人來少
	In the high pine cranes do not flock.	高松鶴不羣
	A single monk—eighty in years,	一僧年八十
8	Has never heard of the affairs of the world.	世事未曾聞

(QTS, j. 573, pp. 6669–70)

The ordinariness of the lines surrounding the second couplet is strikingly obvious, even in translation. Although the title does not reveal this poem as part of social exchange, the reader may suspect that it is; the closing couplet hints that it was addressed to some old monk and is meant as a form of social flattery.

It is not surprising, then, that later critics most often quote the work of Jia Dao and the poets of his circle in couplets. For later readers, no longer recipients of a poem at a social moment who might be overwhelmed by the brilliant flash of the couplet in its bland surroundings, the lone pair of lines alone seem worth the attention:

In stone chambers a man's heart grows calm; In icy pools the moon's reflection fades.	石室人心靜 冰潭月影殘
The sound of reeds blends with the rain; The scent of caltrop and lotus circles the lamp.	蘆葦聲兼雨 芰荷香遶燈
From time to time we fall silent— So slightly the rain soaks the pines.	往往語復默 微微雨灑松
Wild fires burn the ridge grass, And broken mists give rise to stony pines.[9]	野火燒岡草 斷煙生石松

The predilection of Jia Dao and many of his circle for five-character lines may result from demands of this labored simplicity. Two additional characters in a line would force the poet either to make grammatical relations more explicit by adding particles ("empty words") in the extra positions or to add to the line's density and syntactic complexity. The precision and simplicity of Jia's verse precluded such expansions. When he did write seven-character verse, he usually took the first option, making his poem flabby.

On Adept Tongzhen   題童真上人

By the river you cultivate control over your accumulated years;	江上修持積歲年
The sound of the shoals is endless, never halting its gurgle.	灘聲未擬住潺湲
You swore from age fifty to don the monk's habit;	誓從五十身披衲
And then sat in meditation, facing the three thousand realms of phenomena.	便向三千界坐禪
Never blocked from Moon Pass or Green Wall,	月峽青城那有滯
Indeed close relations with Tiantai and Mount Wu.	天台廬岳豈無緣

Last night you suddenly dreamed
   you were traveling the green seas,
8 A myriad miles of billows
   were there before your eyes.
     (*QTS*, *j*. 574, p. 6685)

昨宵忽夢遊滄海
萬里波濤在目前

When forced to construct more elaborate parallelisms, Jia Dao ends up matching trivialities in an attempt to be clever or to take up space: "fifty years" against "three thousand worlds" (a Buddhist term for the experiential universe) is a valid juxtaposition only because it matches number for number; it gives us no real insight into the monk's religious inspiration. The names of various famous holy places placed against each other are there for no other purpose than name-dropping.

One poet who could carry through the lucid, simple style into seven-character verse was Yong Tao 雍陶 (fl. 820–30), perhaps the most talented of the Jia Dao circle and probably a major influence on Late Tang poets, despite the small number of his poems extant today.[10] By adding new elements to a scene or by creating "evidence tropes" that relate two elements within a line to each other as well as to their opposites in the parallel line, he could devise more complex units of signification.

Recalling the Mountains, I Send This to a Monk   憶山寄僧

On the traveled road, who recognizes
   your footprints in the snow?
When I arrive, I vainly recall
   the peak where clouds emerge.
Sky is clear—afar I see
   the trees against the moon;
4 Wind is light—I vaguely hear
   bells on mist's edge.
Tasting the world, several times
   I've longed for monks arrayed in courtyards;
Remembering these mountains, long I've envied
   the crane's return to his pines.
Fresh grief, old resentment
   so much, so hard to tell:
8 Half of it is in my brow,
   the other half in my heart.
     (*QTS*, *j*. 518, p. 5915)

塵路誰知蹋雪蹤
到來空認出雲峯
天晴遠見月中樹
風便細聽煙際鐘
閱世數思僧並院
憶山長羨鶴歸松
新愁舊恨多難說
半在眉間半在胸

1/ "Traveled road": the line literally reads "dusty road," but since dust (*chen* 塵) is often used metaphorically to represent bustle or the confusions of the physical world, I have altered the translation to avoid the seeming contradiction of snow and dust.

The second couplet is constructed in Chinese as follows:

天	晴	遠	見	月	中	樹
sky	clear	far	see	moon	middle	tree
風	便	細	聽	煙	際	鐘
wind	light	slight	hear	mist	edge	bell

It is because the sky is clear, of course, that Yong can see the trees set against the moon (clarity allowing for both moon and distant viewing); and the wind is substantial enough to carry sound but gentle enough not to drown out the bells. Hearing is juxtaposed against sight, weather against weather, faintness against faintness. The use of the seven-character line to create implied "because... then" relations enables Yong to say more in the parallel couplet while maintaining a simplicity of speech.

Yong can, however, display an inclination to cleverness and to the imagistically bizarre; the result can be a scene that is more difficult to fathom or more artificially aesthetic.

For all time, just because you [the poet Du Fu] stayed in this old lodging,	萬古只應留舊宅
A thousand in gold will no longer be traded for fresh verses.	千金無復換新詩
Deserted eaves, a few butterflies hang in spiders' webs;	荒簷數蝶懸蛛網
Empty rooms, a single firefly enters a swallow's nest.	空屋孤螢入燕巢
Filling a courtyard in a poetic realm the red leaves flutter about;	滿庭詩境飄紅葉
Circling the stairs the sound of the zither drips on the hidden stream.	繞砌琴聲滴暗泉
Beyond the gates the evening clears, the autumn scene grows old;	門外晚晴秋色老
Myriad branches of cold-jade bamboo— one creek filled with mist.[11]	萬條寒玉一溪煙

The first example is taken from an octet written on the remains of Du Fu's grass hut in Sichuan; it shows the type of elaborate rhetorical reasoning we have already seen in Late Tang poems on history. The second example comes from a poem written while Yong was ill; the hypersensitivity and queasiness of a sick man are captured in unusual and disquieting imagery. The last example, a quatrain, shows an increasing artificialization of a natural scene: the site becomes a "poetic realm" (*shi jing* 詩境), the zither's sounds "drip" on the sounds of the stream, which is surrounded by jade-like bamboo.

From Yong Tao, it is a mere step to the aesthetic artificiality of Du Mu or the dense, rich "baroque" imagery of Li Shangyin.

Du Mu: *Egrets*   鷺鷥

Snowy robes, snowy hair,
   green-jade beaks;   雪衣雪髮青玉觜
In flocks they pluck fish
   in the stream's reflection.   羣捕魚兒溪影中
Startled they fly, departing
   set against the green hills: 驚飛遠映碧山去
One tree of pear blossom
   falls in the evening wind.   一樹梨花落晚風
    (*QTS*, *j*. 522, p. 5973)

Li Shangyin: *Frosty Moon*   霜月

When I first heard the migrating geese
   the cicadas had already ceased;   初聞征雁已無蟬
From the height of a hundred-foot tower
   water touched the sky.   百尺樓高水接天
The Blue Girl and the White Maid
   both endure the chill   青女素娥俱耐冷
So that in the frost, in the moonlight
   they can both flaunt their charms.   月中霜裏鬭嬋娟
    (*QTS*, *j*. 539, p. 6146)

3–4/ The Blue Girl is the deity in charge of the frost; the White Maid is Chang'e, Goddess of the Moon.

In Du's quatrain, the egrets are clothed metaphorically in human apparel; they seek not the real fish but their reflections. Then, when they fly off, the flash of white against the hills is indistinguishable from the falling flowers. The fragility of this heightened aesthetic sensitivity emerges in Li Shangyin's poem as well. At first, an ordinary, natural scene is portrayed; but through mythological substitution, Li's vision becomes erotic and artificial, as well as eerily supernatural.¹² It is easy to realize how the increasingly sensitive vision of a Yong Tao encouraged poets to write in an even more distorted perspective that can produce fictional visions. It should be stressed, however, that this tendency represents a move into the "distinctive" area of late Tang poetic production and indeed is partly responsible for the exceptional fame of Du Mu and Li Shangyin at the expense of other poets. Neither can contribute much to the present analysis because, although they belonged very much to their age, they are far too original, even in their occasional verse, to be employed in constructing a model of the late Tang poem. The intense but disarmingly simple style of Jia Dao created important guidelines for many more poets. Numerous minor figures carried on the tradition during Wen's life and long after his death—poets like Zhao Gu 趙嘏 (fl. 850's), Xu Hun 許渾 (fl. 830–50), Wei Zhuang 韋莊 (836–910), and Luo Yin 羅隱 (833–909).

Beyond the growth of interest in couplet craft, the anxiety of literati poets made itself felt in other ways. One increasingly important theme in the ninth century is the refuge or utopia, the "safe space" unreachable by the concerns and disasters of the everyday world. Of course, the safe space had preoccupied Chinese literati since Tao Qian's utopia of the Peach Blossom Spring. Moreover, garden and villa poetry (often written as elaborate compliments to wealthy landowners) came to be a major subgenre in the High Tang. But by Mid-Tang times, poets displayed a greater need to *create* such a space, often through gardening and collecting natural objects. Even the ever-confident Bai Juyi, for example, pretended to be in nature even while he served in government—as when he plants bamboo around his district office.

Serving in the city, I cannot satisfy my inclinations	佐邑意不適
So I shut the gate while autumn grass grows.	閉門秋草生
How do I please my wild nature?	何以娛野性
I plant bamboo—around a hundred stems.	種竹百餘莖
When I see its color by the stream,	見此溪上色
I think I've got the feeling of dwelling in the hills;	憶得山中情
Sometimes, when at leisure from official duties,	有時公事暇
I'll stroll all day on my veranda.¹³	盡日繞闌行

The great "Confucian" poet Han Yu was also not immune from the inclination to create safe microcosms. In one series of quatrains, he describes the building of a little pond in his garden, which gradually comes to replace the world (*QTS*, *j*. 343, p. 3847). Yong Tao as well wrote six poems on the theme of the microcosmic refuge, describing the garden of an aristocrat that was constructed within Chang'an.

Matching Six Poems by Liu, Rectifier of Omissions: 和劉補闕秋園
Feelings Stirred by an Autumn Garden (no. 3) 寓興六首之三

   I got the feeling I was in my home forest— 自得家林趣
   Such ordinary times are rare outside! 常時在外稀
   I meet a monk eating rustic fare, 對僧餐野食
4 Greet a traveler wearing mountain robes. 迎客著山衣
   Sparrows squabble, flutter from the eaves, depart— 雀鬥翻簷散
   Crickets startle, fly out from the trees. 蟬驚出樹飛
   Achievement earned in some future day, 功成他日後
8 What need have I to retire to the Five Lakes? 何必五湖歸
     (*QTS*, *j*. 518, p. 5912)

   8/ The statesman Fan Li, after helping the King of Yue conquer the state of Wu, went into reclusion in the Five Lakes area of Jiangsu. He was never seen again.

Underlying this genial and serene praise of a patron's garden may be an unconscious unease and desire for refuge; the images are conventional, of course, but they are evoked in a context of escalating disasters and invasions. Yong Tao, after all, was also the poet of six brilliant quatrains describing the grief of Han captives as they were carried off by the Nan Zhao 南詔 army to the wilds of Yunnan (*QTS*, *j*. 518, pp. 5924–25).

Beyond gardening and bamboo planting, the Late Tang poet could dream of traveling to some refuge in the real world. Parting poems were a standard excuse for the expression of grief, but for an anxiety-ridden lower bureaucrat in the capital a chance to escape to the relatively safe area of the Yangzi delta must have seemed a welcome vacation. The envious poetry extolling the pleasures awaiting the traveler to Jiangnan became almost a subgenre of its own in the ninth century.

Yong Tao: *Seeing Someone off on* 雍陶: 送人歸吳
His Return to Wu

   I distantly cherish the spring waves, 遠愛春波正滿湖
     just now filling the lakes:

So I'm jealous that your eastward journey
   happens to be your homeward road.
Chant a poem, just during
   a moonlit sojourn—
A single cry mid water and sky,
   a sandy crane alone.
     (*QTS*, *j*. 518, p. 5921)

羨君東去是歸途
吟詩好向月中宿
一叫水天沙鶴孤

The increasing interest in the Jiangnan area as a subject for poetry (seen not only in these parting poems, but in many of Wen Tingyun's *yuefu*) may thus represent not just a love of beautiful surroundings but of the desire for a haven not subject to the political and social strains of more "civilized" districts.

One more safe space was the monastery and the mountains that contained it. Of course, the poetic tradition of temple visiting precedes even Wang Wei, but the sheer volume of monastery poetry in the ninth century suggests it had a special appeal beyond the conventionalized wish for a hermit's life. Longing and envy for the monk's existence no longer represent decorous wishes for reclusion or a need for religious transcendence but arise from a very real fear of life on the outside and a romanticization of the safe spaces on top of mountains and in remote forests.

Yet another way of creating the safe space is to turn away from the things around oneself to the small scale and the intimate. This may lie at the heart of Jia Dao's poetics, the intense stare that elevates the banal. It may also be the root of Yong Tao's, Li Shangyin's, and Du Mu's isolation of the striking detail into a self-contained aesthetic artifact or into a brief aesthetic experience that can be privately savored. The poet seeks out the special moment that he can control or fashion; even the loss of such a special moment—as trivial as the sound of rain on a window—can become a subject for a poem.

Du Mu: *The Southern Tower at Kaiyuan Temple in Xuanzhou*

杜牧: 宣州開元寺南樓

This little tower can only
   hold one bed across;
All day I view the hills;
   cups are filled and emptied.

小樓纔受一牀橫
終日看山酒滿傾

A pity, last night's rain
   that came with a warm wind—
Drunk, I missed hearing
   its sound upon the pane.
    (*QTS, j.* 524, pp. 5993–94)

可惜和風夜來雨

醉中虛度打窗聲

There are complex factors, then, that create the special qualities of Late Tang occasional verse; at times they can make it more than the merely polite exchange of generic emotions. The growing anxiety over individual safety and the well-being of the polity, combined with the collapse of belief in the social order, worked to make a poetry that was concerned with small accomplishments: the well-polished parallel couplet, the artificially induced epiphany, the imagistically distorted landscape, or the small, intimate capture of a fleeting emotion or scene. Poets worked harder at their craft than at any other time in Chinese history, because they knew that if they looked up from their worktables they might be forced to acknowledge a much more unpleasant reality. For later critics, of course, this was a heinous fault; but if we embrace the values of this quintessentially "anti-realistic" approach to poetry, we will find qualities to savor and admire. At the same time, our understanding of the poets' predicament will lead us to a greater understanding of historical and social conditions as they speak unwittingly through the poets.

Wen's Occasional Regulated Verse

I ended Chapter 4 with "Rain on a Spring Day," a quatrain in which Wen sees himself as a writer and voices his frustration over the failure of that role to provide recognition. His evident continued participation in the examination system accentuated his awareness of this situation. Although he accepted the role of "mere" poet with good grace and humor, he would always be aware of his state of perpetual waiting: his society expected him to at least attempt to gain public office. Although the conventions of occasional poetry, as I have suggested, were pervasive enough to warrant skepticism of the sincerity of the emotions expressed in a poem, we may still expect to see signs of the strain and complexity of Wen's position in society. Many of his poems deal with expected, polite sentiments, and most seem to suppress the poetic ego to a point unusual even in perfunctory social poetry. Certain characteristics emerge, however, that point to the individual creative personality.

As Wen wandered from patron to patron and eked out a living while waiting for an opportunity to enter the system, his sense of participation in public life evolved differently from that of a typical poet of a century earlier. For the latter, the values of government service were set in contrast with those of eremitism; the central issue was whether to participate in public life or to retire. For Wen, so simple a choice was impossible. By his time, public life had come to be understood as the social relations inherent in the leisure activities through which one made a living and established contacts with people in power. A visit to the country estate of a patron was not an opportunity for Wen to relax in Buddhist or Taoist reclusive pleasures; rather, it threw him into a situation where he was expected to play to the fullest his role as wit, amusing companion, and talented versifier. For poet-officials, poetry was often a release from public duty; for Wen, who was primarily a writer, poetry itself became a duty. Wen's need to please and entertain accounts in part for his tendency to withdraw as an explicit presence in many of his poems. In others, especially in his occasional verse, he emerges as himself but defines his role in social terms. Like his contemporaries, he often writes of friendships, leisure activities, and small aesthetic delights and avoids pressing political problems and ultimate values. Even more so than his contemporaries, however, he is willing to portray himself as the socially inferior companion, eager to please. In more private occasional poetry (works without an addressee, or with an addressee who was obviously close to him) Wen seems to speak more as himself, although his voice is still controlled by convention and aesthetic demands.

A comparison of Wen's poems to one by Wang Wei will reveal these aspects of his work.

Wang Wei: *Reply to Secretary Guo* 王維: 酬郭給事

Gates in series, lofty chambers 洞門高閣靄餘暉
   darken the last rays of the sun.
Peach and plum produce thick shade, 桃李陰陰柳絮飛
   while willow catkins fly about.
Scattered bells in the imperial precincts, 禁裏疎鐘官舍晚
   evening in public offices.

4　Chirping birds in the department bureau, 　　　the clerks grow few. 　　At dawn, letting your jade pendants shake, 　　　you hasten to golden halls; 　　At evening, offering imperial writs, 　　　you bow at the chain-patterned gates. 　　I would force myself to go with you, 　　　but can do nothing about old age. 8　Since I'm abed, sick, 　　　I'll cast off my court robes. 　　　　(*QTS, j.* 128, p. 1296)	省中啼鳥吏人稀 晨搖玉佩趨金殿 夕奉天書拜瑣闈 強欲從君無那老 將因臥病解朝衣

5/ Officials wore jade pendants at their waist, which would shake and jingle as they walked.

6/ Gates and doors of the imperial palace were often decorated in a chain pattern.

Wang describes the routine of palace officials as he imagines his friend Guo going about his tasks; then he explains to Guo that he can no longer join this scene and must instead retire. Wang could also write eremitic poems while serving in office, lamenting that he could *not* take off his court robes and become a recluse, as he often longed to do. These two intellectual stances may seem contradictory, but in fact they make perfect sense within the world that Wang inhabited. Since he was a member of one of the great clans prominent in Tang politics, he felt at ease in a court setting; although he was by no means one of the more powerful ministers, he could take pleasure in the attitude of *noblesse oblige* that accompanied public service. This almost altruistic concept of office made reclusion not an abandonment of his public role but merely its temporary alternative; returning to his country estate, Wang would still remain an important social figure, and his social and political connections would remain intact when he did so. He may even have felt that in retirement he continued to contribute to the well-being of the state through the cultivation of his *virtù*.[14]

This sense of continuity and order is reflected in the poem, which has inherited the celebratory and elevated diction of Early Tang court poetry. The natural order works in harmony with the political order, not against it; the middle couplets picture government offices nestled among trees and birds and an official whose duties are as ordered as the seasonal cycles. If Wang's perception of administration can encompass such a perspective, we can easily understand how a poem like this can stand in a comfortable relation with eremitic poetry.

For Wen, however, no such easy relation exists.

Sent to Secretary Xiao of the Hanlin Academy 投翰林蕭舍人

   The ducks and egrets of the human world 人間鴛鷺杳難從
      are distant, hard to follow;
   Alone, you resent the golden doors 獨恨金扉直幾重
      that stand upright, layer upon layer.
   The myriad images at dawn return 萬象曉歸仁壽鏡
      to the Renshou Hall mirror;
4 And a hundred flowers of spring cut off 百花春隔景陽鐘
      the bells of Jingyang Palace.
   Writing brushes stir in the Secretariat, 紫微芒動詞初出
      as reports are first sent forth;
   Red candle incense fades away 紅燭香殘誥未封
      before the edicts can be sealed.
   Each time you pass the vermilion gates 每過朱門愛庭樹
      you cherish the courtyard trees.
8 What day will a single branch 一枝何日許相容
      permit you its respite?
      (*WFQ, j.* 4, pp. 88–89)

   1/ "Ducks and egrets" is a standard kenning for the ranks of officialdom. Here, Wen puns on its meaning: although Xiao is a member of the "heavenly" [court] ranks, he cannot participate in the world of nature, out in the human world.[15]

   3/ The Jin Dynasty Poet Lu Ji 陸機 (261–303) writes of a large mirror hung on the front of Renshou Hall in Luoyang that reflected people's forms in unusual and startling ways. The "myriad images" are all the appearances of the phenomenal world, which the mirror displays—reflections of intangibles.

   4/ Jingyang Palace: as noted previously, the consorts' quarters.

   5–6/ There are no pronouns in this poem, but since lines five and six imply an official of some rank, Wen cannot be speaking about himself.

   7/ Vermilion gates: those of the imperial palace (like the golden doors of line 2).

   8/ I.e., when can he rest in their shade?

From the first line of this languid, world-weary poem, Wen insists on Xiao's discontent. He imagines him going about his duties, as Wang did with Guo, but Xiao is restless and unwilling, pausing in the end to gaze at the trees, which have become indices not of a unity of the natural and the social but of a longing to escape to a limited and private space. Wen would certainly be careful enough to write such a poem only if he knew Xiao was discontented, but the traditional Chinese poet could write about himself in this manner, and the absence of pronouns creates the impression that Wen is describing himself as well.

By themselves Xiao's emotions are not surprising in the Chinese context: there is, of course, an outright rejection of public values implied in the works of poets like Tao Qian, who was a considerable influence on Wang Wei and his contemporaries. Wen's poem is more subversive on two accounts: first, he aestheticizes court routine, rather than making it seem natural, as had Wang Wei. The whole world, both natural and bureaucratic, already mere "images," becomes a distorted reflection in a mirror, a "seeming" that has only a transient reality; flowers cut off the bells rung at Jingyang, which mark the lofty routine not of officials but of concubines; and documents are prepared amid the fragrance of scented candles. Second, by speaking for Xiao in the poem, Wen turns the verses into both a persuasion and an act of sly complicity. He presents to Xiao his own thoughts and demands that he realize that his true desires lie in retirement from office. Wen invites Xiao away from public values and into his own realm of individualized social relations, where a single person is more than a distorted reflection in a palace mirror.

Wen reduces public life to an aesthetically attractive but fragile routine cut off from larger significance. In doing so, he is representative of many Late Tang literati, who, despite their continued participation in the bureaucracy, had lost their sense of moral commitment. Ambitious public service might still be attractive as a road to personal advancement (albeit a dangerous one), but no one could really believe that such effort contributed clearly and unproblematically to the success of the imperial order. As I have suggested, many literati were indifferent whether they served the emperor or the regional military governors. Whereas some poets, like Li Shangyin, reacted to these circumstances by turning inward, Wen remains in the world but replaces public life with that of leisure and personal cultivation.

With these comments in mind, we can begin a brief investigation of Wen's occasional verse; we will find in them further manifestations of Late Tang concerns (interest in poetic craft and in the search for the safe space) as well as Wen's own awareness that his poetry had become a career, even as it spoke of leisure and entertainment. Although Wen wrote a number of poems on his thwarted political ambitions,[16] he wrote many more on visits to monasteries, on meeting and parting with recluses, and on general depictions of the landscape. What is unusual, however, is Wen's ability to master all the available regulated-verse styles. He could write in the imagistically dense and obscure style of Li Shangyin and evoke eroticism with the same use of imagery as Li could; he could write aesthetically light and brilliant quatrains like Du Mu's or Yong Tao's; and he could write transparent, deceptively simple five-character octets similar to Jia Dao's. Unlike these other poets, who developed a personal style in response to their own circumstances and predilections, Wen not only tailored style to his recipient but also chose from a catalogue of available voices of contemporaries and predecessors, depending on the kind of poem he was writing. Although genre and subgenre have always had a role in determining style in Chinese poetry, most poets seemed to gravitate toward a limited range of genres; Wen was unique in being able to play almost all available stylistic variations. For example, when landscape scenes were required, especially those that might hint at the values of reclusion, he employed a Jia Dao voice.

Spending the Night by a Friend's Pool　　　　　宿友人池

　Against the wall the lamp darkens;　　　　　　背牆燈色暗
　The dream of the sojourning traveler just finishes.　宿客夢初成
　In the middle of the night, rain on the bamboo window;　半夜竹窗雨
4　Filling the pool, the sound of the lotus leaves.　　滿池荷葉聲
　The mat is cool—longing in an autumn room;　　簟涼秋閣思
　Leaves fall—cherishing my home country.　　　木落故山情
　At daybreak, I rise yet again, grief-ridden,　　　明發又愁起
8　While cassia flowers and the stream water turn clear.　桂花溪水清
　　(*WFQ, j.* 9, pp. 180–81)

  Title/ Alternative title: "Sending Someone off on a Journey to the Huai near the Sea" 送人遊淮海.

The gloom of the traveler readying for a morning departure is captured nicely in the first couplet: at some point before dawn, he wakes from a dream to the gloom of the fading lamp and the sound of rain on window and lotuses. The next two lines take up the burden of the outstanding couplet, although Wen does not let the rest of the poem sag quite as much as Jia Dao usually does. The third couplet is deceptively simple, with its bald placement of emotions against scenic detail; it allows the poem to mimic Wen's own supposed thought processes, from a simple reaction to sensory phenomena upon waking up to a self-conscious linking of those phenomena to his emotional state. The last couplet, usually merely conventional in Jia Dao–style verse, has added meaning here by creating a paradox, the poet's grief set against the beauty and clarity of the scene. Wen handles the landscape and travel conventions so smoothly and elegantly that a traditional reader would doubt that this is a product of spontaneous self-expression, but the poem is a little masterpiece nonetheless.

Early Autumn: Sent to a Friend 初秋寄友人

   Just now an idle dream grows melancholy, 閒夢正悠悠
   While a cool wind is born near a tower in bamboos. 涼風生竹樓
   My zither at night lets me know it will rain; 夜琴知欲雨
4 My mat at dawn makes me feel the new autumn. 曉簟覺新秋
   A solitary bird, far away in Chu mountains; 獨鳥楚山遠
   A single cricket grieves in the trees of the pass. 一蟬關樹愁
   I plan to send you this sorrow of parting 憑將離別恨
8 And ask after my fellow wanderer mid Yangzi waters. 江水問同遊
     (*WFQ, j.* 7, p. 150)

   3–4/ These are epistemological tropes that indicate the change in weather. The zither has made some sound in reaction to the rise in humidity or air pressure (perhaps a string has snapped); the chill mat indicates the coming cool weather.
   7–8/ Wen is describing the poem itself, sent as a letter.

This is a more sociable poem, with epistolary conventions in force. Wen and the friend to whom he writes are both on journeys (if we take the "fellow wanderer" in the last line literally); the poet is probably near one of the passes around Chang'an, and the friend is traveling to southern China, nearer to Wen's spiritual home. The wind blows through the bamboo outside the building where Wen sleeps, and the rustling awakens him; he hears his zither responding to the change in weather. As morning dawns and he feels the chill of his mat, he knows autumn has come, a sign of his increasing age. He pictures his friend, a solitary bird, free and migrating away from the north and the approaching cold to a land in which Wen longs to be. He hears a cricket, and it becomes a symbol for himself: like his friend, equally alone, but facing eventual death with the frost. Again, the emotional response at the end is conventional, but the poem succeeds in its goals.

Autumn Rain 秋雨

Clouds fill, paths of birds vanish.	雲滿鳥行滅
The pool chills, as the dragon-stench grows strong.	池涼龍氣腥
I see it as it blows across my chessboard and mat,	斜飄看棋簟
4 Gaze toward scattered downpours at a mountain pavilion.	疎灑望山亭
Small sounds sigh in the forest leaves;	細響鳴林葉
Round wavelets break up the pond duckweed.	圓文破沼萍
Autumn darkness stretches far without end,	秋陰杳無際
8 And all the level wilds turn to a single gloom.	平野但冥冥

(*WFQ, j.* 9, pp. 179–80)

When Wen is not necessarily writing for a specific audience, he can avoid polite compliments. Here he turns his formidable descriptive powers to an autumn storm, evoking it with a strong sense of increasing foreboding and violence. His ability to manipulate Jia Dao's couplet craft in the service of creating sensual *frissons* comes to the fore; one might compare it to "Written on the Shrine to the Bamboo Grove Spirit" (see Chapter 1).

Wen was also capable of fine seven-character quatrains, in the Yong Tao or Du Mu style, although they play a relatively small part in his collection overall.

Encountering Rain in Xianyang 咸陽值雨

Over Xianyang's bridges the rain hangs down;	咸陽橋上雨如懸
Myriad drops of empty drizzle cut off the fishing boat.	萬點空濛隔釣船
It's just the color of springtime waters on Dongting Lake,	絕似洞庭春水色
When evening clouds begin to enter the sky over Yueyang.	晚雲將入岳陽天

(*WFQ, j.* 5, pp. 112–13)

Title/ Xianyang was the old Qin imperial capital, located not far from Chang'an.
3–4/ Lake Dongting, in northern Hunan, was a scenic area associated with the old kingdom of Chu. Yueyang, located where the lake flowed into the Yangzi,

was the site of a famous tower from which hundreds of Chinese poets have composed poems.

Wen's ability in quatrain form is well exemplified here, especially his epigrammatic wit. The poem begins with a fine landscape scene and then compares it to an imaginary vision. There may be a touch of Wen's inclination to fictionalization here in his desire to see absent scenes against present ones, and the overall effect is to hint at his homesickness and loyalty to southern China against the attractions of the capital area. The Xianyang rain is beautiful, but it only reminds him of the more famous scenery seen from Yueyang.

The imagistically heavy and syntactically more complex style that we have come to associate with Li Shangyin also found a place easily in Wen's regulated poetry, although it emerges more prominently in his *yuefu*. Sometimes, though rarely, an ordinary occasion elicited a highly artificial mood painting, such as "Written Offhand on a Forest Pavilion" (see Chapter 1), or the following.

Matching a Friend's Poem: "Country Villa by a Stream" 　　和友人溪居別業

The deep slickness begins to melt, 　　積潤初銷碧草新
　　jade grass is renewed.
With phoenix brilliance, the clear sun 　　鳳陽晴日帶雕輪
　　carries its carved disk.
Silk blows from pliant willows, 　　絲飄弱柳平橋晚
　　evening on the level bridge;
4 Spots of snow on cold plums, 　　雪點寒梅小院春
　　spring in the small courtyard.
On the screen, buildings and terraces 　　屏上樓臺陳後主
　　of Chen Houzhu;
In the mirror, gold and kingfisher feathers 　　鐘中金翠李夫人
　　worn by Lady Li.
In the flower's calyx dew seeps in, 　　花房露透紅珠落
　　the red pearls drop;
8 Butterflies, pair by pair, 　　蛺蝶雙雙護粉塵
　　hoard their powdery dust.
　　(*WFQ, j.* 4, p. 91)

1/ "Deep slickness": ice on the stream.
6/ Lady Li is the famous consort of Emperor Wu of the Han.
7/ The red pearls are the dew drops stained with pollen. The image has metaphorical relation to a woman's tears stained by rouge.

By evoking erotic overtones (not only in the imagery but also in the references to Chen Houzhu and Lady Li), Wen brings his experiments with palace poetry into the realm of regulated incidental verse. We do not know why he should portray a natural scene surrounding a friend's garden in language more befitting a boudoir; usually such poems are written more in the Jia Dao style. It may be that the recipient wanted something in the lush manner Wen was most famous for; without the matching poem, we have no way of knowing.

However, the "lush style" emerges most frequently in his regulated verse in *yongwu* poems or in palace-poetry imitations; many of these are explicitly occasional or suggest an occasion. For Wen (more so than most Late Tang poets) the boudoir, its surroundings, and its accoutrements served as his own peculiar "safe space," a world that he animated with great attention to imagery and sensuality.

On Willows 題柳

A thousand branches of willows, 楊柳千條拂面絲
   silk that strokes the face;
Their green mist and golden grains 綠烟金穗不勝吹
   cannot bear the wind.
Fragrance follows Jingwan, 香隨靜婉歌塵起
   dust rises with her song;
4 Her shadow accompanies Jiaorao 影伴嬌饒舞袖垂
   as her dancing sleeves droop.
One trill from northern pipes: 羌管一聲何處曲
   whence comes this tune?
Flitting orioles—a hundred warbles 流鶯百囀最高枝
   from the highest branch.
In the thousand gates and nine lanes, 千門九陌花如雪
   flowers like snow;
8 They fly past the palace walls 飛過宮牆兩自知
   and only we two know.
   (*WFQ*, j. 4, p. 93)

3–4/ Zhang Jingwan and Jiaorao have turned up previously in poems translated above; both names can also be read as binomes: *jingwan*, "quiet and gracious," *jiaorao*, "femininely attractive." Both women are metaphors for the willows.

8/ Wen gives us no information of who the "two" are; perhaps this poem was originally occasional in nature, and the occasional title was lost.

It was highly conventional for *yongwu* of this sort to make an identity between object and woman at some point in the verse; here we have such identification, not only in the second couplet but in the final lines, whose flying floss seems to hint at some love tryst or at least at privately shared secrets of an amorous nature.

Peonies were another popular subject for *yongwu* throughout the Tang, and here too implicit or explicit comparisons with women were common; in particular, the expense of raising and showing such plants was so considerable that the use of the peony as an emblem for the highly trained and expensive courtesan was inevitable. The wilting of peonies as a symbol for the fading of a woman's beauty was common also, as seen most brilliantly in the Tang courtesan Yu Xuanji's poem, "Selling Wilted Peonies" 賣殘牡丹 (*QTS, j.* 804, p. 9048). Wen left two impressive verses on the subject.

Peonies: Two Poems 牡丹兩首

I

Light shadows—covered by the green paper covers; 輕陰隔翠幃
Last night's rain—they weep clear light. 宿雨泣晴暉
After drunkenness the good times remain; 醉後佳期在
4 The songs linger, but old feelings are gone. 歌餘舊意非
Butterflies pause, trailing the powder they've crossed; 蝶繁經粉住
Bees return, heavily toting their fragrant pollen. 蜂重抱香歸
Don't regret, on the night of scenting clothes 莫惜熏爐夜
8 That they are blown by the wind to your dancing robes. 因風到舞衣

1/ Several days before blooming, peonies were covered with paper covers to enhance their color and to prevent damage from sunlight.

7–8/ I.e., don't regret the falling blossoms, for as they blow into your robes they, rather than any artificial perfume, can serve to scent your gown.

II

Water-rippling clear red 水漾晴紅壓疊波
  hangs down over doubled wavelets;
When dawn comes, golden pollen 曉來金粉覆庭莎
  covers the courtyard sedge.
Cut, they by chance ought to 裁成艷思偏雁巧
  perfect a seductive thought;
4 Thinned, they are most evident 分得春光最數多
  in obtaining the radiance of spring.

About to open, buds seem 　a pair of smiling dimples;	欲綻似含雙靨笑
When in full bloom, something like 　lips in song.	正繁疑有一聲歌
In splendid halls the guests disperse— 　curtains hang to the ground;	華堂客散簾垂地
8　Lost in thought, she leans on the railing, 　contracts her green moth-brows.	想凭闌干斂翠蛾

(*WFQ*, *j*. 9, p. 200)

1/ This complex line seems to describe the blossoms hanging down on the green leaves of the plant.

Both peony poems subtly interweave description of the peonies with description of sexual affairs or flirtations. In the first poem, Wen suggests a context for the peony viewing; a woman, despairing over the loss of her lover, compares the still-fresh blooms, renewed by the night rain, to his fading attentions. Wen enters the poem in the last couplet to offer consolation in the form of the flower's attentions, a witty use of the cliché of the lonely woman left alone to scent and iron clothes (compare Li Shangyin's "Presented to a Serving Maid" in Chapter 3).

The second poem is more interesting in the way it rereads the development of the flower in the progress of a flower-viewing party at a courtesan's establishment. Like Wen's "A Night Banquet" and "A Dancer's Robe" (see Chapter 3), an attention to things hints at the progress of some event. The brilliant images of the third couplet juxtapose a simile for the flower against a possible, real singing performance; here are further suggestions of the courtesan's career (from virginal "bud" to full-blown [overblown?] flowering) and of the sexual experience itself, with the erotic associations of the open, red-lipped mouth.[17] The end of the party in the last couplet is a literal scene as well as an image for the wilted flowers, the aging courtesan, and a post-coital desolation.

The following poem, with woman as object, is probably the closest Wen ever came to writing a palace poem, with its voyeuristic movements and its quotation of the woman's "personal" response.

Composed at Random 　　　　　　　　偶題

A faint breeze, gentle and warm, 　the sun fresh and bright;	微風和暖日鮮明

The hue of the grass bewitches, across from Wei city.	草色迷人向渭城
A Wu girl rolls up her curtains, idly, without talking;	吳客卷簾閒不語
4 A Chu lady pulls at a branch— only she is heartstruck.	楚娥攀樹獨含情
Red, the fruit stems droop; cherry and peach grow heavy.	紅垂果蒂櫻桃重
Yellow-stained flowers cluster, their pollen drifts lightly.	黃染花叢蝶粉輕
"I regret that no news comes here to the blue mansions—	自恨青樓無近信
8 I didn't speak my full heart to my own beloved."	不將心事許卿卿

(*WFQ*, *j*. 4, p. 85)

2/ Wei City: a later name for the Qin capital of Xianyang.
7/ The blue mansions are the brothels.

Was such a poem a mere exercise in style, or did it have a place among other occasional poems? Its title, "Composed at Random," is obviously meant as a belittling of its accomplishments, to make it seem a frivolous game tossed off when the poet felt like it; such defensive strategies are common with morally questionable poetry. However, Wen's liaisons with courtesans and the demimonde (implied by his *ci* output and by the anecdotes surrounding him) suggest that poems like this were written during excursions to the brothels, perhaps in the company of friends or the rich sons of the more important families. A hint of this social context may be given by another poem.

Presented to a Close Friend

	贈知音
With turquoise feathers and flowered crest, the cock of the jade tree	翠羽花冠碧樹雞
Cries out before morning light across from the low wall.	未明先向短牆啼
In the window, a daughter of the Xie family wrinkles her emerald moth-eyebrows;	窗間謝女青蛾斂
4 Beyond the gate, the Xiao lad's white steed neighs.	門外蕭郎白馬嘶
In the lingering dawn, the faint stars sink, opposite the doorway;	殘曙微星當戶沒

198 Small Ambitions

> In pale mist, a setting moon,
>   low, shines on the tower.
> Within Shangyang Palace
>   the bells begin to toll;
> 8 Silent, he lets his whip droop
>   as he crosses Willow Bank.
>   (*WFQ*, *j*. 4, pp. 96–97)

澹烟斜月照樓低

上陽宮裏鐘初動

不語垂鞭過柳隄

3–4/ By Tang times, "Xie daughter" was an elegant term for a beautiful woman or courtesan. Although commentators have tried to identify the "Xiao lad," the Xiaos were one of the great clans of the Six Dynasties period and this probably signifies only a handsome aristocratic gallant.

7/ The Shangyang Palace was built in Luoyang by the Tang emperor Gaozong 高宗 (r. 649–83); the emperor held audiences here. Probably the bells announce an audience that the "Xiao lad" must attend, calling him away from the woman.[18]

This scene of a lover leaving his mistress is aesthetically relocated in the Six Dynasties, but "Xiao lad" may be a polite complimentary designation for one of Wen's companions (the "close friend" of the title) who accompanied Wen on such an excursion. Wen may have composed the poem the next morning to "memorialize" the event.

In the following poem, a real social context for palace-poetry imitations seems even more likely.

> *Two Poems Sent to Supernumerary*
> *Retainer Li of Yuezhou (no. 1)*
>
> Soft and pliant the willows before the tower;
> In the light air, a window beyond the flowers.
> Butterflies soar high in pairs;
> 4 Orioles chatter in the morning, companionless.
> She trims a paper cutout in the form of "spring";
> She opens the screen and sees the river in dawn light.
> In this battle of love they're fighting,
> 8 Today she is about to surrender.
>   (*WFQ*, *j*. 7, pp. 159–60)

寄岳州從事
李員外二首之一

荏弱樓前柳
輕空花外窗
蝶高飛有伴
鶯早語無雙
翦勝裁春字
開屏見曉江
從來共情戰
今日欲歸降

6/ Paper ornaments, often in the form of characters, were used to adorn ladies' coiffures.

The title suggests that the woman so voyeuristically described may be a courtesan known to both the poet and to the addressee Li. The last couplet is wittily ambiguous; without pronouns, it could mean "she" is about to surrender to "you," or "you" are about to surrender to "her," or, if Wen is competing with Li for the attentions of the woman, then perhaps he is the one giving in to Li's more impressive wooing.

These poems should further disprove the generally accepted notion that Wen wrote *shi* in a transparent, non-erotic style; he often did, of course, but his sexual preoccupations do appear in his regulated verse. Once again, this is most probably because, as the talented poet of social occasion, Wen could tailor style to the needs of the moment. However, Wen explored other prominent worlds in his poetry, particularly when he desired to emphasize his role as self-conscious aesthete. The most important explication of these alternative values could be found in the *Shishuo xinyu*, the fifth-century collection of anecdotes describing the lives of literati from the late Han to the Liu Song. This text provided more allusions in Wen's occasional poetry than any other; he constantly compares himself and the addressees of his verse to Jin dynasty aristocrats, hermits, and literary figures. Perhaps he saw the *Shishuo* as a manifesto for a system of social values that stood outside the bureaucratic world he could not enter and did not wholly respect. It demonstrated the possibility of defining the self in a dangerous world through willful eccentricity, lofty (if unconventional) moral standards, and a disregard for Confucian concepts of success. Even when the *Shishuo* idealized a powerful minister such as Xie An, it saw him as an intellect capable of maintaining his individualism within the framework of a hazardous public career. We have already seen that Wen glorifies just this view of Xie in one of his historical songs (see "Duke Xie's Villa" in Chapter 4); and in other poems as well it is clear that Xie was his ideal of the truly public man.

But the *Shishuo* also allowed for the complete disregard of public matters, and Wen welcomed this too. He could invite his patrons and friends, members of the more staid and proper Confucian imperial order, into this countercultural realm where unnecessary concern for career and advancement was a sin of bad taste. Wen could thus create middle ground between public life and reclusion, a "safe space" where he could practice his own tenuous occupation for the amusement and appreciation of literati in general. Such a space also permitted him to maintain his self-respect under the gaze of the public order: in the world of *Shishuo* values, he was the equal of anyone high-minded enough to join him in his own artistic pursuits. In other words, when Wen discreetly compared an official to a noble-spirited and cultured Jin aristocrat, he was both complimenting the official and elevating himself to the official's level.[19]

With a Swift-Flowing Brush I Playfully Thank Retired Scholar Li Yu for His Gift of Freshly Brewed Wine   李羽處士寄新醅走筆戲酬

When I have friends in lofty debate,
   I turn into "a wooded swampland";   高談有伴還成藪
Drunken oblivion, ignorant of time—
   this has become my country.   沈醉無期即是鄉
Because I've long resented the warbling orioles
   who tormented "Xie the Guest,"   已恨流鶯欺謝客
4 You've again sent these floating lees
   to Master Liu.   更將浮蟻與劉郎
Before the eaves, willow color
   expands its green shades;   檐前柳色分張綠
Outside the window, the flowered branches
   add to each other's fragrance.   窗外花枝借助香
What I resent, in this evening of
   red candles and tortoiseshell mats: 所恨玳筵紅燭夜
8 The fact that you, sketching out the "Great Mystery,"
   are alone, near a curve of a pool.   草玄寥落近回塘
   (*WFQ*, *j*. 4, pp. 81–82)

1/ The *Shishuo xinyu* tells of Pei Wei 裴頠, whose arguments were so profound and obstruse that his contemporaries called him "the wooded swampland of conversation."[20] Since Pei himself was a morally serious philosopher, Wen's comparison of Pei to himself is obviously ironic.

2/ The Early Tang poet Wang Ji 王績 (585–644) wrote "An Account of the Country of Drunkenness" 醉鄉記 to supplement the famous Jin drinker Liu Ling's 劉伶 "Ode to the Virtue of Wine" 酒德頌.

3/ "Xie the Guest" is an appellation for Xie Lingyun. One of his more famous lines is "The garden willows cause the singing birds to change"—a line that reflects his distress over the changing seasons and his own homesickness. The *Wen xuan* commentator Li Shan identifies Xie's birds as orioles.

4/ Probably a reference to Liu Ling (see note to line 2).[21] "Floating lees" is a common synecdoche for wine.

8/ Yang Xiong, often a metaphor for the ideal Confucian recluse, gave his retirement over to the authorship of a massive revision of the *Yi jing*, the *Great Mystery* 太玄.

Wen resents the fact that Li is far away and can send only wine, not his presence. There is little, however, of the conventional wish to join Li in his reclusion; rather, he wishes to bring Li into his convivial drinking group, to have him participate in his "wooded swampland of conversation." In failing to serve in office, Wen preferred to see himself not as a Tao Qian, but as one of the Sages of the Bamboo Grove, eminently sociable and active in his culture, even though unemployed.

Sent to Magistrate Yan of Xiangyin: 寄湘陰閻少府乞釣輪子
Begging for a Fishing Reel

The form of the fishing reel 釣輪形與月輪同
  is like the moon's;
Its single cocoon strand merges into mist— 獨繭和烟影似空
  a seemingly intangible outline.
If, at the three Xiangs, you happen upon 若向三湘逢雁信
  this wild-goose letter,
4 Don't refuse to send one a thousand miles 莫辭千里寄漁翁
  to this old fisherman.
Sound on the boat canopy, a dripping at night 篷聲夜滴松江雨
  from rain on Pine River;
Caltrop leaves turning in autumn 菱葉秋傳鏡水風
  by the breeze over Mirror Lake.
The whole day I drop my hook, 終日垂鉤還有意
  always with intent;
8 Letters can be usually found 尺書多在錦鱗中
  in the brocade scales.
    (*WFQ*, *j*. 4, p. 85)

Title/ Xiangyin is near Changsha in Hunan.
2/ From the *Liezi*: "Zhan He made a fishing line from a single thread of silk out of the cocoon, a hook from a beard of wheat, a rod from one of the pygmy bamboos of Chu, and baited it with a split grain of rice. He hooked a fish big enough to fill a cart, in the middle of a swift current in waters seven hundred feet deep."[22]
3/ Three Xiangs: the area of the lakes around Changsha, it is said to be the area where geese (who often carry news from distant loved ones) halt their winter migration.
5/ Pine River is in Wu (Jiangsu), where Wen was evidently living when he wrote the poem.
6/ Mirror Lake is near Shaoxing, in Jiangsu. It received its name from the clarity of its reflections.
8/ A standard *yuefu* trope describes the discovery of a letter within a fish that has been caught. Letter cases were often made in the shape of fish.

Wen writes from his beloved area of Wu, where he plays at being a hermit. Yan is serving as a minor official in Hunan, far enough south to be considered an exile by most bureaucrats. The humor and wit here lie largely in Wen's ability to make literal the clichés of poetic usage. He begins the poem with a *yongwu*-style line describing the reel itself; the magical nature of the fisherman's existence is subtly emphasized as he imagines the fishing line etherealizing into mist. In the context of the poem, he is using the reel as metonymy for himself and thus lays claim to the status of recluse. It is only to be expected, then, that Yan should receive messages from him from the geese, who are heading in Yan's direction anyway; and once Yan sends the reel Wen will find it easy enough to receive letters from his distant friend: all he has to do is catch the fish that Yan sends down the Yangzi for him. All of this is a clever reworking of a stock situation for Chinese poetic composition—the need to establish correspondence with a distant friend, perhaps to enquire why he has not written.

In the middle there is a lovely parallel couplet of eremitic landscape description; although it bears no comment from Wen, it is obviously an account of his experiences as a recluse (the rain at night, the wind on the water in the day). In a poem almost free of imagery and depending largely on witty rhetoric for effect, the couplet constitutes a sort of travelogue. Like the closing couplet of the poem to Secretary Xiao, it is a subtle dig at Yan, who is trapped at his duties in the distant south. Wen is again calling on his addressee to forgo office and follow other pleasures. No matter that Wen is hardly the model recluse; his role here is an exercise in conventions, meant to amuse his recipient.

Most of these poems we have seen so far portray Wen in a network of social relations; as friend, as flattering social inferior, as witty epigrammatist. Such a poetic production was inevitable for a failed literatus who depended partly on the patronage and assistance of others for his livelihood. I have suggested that this lifestyle has defined both the content and the approach of these poems. First, Wen describes and defends eccentricities of all kinds not only to amuse his audience but also to create a role for himself as social equal of more distinguished men within a safe world of *Shishuo* geniuses.[23] Second, the demands of his audience encouraged him to write an extroverted poetry in which he experimented with radically different styles to match the mood of the subject and the character of the poem's recipient.

I mentioned the frequency of refuge themes in ninth-century poetry: whether it be a monastery, some mythical vision of the south, or a district magistrate's garden, poets sought places where they could relax from the stresses of politics. Although Wen was too extroverted to write seriously of escaping the world, this underlying anxiety emerges from time to time in his poetry as well, although it is hard to discover under the veneer of sociability. Like Jia Dao, Wen created a language of "escape" from his association with Buddhist and Taoist monks, but it is still well within the framework of relations he set for himself. Just as playing the fisherman enabled him to engage in poetic banter with his friends, so the role of religious layman gave him new opportunities for artistic sensitivity. It is true that he could express lofty Buddhist sentiments at times:

. . . . .

In the incense fire is a noble aspiration;	香火有良願
The fame of office is not my pure heart's wish.	宦名非素心
If the way to Vulture Peak has not been blocked,	靈山緣未絕
Then another day I'll come seeking it again.[24]	他日重來尋

But these are more part of the conventions of temple-visiting poems than they are sincere resolutions to leave the world. Much more typical is another poem, in which the pleasures of the monastery are somewhat more earthly.

Written on the Monk's Courtyard at West Brightness Temple	題西明寺僧院
It once knew Master Huiyuan from Mount Kuang;	曾識匡山遠法師
Scrub pines and rocky benches face the front altar.	低松片石對前墀
I stopped by the temple to seek out its famous paintings;	為尋名畫來過寺
4 And because I visited people at peace I got to watch a game of chess.	因訪閒人得看棋
Newly arrived geese in straggling groups where the clouds are jade-green;	新雁參差雲碧處

Cold crows from a distance, in disorder 寒鴉遼亂葉紅時
  at a time when leaves turn red.
Yet I know in the end that I'll 自知終有張華識
  make the acquaintance of a Zhang Hua;
8 So I won't set up my hook and line 不向滄洲理釣絲
  on some Canglang islet.
    (*WFQ, j.* 4, p. 84)

1/ Mount Kuang: another name for Mount Lu, the home of the fifth-century Buddhist monk and philosopher Huiyuan. "It" is the courtyard.

7/ The Jin poet Zhang Hua 張華 was noted for his patronage of gifted men.

8/ The Canglang River was the home of the fisherman-recluse who castigated Qu Yuan for his excessive rectitude in public service; the river consequently came to be associated with recluses in general.

Wen's poem is an example of a transition stage in temple-visiting poetry. When Wang Wei visited a temple, a very real pilgrimage was taking place—the site becomes literally "not of this world." By Wen's time, the monastery had become a social center divorced from demanding literati relationships, a sort of vacation spot. Wen enjoys the company of monks, and he pictures their temple as a place of relaxation, where he can take time to examine paintings or watch a chess game. These acts serve to strengthen his ties to his own secular (albeit bohemian) world. Wen can relate to the monks as intellectuals who stand outside the world of public Confucian affairs, but he does not stress their possession of a valuable religious knowledge that could teach him to transcend his desires; even his implied identification of the monks as Huiyuan's disciples bespeaks more his politeness than their theological sophistication. The natural descriptions of lines five and six imply another act of aesthetic appreciation to be found at temples: the pleasurable investigation of the landscape. The coming winter and the restless birds do not remind him of old age and the passing of time (as they might another poet) and are probably meant merely as a descriptive touch. In the end, the poet politely rejects reclusion: better to find a powerful poet-minister who can appreciate him for his artistic accomplishments.

Nonetheless, Wen knew Buddhist discourse well enough to participate in it and to respect monks for what they represented. Despite the persecutions of 845, Tang intellectuals could still recognize the Buddhist way of life and perhaps envy it for the alternative it offered. Wen refuses the life of a monk, but he takes the option seriously. When Confucian literati regain their self-confidence in the Song dynasty, the role of monastery as a legitimate refuge is even more reduced, and its place in tourist economics becomes even more apparent. Su Shi 蘇軾 (1037–1101) writes:

First day of the twelfth month: no return to wife and children;	臘日不歸對妻孥
In name I'm seeking the men of the Way, but really I'm pleasing myself.	名尋道人實自娛
. . . . .	
The day cold, the road far: it grieves my manservant;	天寒路遠愁僕夫
He readies my carriage, urges me to return before it gets too dark.	整駕催歸及未哺
Emerging from the hills, I turn and look: clouds and forest join;	出山迴望雲木合
I only see a wild falcon wheeling over the pagoda.	但見野鶻盤浮圖
This trip has been simple but has been fun enough;	茲遊淡薄歡有餘
Getting home, I was dazed as though waking from a dream.	到家怳如夢蘧蘧
I wrote a poem as swiftly as fire in pursuit of the swiftly fading;	作詩火急追亡逋
A pure landscape, once lost, cannot be seized again.[25]	清景一失後難摹

Wen's respect for religious accomplishments was often combined with a teasing good humor; in the following poem, he also adds some of his customary Six Dynasties posturing.

I Went to Visit Master Zhixuan [Knowledge-of-Mystery] and Found Him Airing out His Sutras; So I Presented Him with This	訪知玄上人 遇暴經因有贈
The light-blue scroll covers are free of dust; they fill the painted veranda.	縹帙無塵滿畫廊
The disciple from Mount Zhong burns incense in the stillness.	鍾山弟子靜焚香
Since Huineng had no method for transmitting his mind,	惠能未肯傳心法

4 It's wasted effort for Zhang Zhan 張湛徒勞與眼方
    to give you a regimen for your eyes.
  Sandalwood smoke wafts on the breeze, 風颺檀烟銷篆印
    while the seal-cake melts away.
  The sun moves pine shadows 日移松影過禪牀
    across the meditation couch.
  Xie Lingyun has his own place 客兒自有翻經處
    to translate the sutras—
8 While autumn comes to the riverbank 江上秋來蕙草荒
    and marsh orchids go to seed.
    (*WFQ, j.* 9, p. 183)

1/ That the sutras are without dust is both a description of the results of the airing and a compliment to Zhixuan, who is above the dust of earthly affairs.

2/ Most likely Mount Zhong north of Jinling.

3–4/ Huineng was the famous Sixth Patriarch of the Southern School of Zen. His teaching involves the transmission of wisdom without reliance on a written text (the patriarch himself was illiterate). When the Jin minister Fan Ning 范甯 complained of sore eyes, Zhang Zhan jokingly offered him a regimen that would cure them; it included abandoning the reading of books. Wen facetiously suggests that since Huineng was unable to transmit his teaching personally to Zhixuan, the latter must rely on an extensive library; thus, since his love of sutras is so great, Zhang Zhan's advice would be lost on him.

5/ Incense was often molded in the form of a seal-cake. This may be the fumigating incense used to drive out pests from the sutra scrolls.

7/ Xie Lingyun: The text has "Ke-er," or "guest-lad." Xie Lingyun received this nickname as a boy because he was raised by an acquaintance of the Xie family. Xie was an admirer of Huiyuan's, and once while visiting his temple he was so inspired he remained there to help translate sutras.

8/ Marsh orchids are flowers associated with Qu Yuan, and, consequently, with the virtuous minister in retreat and/or exile. Here they may refer to Wen in his Xie Lingyun persona (Xie himself often employed *Chu ci* imagery in his poetry).

Wen both makes fun of and flatters his friend, ironically taunting his erudition (so prominently displayed during the airing) yet admiring the quiet transcendence of his surroundings (capturing this in the descriptive third couplet). As is often typical of Wen's allusions, line seven reinterprets the poet's life in Six Dynasties terms and Zhixuan becomes the present-day Huiyuan only in the act of making Wen a present-day Xie Lingyun: elegant sophisticate, talented poet, and ideal Buddhist layman. Of course, once again the ties of friendship seem more of interest to Wen than abstruse philosophical insights, although the last line has him poring over

Zhixuan's sutras while autumn deepens around him—perhaps with a renewed awareness of life's transience.

Monasteries and monks, then, did provide Wen with one of his needed safe spaces, but by reinterpreting Buddhist life in conjunction with Six Dynasties allusions, he co-opts it once again into his own *Shishuo* world of eccentrics and wits. Moreover, even in his Buddhist poetry he shows a consciousness of himself as flamboyant master-poet: both of these poems, like Wen's poems on the fishing reel and on the gift of wine, place a Jia Dao–style couplet of landscape description amid largely non-descriptive rhetoric and narrative. Wen is still the craftsman at work.

Allusions to eremitism in Wen's poetry are common enough to make us wonder if he did perhaps seriously consider retirement as an option.[26] For example, one of his most beautiful landscape poems ends on a reclusive note.

The Southern Ferry at Lizhou	利州南渡
Tranquilly, the empty water faces the slanting sunlight;	澹然空水帶斜暉
The twisting islets, vast and green, touch the mountain's azure.	曲島蒼茫接翠微
Across the waves a horse whinnies as I see the oars depart;	波上馬嘶看櫂去
4 By the willows, people rest, awaiting the boat's return.	柳邊人歇待船歸
In a few clumps of sandy grass the flock of gulls disperses;	數叢沙草羣鷗散
Over a myriad acres of river paddies one egret flies.	萬頃江田一鷺飛
Who knows how to take a boat and seek out Fan Li,	誰解乘舟尋范蠡
8 And over misty waters of the Five Lakes alone forget the world's affairs?	五湖烟水獨忘機
(*WFQ*, *j*. 4, p. 80)	

7/ Fan Li: see note to line 8 of "Matching Six Poems by Liu, Rectifier of Omissions."

Compare this to a Du Mu seven-character octet, with a similar reference to the recluse Fan Li in the last couplet:

Du Mu: *Written on the Water Pavilion of the Kaiyuan Temple in Xuanzhou; Below the Pavilion Is the Wan Stream, Lined with the Homes of People* 題宣州開元寺水閣
閣下宛溪夾溪居人

The cultured things of the Six Dynasties:
   now grass stretches to the sky. 六朝文物草連空
Heavens broad, clouds move leisurely,
   past and present are one. 天淡雲閒今古同
Birds come and go
   amid the mountain colors; 鳥去鳥來山色裏
4 People sing and weep
   within the sound of water. 人歌人哭水聲中
Curtains in the deep autumn,
   rain on a thousand homes. 深秋簾幕千家雨
Sinking sun on the terrace,
   one flute in the wind. 落日樓臺一笛風
I'm depressed that there's no way
   to meet with Fan Li; 惆悵無因見范蠡
8 Scattered, the misty trees
   east of the Five Lakes. 參差煙樹五湖東
   (*QTS*, *j*. 522, p. 5964)

Du Mu arrives at the Fan Li allusion as a response to the recognition of the transitory nature of human endeavor; great, cultivated achievements sink into the grass, while the dreary lives of ordinary humans continue endlessly in a natural and unstoppable cycle. Wen's vision of the ford is seductively beautiful; the poem remains on a positive, optimistic level that argues against the sentiments at the end. Du Mu may not have been serious in his reclusive leanings, but in comparison to Wen he seems a model aspirant.

In poems in which Wen seems to consider reclusion more sincerely, the intensity of his aesthetic vision gets in his way.

Randomly Composed on a Spring Day 春日偶作

In the western garden, a single
   song of lush spring; 西園一曲豔陽歌
In the noise, the carriage dust
   makes me betray my hermit's weeds. 擾擾車塵負薜蘿
My desire to put anxieties to rest
   has yet to be fulfilled; 自欲放懷猶未得

4 And I can't know if my plans for the world 不知經世竟如何
   will come out in the end.
  At night I hear a fierce rain, 夜聞猛雨判花盡
   and judge that flowers are spent;
  In the cold, I cherish my double-layered quilt 寒戀重衾覺夢多
   and wake often from my dreams.
  Since I left the fishing islet 釣渚別來應更好
   it certainly must have grown even better—
8 With a spring wind still 春風還為起微波
   stirring up the light ripples.
     (*WFQ, j.* 4, p. 89)

As in "Encountering Rain in Xianyang," Wen employs the artistic trick of closing with an imagined image rather than a real one; here, the vision is an index to unfulfilled desire, placed in opposition to the opening images of the "lush song" and the "dust of carriages," themselves perhaps indications of Wen's popularity as participant in parties and outings. He does speak conventionally of his "plans for the world," but his exhaustion seems from service as entertainer than as potential statesman.

When occasionally he becomes a sort of mock-recluse, doing a bit of farming at city's edge, he is taken up with the satisfactions of fishing and gardening rather than with the seriousness of the moral commitment.

While Dwelling in the Imperial Suburbs, 郊居秋日有
I Think of One or Two Close Friends on 懷一二知己
an Autumn Day

  Through the rice fields, geese and ducks 稻田鳧雁滿晴沙
   fill the clear sand
  While I come home from a fishing islet 釣渚歸來一徑斜
   by a single slanting path.
  The gate is lined with fruit trees 門帶果林招邑吏
   that call out to the city clerk;
4 The well divides me from the vegetable plot 井分蔬圃屬鄰家
   that belongs to the neighboring house.
  The paddies and plains turn quiet now, 皋原寂歷垂禾穗
   the grains droop in their ears;
  Mulberry and bamboo grow scattered everywhere, 桑竹參差暎豆花
   set against the bright bean blossoms.

> I mock my self-deception,
> my noble world-saving plans;
> 8 I won't commit my mind's concerns
> to the smoke and mist.
> (*WFQ*, *j*. 4, p. 82)

自笑漫懷經濟策
不將心事許烟霞

As with Wen's Buddhist poetry, however, love of wit and of beautiful description does not necessarily preclude an underlying belief in reclusion as a possibility. True, it was conventional to long to join the recluse, and so often for a Chinese poet what was out of reach was poetically the most desirable. Occasionally, though, the beauty of description coincides so magically with the emotional content that a real intention seems to come through, unblocked by the artistry of the poet.

> *On West River, Seeing off a Fisherman*
> You followed Yan Guang back
> toward Ruoye Creek,
> Where you gave your life over to
> a fishing reel and caltrop oars.
> In mid-autumn, mid rain on the plum trees,
> you grew sad for the maple leaves;²⁷
> 4 Then, one night, your canopied boat
> lodged amid the reed flowers.
> When you can't see water and clouds,
> things seem but a dream to you;
> So you'll follow at random the misty birds
> and make of them your household.
> A wind rises over the white duckweed,
> evening on the storied ship;
> 8 River swallows, pair by pair,
> just as the rain blows aslant.
> (*WFQ*, *j*. 4, pp. 98–99)

西江上送漁父
卻逐嚴光向若邪
釣輪菱櫂寄年華
三秋梅雨愁楓葉
一夜篷舟宿葦花
不見水雲應有夢
偶隨烟鳥便成家
白蘋風起樓船暮
江燕雙雙正雨斜

1/ Yan Guang was a childhood friend of Emperor Guangwu 光武 (r. 25–58) of the Eastern Han. Originally named Zhuang Zun 莊遵, he changed it on Guangwu's succession and fled to Fuchun Mountain in order to escape the emperor's invitations to serve the dynasty. Yan Guang's refuge at Fuchun Mountain was close to Ruoye Creek (both in Zhejiang).

Wen's meeting with this nameless fisherman seems to have been by accident; the poem frames a brief moment of encounter, as it traces the recluse's arrival and then anticipates his departure the following morning. The poet himself is traveling in the "storied ship," probably on some pleasure excursion, but he is forced to ignore these social ties—the ties that define his life—as he stares out onto the river, imagining the recluse's departure, the continuation of random wandering in his canopied boat, guided only by the lack of intention that allows him to befriend the birds. Instead of ending with the fisherman's disappearance, however, he returns to his own life, pausing to watch the swallows before he returns to his own affairs and commitments: the bit of artistic sensitivity that here gives meaning to the experience, rather than contradicting its sincerity.

Without writing a detailed history of regulated verse of the ninth century, it is difficult to speak precisely and comprehensively of the regulated verse of Wen Tingyun. Unlike his *yuefu*, it is thoroughly typical of the ninth century, and it participates actively and intricately with the social world of the time and its literary manifestations. Above all, its interpretive problems lie within an aspect of traditional poetics—the reading of poetry in order to discover the poet. The lives of most Late Tang poets are largely hidden under the conventionalized sentiments of their own poetry. With Wen, the problem is doubly difficult: his role as primarily a social poet, hired to please and entertain, makes almost all sentiment, opinions, and attitudes expressed in his poetry questionable. This survey, however, brief as it has been, should sketch a few probable qualities of Wen as poet and as individual: his glorification of bohemianism, often expressed through the use of Six Dynasties figures; his constant proclivity for aesthetic flash and surprise in his poetry, even in the simpler, Jia Dao–style verses; and his continuing admiration for recluses and Buddhist monks, despite his refusal to join their world. In this he represents, though in a somewhat obscured way, the anxiety-ridden concerns of his generation, who employed craft and small subjects in an attempt to mask a fear of a crumbling world or who sought out refuges, "safe spaces" where they could take their leisure for a time. It is thus appropriate that the last word I give to Wen reflects his love of the safe, semi-mythical south and his ever-present desire to create imagined landscapes so much more satisfying than present reality.

Seeing off Retired Scholar Lu on His Travels to Wu and Yue 送盧處士游吳越

I envy your departure east, where you'll see
   the lingering plum flowers; 羨君東去見殘梅
Only you are the Prince
   who will never return. 唯有王孫獨未回
Evening light in the gardens of Wu
   will brighten the ancient ramparts; 吳苑夕陽明古堞
4 And spring grass by Yue Palace
   will ascend the lofty terraces. 越宮春草上高臺
Waves will be born in the wilderness waters,
   geese will begin to alight; 波生野水雁初下
A breeze will fill the post-station buildings
   while the tide will start to come in. 風滿驛樓潮欲來
Then try to follow the fishing boats,
   watch the snow-capped waves; 試逐漁舟看雪浪
8 So many swallows, so many
   caltrop flowers open. 幾多江燕荇花開
   (*WFQ*, *j.* 8, p. 168)

2/ An allusion to "A Summons to the Recluse" 招隱士 from the *Chu ci*: "The prince, he wanders, and returns not; / Fragrant herbs grow, how lush and green." Wen recognizes that Lu will never return to the capital and participate in public service again.

Wen usurps Lu's experience and creates it completely out of his imagination, telling Lu what he will see. The description of the ruins of Wu and Yue in the second couplet could be taken from Wen's *yuefu*, but what was there objective description becomes here a scene of desire and an urge to reject his compulsive allegiance to society and the forces of history—just as the inhabitants of New Feng and the poet He Zhizhang managed to do. You will dwell amid the ruins of splendor, says Wen, but you must take pleasure instead in the simple moments of the season, as you follow the fishing boats to a place where names are forgotten.

Appendix

APPENDIX

A Note on the Tonality of Wen Tingyun's Seven-Character *Yuefu*

Although tonal regulation in octets and quatrains is now explained through the use of models, tonality in the Tang evolved as a series of rules that produced "correct" verse when incorporated in toto. Since these rules increase the scope of their restrictions from regulation of the individual line to regulation of four-line units, one may measure the degree of tonality in Wen's *yuefu* by observing their fidelity to each of these laws in turn.[1]

The pool for statistical observation consists of the sixteen seven-character *yuefu* translated in the course of this study (ordered below by page number in *WFQ*). All of these poems are homogeneous in language and imagery, reflecting the distinctive "song style" that Wen developed from Li He.

1. "Song: Cockcrow Dike" (20 lines)
2. "A Night Banquet" (16 lines)
3. "Lotus Bank Song" (8 lines)
4. "Song: Retired Scholar Guo Strikes the Musical Bowls" (22 lines)
5. "Dawn Immortal Song" (16 lines)
6. "A Dancer's Robe" (16 lines)
7. "Zhang Jingwan Picks Lotus" (20 lines)
8. "The Reflection" (8 lines)
9. "Song of Wu Garden" (8 lines)

10. "Song of Huyin" (16 lines)
11. "Song: The Han Emperor Welcomes Spring" (14 lines)
12. "Song: Naval Battle on Kunming Lake" (16 lines)
13. "Song: Duke Xie's Villa" (12 lines)
14. "Lament for Spring" (8 lines)
15. "Song: Nights of Spring Rivers and Flowered Moons" (20 lines)
16. "Spring Dawn Song" (8 lines)

Tonal rules

Rule One. Rhyme scheme. In regulated verse, characters at the end of even-numbered lines rhyme, with allowance for a rhyming couplet at the beginning of a seven-character octet or quatrain.

As I note in Chapter 2, many seven-character *gushi*, especially Wen Tingyun's *yuefu*, adopt regulated quatrain structure with stanzas of rhyme scheme *aaba*; however, a rule that developed during the High Tang demands that stanzas alternate level and deflected rhymes, with the non-rhyming end word always the opposite tone category from the rhyme. Although deflected rhymes are not allowed in regulated verse, the creation of a rigid rule *demanding* deflected rhymes in certain situations argues against the common perception of all *gushi* as "tonally ruleless."

Rule Two. Line tonality. In a tonally regulated seven-character line, the second, fourth, and sixth characters should be deflected-level-deflected (D-L-D) or level-deflected-level (L-D-L). These patterns restrict the writer to two of the eight possible combinations for such a line.

Rule Three. Couplet tonality. In a tonally regulated seven-character couplet, the second, fourth, and sixth characters of each line should be opposite tonally from the corresponding characters of the other line. That is, a D-L-D line should be matched with an L-D-L line, and vice versa. Because I am interested in shades of tonality and not rigid adherence, I am also looking for couplets in which changing the tonality of one character would result in tonal correctness.

Rule Four. Quatrain tonality. Ideally, within a tonally regulated seven-character quatrain, the second couplet should be a mirror-image of the first couplet; that is, the tonality of the first and fourth lines, as well as that of the second and third, should be identical. Stimson has pointed out, however, that independent quatrains have less stringent tonality laws than other regulated verse and often violate this rule.[2] With this in mind, I also searched for quatrains that follow a "mirror" structure or a "back-to-front" structure (where the two couplets are metrically alike—e.g., L-D-L / D-L-D / L-D-L / D-L-D), as well as for quatrains where changing of one or two characters would result in tonal correctness.

Application of tonality rules to test poems

Rule One. All but three of the sixteen poems follow the formulated rule of rhyme changes at quatrain intervals (*aaba*, with alternating level and deflected rhymes). Number 4 has a couplet added to the fourth quatrain, with a rhyme scheme *aabaca*; No. 11 begins with a rhyming couplet (level rhyme), followed by a quatrain with deflected rhymes; No. 16 follows the rhyme scheme of a regulated seven-character octet (*aabacada*), although the rhyme itself is deflected.

Rule Two
Total number of test lines: 228
Number of tonally correct lines: 168 (73.7 percent)

Rule Three
Total number of test couplets: 114
Number of tonally correct couplets: 56 (49.1 percent)
Number of couplets short one character for correctness:
    38 (33.3 percent)
Total: 94 (82.4 percent)

Rule Four
Total number of test quatrains: 56 (eliminating extra
    couplets in Nos. 4 and 11)
Number of tonally correct quatrains: 6 (10.7 percent)
Number of quatrains short one character for correctness:
    13 (23.2 percent)
Number of quatrains short two characters for correctness:
    10 (17.9 percent)
Total: 29 (51.8 percent)

Conclusions

This admittedly limited survey leaves many questions unanswered. I have examined only seven-character *yuefu* because of their primacy among Wen's corpus and because of the broader statistical base they allow (three variable positions per line as opposed to two). A more detailed examination of tonality in non-regulated verse—one that could easily approach book-length—ought to examine the following issues:

1. Tonality or near-tonality in five-character *yuefu*;
2. Tonality or near-tonality in non-*yuefu gushi*;
3. The possibility of a poet using the contrast between regulated and non-regulated passages for aesthetic effect;
4. Possible patterns that suggest autonomous rules for tonality in *yuefu*, or patterns that suggest the occasional deliberate avoidance of exact tonal correctness;
5. Evidence of greater or lesser tonality in certain subgenres or subjects.

These last three questions are the most interesting for further exploration, and this statistical survey hints at some possible directions such exploration might take. For example, although most of the individual poems fall very close to the statistical average, some stand out as either adhering more closely to regulation or as avoiding it more. For example, No. 1 has eighteen regulated lines out of twenty (90 percent), eight regulated couplets and one near-regulated couplet out of ten (90 percent), and three quatrains that are regulated, or near-regulated (60 percent). On the other hand, No. 10 has eleven regulated lines out of sixteen (68.8 percent), four regulated couplets and four near-regulated couplets (100 percent, but half are imperfect), and no regulated or near-regulated quatrains.

Granted these statistical limitations, however, we may still reach some tentative conclusions. It seems that Wen treated rules of regulation as guidelines for composition, though not as precise and rigid demands—much as English poets followed metrical rules with a freedom for frequent violations. Another possibility that emerges—though by no means a statistically proved one—is that Wen occasionally moves away deliberately from conventional regulation as a way of indicating that his poem was not to be considered "regulated verse" in the technical sense. An examination of such strategies would require a broader statistical sampling, as well as further proof on how well defined regulated verse was during Wen's lifetime.

At the level of individual line composition, Wen was inclined more to write a regulated line than a non-regulated one. It may be that for a poet accustomed to regulated verse composition, a tonally regulated line was essentially easier to write than one that was not—much as traditionally trained poets in English find iambic pentameter a natural means of expression.

Couplet regulation is also the general rule for these poems; violation is frequent but not widespread. The large number of couplets that are near-tonal suggests the possibility that Wen deliberately inserted a violating character at times as a way of signifying "non-conventional" regulation; however, this is far from being a rule—he is more likely to write a tonally perfect couplet.

It is at the quatrain level that tonality tends to break down most clearly, although a slight majority of quatrains still move toward regulation. The total number of quatrains that *tend* toward a "back-to-front" structure is less (sixteen altogether, or 28.6 percent) than the number of those that tend toward conventional regulation; however, the slightly greater number of perfect "back-to-front" quatrains compared to perfect, conventionally regulated quatrains (eight to six) suggests that Wen may have used this counter-model as a way of signifying "non-conventional" regulation. A greater statistical sampling is needed before any further conclusion can be made.

My purpose here is merely to make statistically clear Wen's use of tonality in many of his *yuefu* and to emphasize the fact that tonality was a mode of composition applied at various levels, rather than a set of iron-clad rules. It should be clear, however, that no true history of tonal regulation can be written without careful and widespread examination of *gushi* in general.

Reference Matter

Notes

For complete author names, titles, and publication data for the works cited here in short form, see the Bibliography, pp. 241–46. For the abbreviations used in the notes, see p. xii.

CHAPTER I

1. Yan Yu is credited with the following common division (Yan, pp. 48–107, esp. 52–58): Early Tang (seventh century); High Tang (the reign of Xuanzong 玄宗, 712–56); Mid-Tang (late eighth century–first quarter of ninth century); Late Tang (remainder of ninth century). Note, however, that Yan does not conceive of a Mid-Tang period as such, but speaks instead of the two styles characteristic of the Dali 大曆 (766–79) and Yuanhe 元和 (806–20) periods.

2. Citations of *WFQ* are to traditional *juan* number, followed by page number in the typeset edition. The nine *juan* of Wen's poetry in the *QTS* follow the *WFQ* arrangement.

3. The best examination of Chinese ways of reading is Owen's *Traditional Chinese Poetry and Poetics*. See also Yu, *Reading of Imagery*, an excellent survey of changing interpretive strategies of the Chinese tradition from the Han through the Tang.

4. Hung, p. 1.

5. Xue Xue, *Yipiao shihua* 一瓢詩話, in Ding, p. 696. The first quote is from "Matching a Friend's 'Streamside Estate'" 和友人溪居 (*WFQ*, *j*. 4, p. 91); the second is from "The Late Spring Banquet Ends: Sent to My Elder, Song Shou" 春暮宴罷寄宋壽先輩 (*WFQ*, *j*. 4, pp. 89–90). The second quote means, roughly paraphrased, "The singing girls at your [Song Shou's] party are enough to seduce a whole city; and you, the host, have a talent equal to the great Han poet, Sima Xiangru."

6. This version of the anecdote is quoted by the Song anthologist Hu Zi (2: 126) from Liu Gong's 劉公 *Jia hua* 嘉話.

7. Wang Fuzhi, *Jiang zhai shihua* 薑齋詩話, in Ding, p. 9. For a more detailed discussion of craft in Late Tang verse, see Chapter 5 below. My translation here is based partially on Owen's in *Readings in Chinese Literary Thought*.

8. Lin Bangjun, "Lun Wen Tingyun he tade shi," pp. 132–44.

9. *Jiu Tang shu*, pp. 5078–79; *Xin Tang shu*, pp. 3787–88 (under biography of Wen Daya 大雅).

10. Xia Chengtao's *nianpu* of Wen Tingyun was first compiled in the 1930's and revised for the publication of *Tang Song ciren nianpu* (pp. 383–412). For Gu Xuejie's various pieces on Wen's life, see *Wenxue lunji*, pp. 188–260.

11. Xia and Gu have assigned a birthdate of 812, basing their arguments on two autobiographical poems (although both agreed that the birth year could be moved several years in either direction). Arguments for different birth years have emerged in the past decade, similarly based on hints in Wen's writings. Note the following: Chen Shangjun, "Wen Tingyun zaonian," and "Ye tan Wen Tingyun shengping"; Wang Dajin; and Mou. All these speculations, though careful, are based on the assumptions that the movements of people who lived over a thousand years ago can be traced as precisely as celestial bodies, that poets possessed extraordinarily accurate memories, and that poems never exaggerated or fudged events for aesthetic or personal reasons.

12. Ji Yougong, p. 823.

13. As for Wen's name itself, the character 庭 appears occasionally as 廷, and the character 筠 as 雲. Gu Xuejie (p. 194) speculates that, after abandoning the name Qi, Wen chose 廷雲, which can be translated as "imperial court clouds," to signify his aspirations for a public career. After repeated failures convinced him he could never become a high official, he changed his name to the more reclusive 庭筠, "courtyard bamboo." Although a tempting explanation, the free substitution of phonetically identical or similar characters is common enough in early texts to make this doubtful without further proof.

14. *Xin Tang shu*, p. 3788: "He could set luxuriant lyrics to the sounds of strings and bamboo."

15. The first is a 100-line *pailü* addressed to a Vice-Director Li (probably Li Deyu; *WFQ, j.* 6, pp. 129–34); the other is a 200-line *pailü* sent to various officials and friends that bemoans his inability to go to the capital for the examinations in 840 (*WFQ, j.* 6, pp. 119–29).

16. For a discussion of Li's relations with both factions and how commentators have interpreted their significance for his work, see Wu Diao-

gong, pp. 43–49. Wu himself thinks that Li was independent of both factions.

17. Ji Yougong, p. 824.
18. Gu Xuejie, p. 250.
19. Xin, p. 238.
20. Although the dynastic histories do not mention that Wen held this office, the preface to the *Huajian ji* refers to him by his professorial title, as does the *Tang caizi zhuan* and a few other early works.
21. Yu Xuanji's two poems addressed to Wen are "On a Winter Night: Sent to Wen Feiqing" 冬夜寄溫飛卿 and "Sent to Feiqing" 寄飛卿 (*QTS*, *j.* 804, pp. 9049, 9053).
22. The history of Wen's edition is complicated; for a brief discussion of its provenance, see Chapter 2 and notes; see also Gu, pp. 207–10, Wan, pp. 308–10, and Xia, pp. 419–24.
23. The *Jiu Tang shu* (p. 5078) states that Li was considered on a level with Wen and Duan Chengshi, and that the three received the nickname "the Three Sixteens"—perhaps because they each ranked sixteenth in age in their extended families. For "Wen-Li," see, e.g., Xin, p. 238.
24. Murakami Tetsumi (*Sō shi no kenkyū*, p. 98) finds Wen to be a more "characteristic" Late Tang poet than Li, but as will soon become apparent, this holds only for his regulated verse.
25. I use *subgenre* here in the sense of Stephen Owen (*Poetry of the Early T'ang*, chap. 1 and *passim*), who uses it to describe a body of poetry linked not by metrical rules but by shared conventions that affect the way poetic content is treated.
26. For the Yu Xin series, see Lu, p. 2395; for examples of Du Fu on painting, see, e.g., "Song on a Landscape Painting by Wang Zai" 題王宰畫山水圖歌 and "Painted Hawk" 畫鷹 (*QTS*, *j.* 219, p. 2305, *j.* 224, p. 2394).
27. The beginnings of the popularity of this couplet may begin with Ouyang Xiu's 歐陽修 (1007–72) *Liuyi shihua* 六一詩話 (in He, p. 267). For an interpretation of this couplet in the context of Late Tang–Early Song poetics, see Owen, *Readings in Chinese Literary Thought*.
28. *Jin shu*, pp. 1228–29.
29. *Nan shi*, p. 1356.

CHAPTER 2

1. For a full discussion of the impact of *Classic of Poetry* interpretation on poetics in general, see van Zoeren, pp. 52–115.
2. For a translation of the borrowed sections from the *Yue ji* 樂記 (Record of music), see Legge 2: 93–94; the argumentative methods of the *Yue ji* in general may be seen throughout the Great Preface.

3. Of course, the *yuefu* of literati poets with known biographies may be interpreted as a mask concealing real, personal concerns.

4. See Ripley. Using a sample of some six hundred poems, Ripley finds that only roughly 25 percent of them follow the rules for regulation set down by Qing dynasty scholars; moreover, he notes that strictness in tonality comes to the fore only in the Late Tang and Song.

5. Some early theorists (and critics) of tonal regulation saw tonality as a compensation for the loss of music in poetry; see Bodman, pp. 121–23; however, this argument was limited to the early polemics on tonality. By the seventh and eighth centuries, attention to tonal regulation was common enough to become an expected quality of "new" poetry. For the appropriateness of regulated verse for song, see Ren Bantang 1: 155–60.

6. For a summary of this argument, see, e.g., Wang Li, pp. 34–35.

7. Xiao, *j*. 19, pp. 264–67.

8. Lu, p. 102.

9. That Xiao Yan's poem is regulated is particularly striking, since we know that he was skeptical of the new rules of tonal regulation; see Mather, *The Poet Shen Yüeh*, p. 38.

10. For Ren's criteria of judgment, see 1: 62–65. The strictness of his requirements disqualifies many poems that may in fact have been sung; for example, Ren rejects any poem with a song-style title that derives from pre-Tang sources if he cannot find additional evidence that it was sung (1: 46).

11. Ren 1: 52–56.

12. Ren 2: 503; *QTS*, *j*. 472, p. 5354.

13. Ren 2: 78; *QTS*, *j*. 636, p. 7300.

14. Ren 1: 341–404.

15. I distinguish here between, on the one hand, quatrains and *changduan ju* written by literati and, on the other hand, the genuine folk *changduan ju* found in the Dunhuang manuscripts. Even early literati poets of the new genre who employed lively and near-vernacular diction never really fully adopted the vernacular; their works show a retrenchment, a desire to bring *changduan ju* up to the level of quatrains in diction and theme.

16. Ren 1: 126. The first example is "Watching the Hunt" 觀獵 (*QTS*, *j*. 126, p. 1278), retitled "Garrison Song" 戍渾辭; the second can be found in *QTS*, *j*. 127, pp. 1286–87, retitled as "Xixi yan" 昔昔鹽.

17. Owen, *Great Age of Chinese Poetry*, pp. 91–95. On pp. 91–92, Owen translates a well-known anecdote concerning the poets Wang Changling, Gao Shi 高適, and Wang Zhihuan. While visiting a tavern, they held a contest to determine whose poems were most often sung by the entertainers there. Obviously, a poet's fame, even in the eighth century, could be largely dependent on his popularity among musicians.

18. Ren 1: 323–26.
19. *QTS, j.* 561, p. 6519.
20. See the Li Bai song translated above for a typical use of this phrase. Historical circumstances have imbued Li's poem with an irony it did not possess when written.
21. Wang Li, pp. 350–62; Wang attributes the use of regulation to the semiconscious influence of regulated verse. But since regulated verse had yet to be precisely defined as a genre at this time, I prefer to see it as another example of the general feeling in the Tang that regulation was appropriate for up-to-date and fashionable poetic forms.
22. Finals based on phonetic reconstructions used in Stimson, *T'ang Poetic Vocabulary.*
23. Ren 1: 125–26. For the Li He poem, see *LHSJ*, p. 245; for the Liu Changqing poems, *QTS, j.* 150, p. 1556; for the Wen Tingyun poems, see *WFQ, j.* 2, p. 47, and *j.* 2, pp. 37–38.
24. The distinction between *yuefu* and *gexing* is not a clear one; *yuefu* tend to be written in voices of persona other than the author's, whereas *gexing* are personal poems, often occasional in nature, written in a *yuefu* style. Li Bai was the first major poet to write many of them; see Stephen Owen, "Li Po," in Nienhauser, p. 549. For a rare example of a *gexing* in Wen's work, see "Retired Scholar Guo Strikes the Musical Bowls," translated later in this chapter.
25. *Jiu Tang shu*, p. 3772.
26. For a discussion of the Jade Consort's appearances in Tang literature, see Schafer, pp. 67–70.
27. For a discussion of music poems, including Li He's, see Owen, *The Poetry of Meng Chiao and Han Yü*, pp. 235–39.
28. Bo Ya was a talented player of the Chinese zither; his friend, Zhongzi Qi, knew Bo Ya so well that he could guess what Bo Ya was thinking just by listening. See *Liezi jishi*, pp. 178–79, and Graham, *Book of Lieh-tzu*, pp. 109–10.
29. Han Yu, "Listening to Master Ying Play the Lute" 聽穎師彈琴, *QTS, j.* 340, p. 3813.
30. Li He, "Song: Hearing Master Ying Play the Lute" 聽穎師彈琴歌, *LHSJ*, p. 350.
31. Zhou Chengzhen (p. 30) points out that Li runs a gamut of responses: phoenixes, goddesses, clouds, stones, fish, plants. It is characteristic of Li, however, not to attempt to put these elements into any sort of perceivable hierarchical order. He mentions them as he thinks of them.
32. *Weizhui* 委壟 is a binome that seems to imply drooping hair, perhaps in a ponytail; hence my translation.
33. Modern Chinese articles and books that present this view are too

numerous to mention. For English works on Wen's *ci* that agree essentially with this perspective, see Chaves, pp. 35–54; Chang, pp. 33–62; and Wagner, pp. 118–27.

34. In addition to the *Wolan ji* and the *Jinquan ji*, the *Xin Tang shu* and *Song shu* list a *shi* collection in five *juan*; other Song sources describe a *shi* collection in seven *juan*, which is probably the source for the edition we have now (see the following note). Interestingly, the twelfth-century poet Lu You 陸游 notes in a colophon to his own copy of Wen's collection that his father possessed an edition that contained "Setting out Early from Mount Shang" (see Chapter 1 for translation); Lu's edition lacked this poem, and he assumed that it had been lost (see Wan, pp. 308–9).

35. Two further points about this final "definitive" version of Wen's edition. First, by Gu Sili's time the ten "Willow Branch Songs" ("Yang liu zhi"; the first eight are found in the *Huajian ji*) were moved to the *shi* collection, obviously because of their ambiguous status as both *ci* (by Qing dynasty standards) and quatrains. They are the only example in the *shi* collection of a series of poems listed under the same tune title (for possible reasons for this, see note 51 to this chapter). Second, Gu Sili reports in the colophon to his edition that he had seen a Song edition of Wen's *shi* (called *Jinquan ji*; it is evident that by this time this name was given to the *shi* collection regardless of the contents of the original *Jinquan ji*) that consisted of seven *juan*, followed by a one-*juan* supplement and a ninth *juan* called *Jinquan ci*. Although Gu does not describe this last *juan*, it probably consisted of the *ci* found in the *Huajian ji*, with possibly the five other currently existing *ci* as well. Gu based his edition on this, removing the *ci* (which by Gu's time would have been considered out of place in a *shi* collection) and replacing them with *shi* he had discovered in other sources. This is the edition apparently preserved in the *Quan Tang shi*; the poem order and chapter divisions are the same, but several poems from the ninth *juan* are missing.

36. Ye, *Jialing lun ci conggao*, pp. 8–10.

37. Another possibility is that certain of Wen's poems were kept out of his official *shi* collection because they dealt with "improper" (i.e., erotic) subject matter. That is the case with Han Wo's 韓偓 (844–923) *Xianglian ji* 香奩集, a specialized anthology of his "palace" style *shi*. The *Wolan ji* and *Jinquan ji* may in fact be such collections.

38. For a skeptical appraisal of Zhang Huiyan's interpretations, see Ye, *Jialing lun ci conggao*, pp. 10–17; see also Ye, "The Ch'ang-chou School of Tz'u Criticism," pp. 119–24.

39. One interesting barometer of his reputation as *ci* and *shi* poet is Cao Xueqin's eighteenth-century novel *Hong lou meng*. I have found five references to Wen in that novel; three mention him in the company of other

shi writers (see Cao, chap. 2, p. 20; chap. 49, p. 525; and chap. 75, p. 854). In another place, the famous couplet from "Setting out Early from Mount Shang" turns up in a drinking game (chap. 28, p. 294). Last, and most interestingly, Jia Baoyu mentions "Master Guo Plays the Musical Bowls" as a fine example of the song form, in conjunction with Bai Juyi's "Song of Lasting Pain" 長恨歌 and Li He's "Song of Kuaiji" 會稽歌 (chap. 78, p. 895). Wen is one of the most mentioned poets in the novel, and it is fairly clear that he is seen as a *shi* poet and not as a *ci* lyricist.

40. Kang-i Sun Chang (pp. 30–32) argues that only the single-stanza *ci* share this conventional style, but I believe that a close reading of both single- and double-stanza lyrics does not bear this out. Again, this style is not Dunhuang style at its "folksiest" but a literati reworking of folk motifs.

41. "South Garden" 南園, first of thirteen; *LHSJ*, p. 62.

42. Many of these qualities are examined in detail in the next chapter; suffice it to say here that the imagery and even the disposition of poetic vision in this *ci* are repeated over and over again in many of Wen's *yuefu* and in not a few of his regulated verses.

43. Chang, p. 36.

44. Quoted in Ye, *Jialing lun ci conggao*, p. 25.

45. For another good example of this approach, see Wen's "Spring Dawn Song" 春曉曲 (*WFQ*, *j*. 3, p. 53), translated in Chapter 3.

46. Ye, *Jialing lun ci conggao*, pp. 18–20.

47. For a detailed consideration for these aspects of eroticism, see Chapter 3.

48. A recent history of the *ci* genre by Yang Haiming does deal explicitly with the performance context of literati *ci*; the author in fact sees sexuality as the dominant theme in Late Tang literature. Yang carries out a similar comparison of a few *shi* from Han Wo's palace-poetry collection (*Xianglian ji*) with the same poet's *ci* and finds them very close in style. It is to be regretted that he did not try to do the same with Wen's poetry.

49. Granted, of course, that a style for *ci* in the mid-ninth century can even be determined. Murakami Tetsumi (*Sō shi no kenkyū*, pp. 99–100) has noted that with the elimination of Wen's collection, of dubious attributions, and of *ci* that are obviously *shi* quatrains, there are only eighteen surviving Late Tang *ci*.

50. Murakami (*Sō shi no kenkyū*, p. 118) mentions the influence of Wen's *yuefu* on his *ci* and the roots of both in Li He and Li Shangyin—although he does not go into details.

51. Wen's *ci* collected in the *Huajian ji* are nonetheless distinct from Wen's *shi* because they are groups of unnamed poems written to the same tune—unlike Wen's *shi*, with the exception of the "Willow Branch"

songs, which are part of both the *shi* collection and the *Huajian ji*. This may be a reflection not of the musical qualities of *ci* (as opposed to the supposedly non-musical qualities of *shi*, which Ren Bantang has disproved) but of the method of collection of the *Huajian ji* and of the nature of *ci* composition. The editors were more interested in *ci* as a new and distinctive kind of song; so they looked for famous examples of Wen's and identified them by the tune they were sung to. This suggests that although Wen's *yuefu* and *ci* share qualities of musicality, Wen would have composed *ci* with a specific existing tune in mind, whereas his *yuefu* (though quite possibly singable) were probably written independent of a pre-existent tune.

52. The *Huajian* poets may simply have used Wen Tingyun as the father of their genre because of his reputation: he was immensely popular as a *shi* poet during the Five Dynasties. The *Caidiao ji* 才調集, a tenth-century anthology of Tang *shi* compiled by Wei Gu 韋縠 from the state of Shu, has more poems by Wen (sixty-one) than by any other poet save Wei Zhuang (sixty-three), who had been a minister of Shu and consequently was worthy of special attention. Out of Wen's sixty-three selected poems, thirty-one are *yuefu*—a greater proportion of *yuefu* to regulated verse than exists in his poetry collection overall. See *Tang ren xuan Tang shi*, pp. 479–94.

CHAPTER 3

1. Li Shangyin, "Imitating Xu Ling's Style: Presented to a Serving Maid" 效徐陵體贈更衣, *QTS*, *j*. 540, pp. 6204–5. The "serving girl" in the title is a "change-clothes" (*gengyi* 更衣), a term that has certain connotations in erotic poetry. Wei Zifu 衛子夫, a singer in the retinue of the Princess of Pingyang 平陽公主, won the emperor's favor when she attended him on his trips to the privy during a drinking party at the Princess's house. *Gengyi* is also a common euphemism for "privy." Here, the story is exploited for its associations with the mercurial rise and fall of court ladies, although, as it turns out, the woman described is quite literally a *gengyi*, employed as she is in the imperial wardrobe. For comparison, see Liu Yuxi's 劉禹錫 (772–842) "Song of a Change-Clothes" 更衣曲 (*QTS*, *j*. 356, p. 3995). The gardenia seeds hanging from her girdle are a kind of love gift and symbolize the desire to find a lover; thus, they have the same implications as the embroidered ducks of the next line. The aloes fragrance of the last line is probably being used as a perfume that the iron seals into the fabric.

2. To some extent the term *palace-style poetry* is nebulous; I conceive of the genre in terms of its later traditional Chinese definition, namely,

poems of the late Southern Dynasties on beautiful women. Technically, however, the borders of the genre are much wider. Zhou Zhenfu (pp. 141–47) has challenged the late traditional view by suggesting that in the view of its practitioners "palace poetry" meant either a new style pioneered by Xu Chi 徐摛 (472–551; Xu Ling's father), in which tonal proprieties were largely observed, or the style championed by Xiao Gang himself, which stressed elegant and sophisticated diction at the cost of serious content. Ronald C. Miao (p. 1) uses this broader conception as well when he defines it as "Chinese verse centered on the life of the imperial residence, and may include such varied but related subject matter as court functions and ceremonies, objects of palace art and architecture, landscape, as well as . . . the palace lady (*kung-nü*)." However, the very existence of *New Verses from the Jade Terrace* proves that the poets of the time did think of erotic poetry as a separate entity, even if they did not apply the term *gongti* to it. While acknowledging the "correct" meaning of the term, I apply it to the erotic theme here out of convenience.

3. For the influence of palace poetry on the palace lament, see Miao, pp. 30–42.

4. Of course, a renewal of interest in, and the use of, past styles is a recurring characteristic of Chinese poetry and is generally of a piece with Chinese cultural interests in "returning to antiquity" (*fugu* 復古). The reanimation of palace poetry tropes and rhetoric among Late Tang poets, however, has little to do with the (highly moral) enterprise of renewing the values of the past—as should be obvious from the rejection of the palace style by *fugu* moralists of the Sui and Early T'ang (see Miao, p. 30 n69; and Owen, *Poetry of the Early T'ang*, pp. 14–26). I borrow the comparison with Stravinsky and Picasso from Cahill, p. 53. He is speaking particularly of the Ming painter Dong Qichang's 董其昌 technique of *fang* 仿 or "imitation" of earlier painters. A poet (or painter or composer) need not, however, engage in a self-proclaimed "imitation" in order to give his work historical depth or in order to comment on his own artistic tradition.

5. By the time of the Liang dynasty, some distinction was made between writing that possessed "ornament" (*wen*)—which, rigidly defined, meant rhyme—and writing that was meant to record events and ideas in a direct way (*bi* 筆). The former emphasized expressing the personality of the writer; the latter was aimed merely at preserving content. See Yu, "Formal Distinctions," pp. 31–36; Qian, pp. 1420–21; and Knechtges, pp. 16–20.

6. For the preservation of northern dialect, see Mather, "Note on the Dialects."

7. Allen.

8. For an attempt to analyze the "psychological profile" of the average woman described in palace poetry, see Birrell, "Dusty Mirror." Although Birrell's reading is perceptive, she seems unwilling to deal with the implications of male authorship in the depiction of women. Only at the end does she make some tentative suggestions concerning the attractiveness of such portrayals to male readers. Incidentally, when I say that the poet addresses his fellow poets, I am describing the general rule. Although there are a few poems in *New Verses from the Jade Terrace* by women that reveal a distinctively female perspective, most poems with female authorship turn the author or other women into objects of contemplation for the man. See, e.g., the poems by "Fan Jing's wife" 范靖婦 (Shen Manyuan 沈滿願) and by Liu Lingxian 劉伶嫻, *YTXY*, pp. 208–10, 255–56.

9. Suggestions of this method can be seen already in the tradition that grows out of Song Yu's "Master Dengtu the Lecher" 登徒子好色賦 (Xiao, *j*. 19, pp. 268–69), in which the poet boasts of his immunity to feminine charms while describing them elaborately. Needless to say, Song Yu's poem is a major source of erotic imagery for the palace poets. More broadly, one may point to the Han *fu* tradition of glorifying sensual pleasures while rejecting them in the end; both *fu* poets and the palace poets were interested in the description of physical phenomena. For this aspect of the *fu*, see Watson, *Early Chinese Literature*, pp. 259–69. Compare this aspect of Chinese poetry to a discussion of the female nude in Western art by John Berger in *Ways of Seeing*. He too suggests that the act of aesthetic distance when viewing a work of art becomes more complex when a male views a female nude. Dynamics of sexual desire and control are still at work in the act of "disinterested" viewing.

10. Lu, p. 329.

11. Zhang Shuai 張率 (475–527), "Distant Appointment" 遠期, *YTXY*, p. 246.

12. Xiao Gang, "Song: Night After Night" 夜夜曲, *YTXY*, p. 510.

13. Wang Taiqing 王臺卿 (fl. 520's), "Moon on the High Tower of a Wanderer's Wife" 蕩婦高樓月, *YTXY*, p. 516. Line 2 literally reads, "Never again will I be fifteen years old." A variant gives *yuan* 圓 for *nian* 年—"Never again will it [the moon] be full." Though illogical, this reading associates the full moon with the fullness of lovers' union; the persona anticipates the loss of her lover's faith.

14. While developing my view of palace poetry, I had an opportunity to read Judith Zeitlin's unpublished paper, "Objects of the Boudoir in the *Yutai xinyong*." Her similar examination of palace poetry has contributed to my presentation of the dynamics described here.

15. For the attraction of the appearance of things, see Liu Xie, "Wu se," pp. 493–501 (trans. Shih, pp. 476–85).

16. There is an interesting philosophical difference between voyeuristic palace poetry and its closest analogy in the West, the Renaissance *blason*. The latter, which enjoyed a brief vogue in the sixteenth century, consisted of detailed eulogies on various parts of a woman's body. Although the most popular collection of *blasons*, the *Blasons anatomiques du corps feminin* (Lyons, 1536, 1543), was organized in such a way as to suggest the eventual consummation of the sexual act (the first poems describe eyes, lips, etc., later verses gradually move down to shoulders, breasts, and other, more intimate locations), the Western emphasis is not on process but on dissection and analysis. The "beloved" becomes nothing more than a generic assemblage of idealized parts that the poet reproduces for the reader's stimulation—in this way, the *blason* is a radical extension of the Platonic/Petrarchan love poem.

17. *YTXY*, pp. 184–85. Shen Yue is technically too early to be considered a "palace poet" (he died before Xiao Gang's court circle had formed), but his poems in *YTXY* are still typical though distinctive examples of the erotic genre.

18. For a description of Early Tang court poetry circles, see Owen, *Poetry of the Early T'ang, passim*.

19. In Waley's translation, the *Shi jing* passage runs: "Where can I get a day-lily / To plant behind the house? / All this longing for Po / Can but bring me heart's pain" (p. 50). This is a very early example of the kind of trope palace poetry was built on.

20. For a description of the Tang entertainment districts, see Wagner, pp. 81–103.

21. For example, Du Fu's "Watching a Pupil of Madame Gongsun's Perform the Jianqi" 觀公孫大娘弟子舞劍器行 (*QTS, j.* 222, pp. 2356–57); and Cen Shen's 岑參 (715–70) "Song for the Lord Governor Tian's Beauty 'Like-a-Lotus' Dancing a Northern Whirl" 田使君美人舞如蓮花北鋋歌 (*QTS, j.* 199, p. 2057).

22. In simple, descriptive terms this banquet could be taking place in an actual palace, but it is more likely that the images elegantly idealize one of the high-class brothels of Chang'an.

23. The poem attributed to Zhuo is "Bai tou yin" 白頭吟; see Lu, pp. 274–75.

24. Orchid Hall here is probably only a modal evocation of the south, since orchids (*lan* 蘭) were associated with Chu and the poet Qu Yuan 屈原. Although the term does appear in Zhang Heng's 張衡 (78–139) "*Fu* on the Southern Capital" 南都賦, the connotations there hardly seem appropriate for the sensuous ambience Wen is creating. See Knechtges, p. 324, l. 157.

25. For a discussion of Jiang Kui's *yongwu ci*, see Lin Shuen-fu.

26. Mention of Zhang Jingwan occurs in *Liang shu*, p. 561; the same passage is repeated word for word in *Nan shi*, p. 1547. In Wen's somewhat romantic reading, Yang composes songs specifically for Zhang.

27. See, e.g., pp. 731–35.

28. Compare to Wen's "Lotus Bank Song" translated in Chapter 2.

CHAPTER 4

1. For a contrasting of Chinese and Western poetics, see Owen, *Traditional Chinese Poetry and Poetics* (esp. chap. 3, "An Uncreated Universe"); and Yu, *Reading of Imagery* (esp. chap. 1, "Setting the Terms").

2. The excerpts quoted below are from Owen's translation in *Poetry of the Early T'ang*, pp. 105–8, with romanization altered; I have benefited from his commentary on the poem as well (pp. 108–11). For Lu's poem, see *QTS*, *j*. 41, pp. 518–19.

3. For a discussion of the applicability of formulaic composition analysis to the *Classic of Poetry*, see C. H. Wang. I believe such analysis would prove fruitful as well when applied to early *yuefu* and anonymous *gushi*.

4. The image of the impersonal city is a common and powerful one; it recurs for example in Du Fu's "Autumn Meditations" 秋興八首, when he thinks of how quickly families rise to and fall from power: "Well said Chang'an looks like a chess-board; / A hundred years of the saddest news. / The mansions of princes and nobles all have new lords: / Another breed is capped and robed for office." (*QTS*, *j*. 230, p. 2510; trans. Graham, *Poems of the Late T'ang*, p. 53 [romanization altered]).

5. The most famous example is "Dream Journey to Tianmu Mountain: A Parting Poem" 夢遊天姥吟留別, *QTS*, *j*. 174, pp. 1779–80.

6. Sima Qian, pp. 295–339; pp. 341–94. Trans. Watson, *Grand Historian*, 1: 37–74, 77–119.

7. Sima Qian, p. 2629; trans. Watson, *Grand Historian*, 1: 231 (romanization altered).

8. Sima Qian, p. 333; Watson, *Grand Historian*, 1: 70.

9. *Jin shu*, pp. 1359–62.

10. In *LHSJ*, pp. 53, 131, and 77, respectively.

11. See, e.g., Cui Hao's (d. 754) famous "Yellow Crane Tower" 黃鶴樓 (*QTS*, *j*. 130, p. 1329) and Li Bai's equally famous imitation of it, "Climbing Phoenix Terrace in Jinling" 登金陵鳳凰臺 (*QTS*, *j*. 180, p. 1836). See also Du Fu's more innovative "Meditations on Ancient Sites: Five Poems" 詠懷古跡五首 (*QTS*, *j*. 230, pp. 2510–11).

12. These subgenres often merge or contribute elements to other poems. At times an occasion for a *huaigu* produces not so much an emotional reaction as the distanced, objective observation more commonly found in *yongshi*. *Yongshi*, on the other hand, may possess a strong emotional con-

tent. If either subgenre stresses the link between past events and the present political and social situation of the poet, then the result may come very close to the *ganhuai* tradition of Ruan Ji, Chen Zi'ang 陳子昂 (661–702), and Li Bai.

13. One may find the origins of such experimentation in regulated verse in Du Fu; the "Autumn Meditations" (*QTS*, *j*. 230, p. 2510) provide an interesting example.

14. Wu Diaogong (pp. 135–37) makes this very point about Li's *huaigu*, arguing that he has (through the use of imagination and removal from the scene of the poem) effectively blurred subgenre distinctions.

15. The King of Wu's obsessions led to such a thorough disregard of state affairs that one of his ministers said that soon he would see deer wandering outside the palace.

16. The image of rats scurrying through the walls of an abandoned palace is probably derived from Du Fu's *huaigu* on Taizong's Yuhua Palace (*QTS*, *j*. 217, pp. 2276–77), line 2: "Gray rats scurry under ancient tiles."

17. Although Liu Yuxi is usually perceived as a highly moral Confucian optimist, other signs in his work point to an uneasiness over the political and social order. See, e.g., Stephen Owen's comments on "Meditation on the Past: Western Pass Mountain" in "Place: Meditation on the Past at Chin-ling," pp. 431–33.

18. Wu Diaogong, p. 35.

19. Sima Guang, pp. 5508–9 (Sui Wendi, ninth year of Kaihuang, 589).

20. My translation here is tentative. *Dingxing* is a problem; if a descriptive binome, it almost certainly refers to the glitter of the ornaments. The *Hanyu da cidian* suggests "face the stars," but its only citation is this very line, and reading *ding* as "to face" is a rather archaic usage.

21. I mean here the traditional Western rhetorical definition of irony as saying one thing but meaning another, usually for comic or witty effect.

22. For Zhang Ruoxu's and other examples of this tune title, see *YFSJ*, pp. 678–80.

23. *QTS*, *j*. 365, p. 4117. The place-names here are all famous sites in Jinling. The Wangs and Xies were the two great noble clans during the Southern Dynasties.

24. See, e.g., Ye Zongqi's reading in *LHSJ*, p. 55.

25. Liu Yiqing, p. 209; trans. Mather, *Shih Shuo Hsin Yü*, p. 192 (romanization altered, translation slightly altered).

26. Mather, "Introduction," *Shih Shuo Hsin Yü*, xvii–xxi.

27. *Jin shu*, p. 161.

28. There is some debate on why Wen refers to Huyin when the history sets the anecdote in Yuhu. Yang Shen 楊慎 (quoted in the Gu Sili com-

mentary) believes that Wen has misread and mispunctuated the text, reading the place name "Yuhu" (in Anhui) as "arrive at Hu-" and reading *yin*, "secretly," the first word of the following sentence, as the second character in the place name. If such is the case, one wonders if the author of the original *yuefu* Wen mentions had made the same mistake. Lin Bangjun ("Wen Feiqing 'Huyin ci' xu bian") believes that Wen is merely saying that Wang Dun "raised a force and arrived on the lake's north shore"—reading *yin* to mean "north side." If Lin is correct, it still seems odd that Wen does not mention which lake.

29. *Jin shu*, p. 398.

30. Ibid., p. 1096; Lin Bangjun ("Wen Feiqing 'Hu yin ci' xu bian") thinks that the poem is referring to the recovery of the Tang after a revolt in the early 840's.

31. Ban, p. 196. Wei Yingwu 韋應物 (ca. 736–ca. 791) wrote a poem on this incident that is yet another precursor to Li's and Wen's narrative songs. See "The Song of Han Wudi" 漢武帝雜歌, *QTS, j.* 195, p. 2006; for a translation, see Owen, *Great Age of Chinese Poetry*, pp. 311–12.

32. *QTS, j.* 181, p. 1846. The soldiers are dressed in the plunder taken from Wu's palaces.

33. Valéry, p. 12.

34. Legge, 1: 253–54.

35. In contrast to this amoral perspective, cf. Du Fu's famous poems on Tang Xuanzong's palace excursions written both before and after the An Lushan rebellion ("Ballad of Lovely Ladies" 麗人行, *QTS, j.* 216, p. 2260; "Lament by the River" 哀江頭, *QTS, j.* 216, p. 2268); the inherent note of moral disapproval here has often been noted. Xuanzong will preoccupy us shortly.

36. See Sima Qian's essay on the Feng and Shan sacrifices, pp. 1355–404; trans. Watson, *Grand Historian*, 2: 13–69.

37. As I have said, these are merely the facts as they came to be popularly understood by the literary tradition. For a more balanced view of the rebellion, see Twitchett, pp. 447–63.

38. See, e.g., Du Mu's "Passing by the Huaqing Palace," translated in Chapter 2.

39. *WFQ, j.* 9, pp. 195–99; this poem is missing from the *QTS*.

40. Reading variant *xue* 血 for *xue* 雪.

41. Sima Qian, p. 2455.

42. These poems are missing from Wen's collection in the *QTS*.

43. A point also made by Murakami Tetsumi in "On Hikyō no bungaku," pp. 31–32.

44. Sima Qian (pp. 1387–88) identifies the consort as Lady Wang; Ban Gu (p. 3954) identifies her as Li and describes the incident in greater detail; later tradition follows Ban.

45. Gu Sili notes that an anecdote in the *Taiping guangji* 太平廣記 states that the tree was named by Xuanzong's grandson Dezong, who passed the tree on a visit and associated it with Xuanzong, Yang Guifei, and Mawei Station nearby. Wen seems to believe that Xuanzong was responsible for the naming.

46. This same technique also makes Li Shangyin's "Mawei," translated earlier, more a portrait of Xuanzong's emotional state than a distanced commentary on his predicament.

47. The poetic popularity of Zhuge Liang begins most probably with Du Fu, who quite obviously saw himself in the role of the noble genius living in reclusion.

48. For his biography, see *Jiu Tang shu*, pp. 5033–34.

49. Many literati of the Mid- and Late Tang tried to find secluded spaces within official life as a refuge from its pressures; see Chapter 5.

CHAPTER 5

1. It may be old-fashioned to talk about "greatness," when the concept of greatness is being critiqued by literary theorists. The fruitful revision of a canon can, however, exist only when a canon has arisen that elicits the acknowledgment (enthusiastic or grudging) of a culture's readers. Even a thoughtful, traditional approach to Chinese literary history, both in modern China and in the West, is still relatively undeveloped; for this reason, some old-fashioned value judgments that act to create a sense of canon are not necessarily out of place at this stage of Chinese literary studies, as long as claims of universal value are avoided.

2. On the other hand, Du Mu and Li Shangyin were canonized because their works possess qualities shared by the admired poets of the High Tang; their positions were guaranteed by late Ming and Qing aesthetics.

3. The best current edition of Kūkai's work is Wang Liqi's; see also translation of the most important sections of the work in Bodman.

4. See Luo, 2: 186–220.

5. *QTS, j.* 634, pp. 7283–88; "Chong dan" 沖淡, ll. 1–6; "Xian nong" 纖穠, ll. 5–8; "Qi li" 綺麗, ll. 5–10.

6. Traditionally, Jia has been linked with Han Yu and especially Meng Jiao, though Arai Ken (pp. 68–76) has pointed out that Meng and Jia have little in common. Instead, he suggests a definition of a Jia Dao "circle" based on inter-poetry communications; specifically, he cites such figures as Yao He 姚合 (775–855), Ma Dai 馬戴 (fl. 800), Zhu Qingyu 朱慶餘 (fl. 820), and Yong Tao 雍陶 (fl. 820–30).

7. The most renowned example of this effort is the famous anecdote recorded in the *Tiaoxi yuyin conghua*; see Chapter 1.

8. In addition to the famous anecdote in the *Tiaoxi yuyin conghua*, one

may note a story concerning his younger contemporary, Li He. The *Xin Tang shu* tells us that as lines of poetry occurred to him in the course of the day, he stuffed them into an embroidered bag; he would later insert these lines in his poems (quoted in *LHSJ*, p. 357).

9. "Sent to Master Mo of Baige Mountain" 寄白閣默公 (*QTS*, *j*. 572, p. 6632), ll. 3–4; "After Rain, Spending the Night at the Pool of Adjutant Liu" 雨後宿劉司馬池上 (*QTS*, *j*. 572, p. 6632), ll. 3–4; "Spending the Night at Jingye Temple with Li Kuo, Former District Defender of Hu" 淨業寺與前鄠縣李廓少府同宿 (*QTS*, *j*. 573, p. 6663), ll. 3–4; "After Snow, Gazing Afar in the Evening" 雪晴晚望 (*QTS*, *j*. 573, p. 6661), ll. 5–6.

10. For the little known about Yong's career and reputation, see the Introduction to *Yong Tao shi zhu*.

11. "Visiting the Former Dwelling of Du Fu" 經杜甫舊宅 (*QTS*, *j*. 518, p. 5915), ll. 3–4; "Autumn Dwelling, While Ill" 秋居病中 (*QTS*, *j*. 518, p. 5916), ll. 5–6; "Recluse Wei's Dwelling in the Suburbs" 韋處士郊居 (*QTS*, *j*. 518, p. 5920).

12. The use of deities as substitutes for cosmological phenomena, while common in the West, is extremely rare in Chinese poetry.

13. "Newly Cut Bamboo" 新裁竹, ll. 1–8 (*QTS*, *j*. 432, p. 4768).

14. The public role of the recluse was also important during the Six Dynasties period; see Holcombe.

15. Du Fu plays similarly on the phrase in the fifth poem of his "Autumn Wilds" 秋野 series (*QTS*, *j*. 229, p. 2500).

16. See, e.g., "On a Spring Day, About to Return East, I Send This to My Elder, Miao Shen, a Recent Graduate" 春日將欲東歸寄新及第苗紳先輩 (*WFQ*, *j*. 4, p. 101); "Seeing off Director Cui on His Way to Office" 送崔郎中赴幕 (*j*. 4, p. 102); and "Spring Grows Late in Chang'an" 長安春晚 (*j*. 5, p. 112; no. 1).

17. Of the representation of a very young courtesan as a bud, see Du Mu's famous "Presented at Parting" 贈別 (*QTS*, *j*. 523, p. 5988): "Graceful and sinuous, a little over thirteen: / At the beginning of March, a nutmeg buds on branch's end."

18. The *Cai diao ji* (see note 52 to Chapter 2) has the variant "Jingyang Palace," the palace of imperial consorts so often seen in Wen's poetry. Here, however, Shangyang Palace makes more sense.

19. For other poems in which contemporaries (friends or superiors) or the poet himself are described through the use of Six Dynasties allusions, see, e.g., "Sent to a Monk of Qingliang Temple" 寄清涼寺僧 (*WFQ*, *j*. 4, p. 78); "On the Secluded Dwelling of the Retired Scholar Li" 題李處士幽居 (*j*. 4, pp. 79–80); "Sent to General Li" 贈李將軍 (*j*. 4, pp. 80–81); "Sent to Yuan, Keeper of Records" 贈袁司錄 (*j*. 4, pp. 83–84); and many others.

20. Liu Yiqing, p. 235; trans. Mather, *Shi Shuo Hsin Yü*, p. 216.

21. Gu Sili thinks this is really a reference to Liu Chang 劉昶, and quotes the following anecdote: "When Wang Rong was a young man of twenty he went to visit Ruan Ji. At the time Liu Chang was also present. Ruan said to Wang, 'I happen to have two dipperfuls of excellent wine which I will drink with you. That fellow, Liu Chang, will not be joining us.' Thereupon the two men proceeded to exchange goblets and drink to each other's health, while Liu Chang never got a single cupful. Nevertheless in their conversation and jokes the three men acted quite as if nothing were out of the ordinary. When someone asked Ruan about it, he replied, 'If it's someone superior to Liu Chang, I have no choice but to drink with him, or if it's someone inferior to Liu Chang, it's improper not to drink with him. It's only Liu Chang himself with whom it's quite all right not to drink at all'" (trans. Mather, *Shih Shuo Hsin Yü*, p. 392 [romanization altered]). Unless this line is some covert reference to the relationship between Wen and Li Yu, however, the less obscure referent, Liu Ling, is more likely.

22. *Liezi jishi*, p. 172; trans. Graham, *Lieh-tzu*, p. 105 (romanization altered).

23. Not that the figures of the *Shishuo* lived peaceful lives—far from it. Rather, in Wen's romanticization of the Six Dynasties, the *Shishuo* past seems preferable to and safer than the present.

24. "Taking Leave of Master Sheng at Dawn at the Temple of Right Seeing" 正見寺曉別生公 (*WFQ, j.* 8, p. 165), ll. 5–8. "Vulture Peak" was one of the dwellings of the Buddha.

25. Su, 2: 317–18.

26. Perhaps the most serious consideration of the hermit theme are Wen's three quatrains on the recluse Lü Shang 呂尚, "Written on the Wei" 渭上題 (*WFQ, j.* 5, pp. 114–15).

27. This line has *meiyu* 梅雨, "plum rain," a term that usually describes the fine rain that falls in southern China in the late spring. However, since this line obviously describes an autumn scene, I can find no other way to read the phrase than simply "rain on the plum trees."

APPENDIX

1. I have based my analysis of tonality on Stimson, *Fifty-five T'ang Poems*, and Downer and Graham.

2. Stimson, *Fifty-five T'ang Poems*, pp. 54–56.

Bibliography

Allen, Joseph Roe, III. "From Saint to Singing Girl: The Rewriting of Lo-fu Narrative in Chinese Literati Poetry." *Harvard Journal of Asiatic Studies* 48, no. 2 (Dec. 1988): 321–61.
Arai Ken 荒木健. "Ka Tō"賈島. *Chūgoku bungaku hō* 中國文學報 10 (1959): 52–95.
Ban Gu 班固. *Han shu* 漢書. Beijing: Zhonghua 中華, 1962.
Berger, John. *Ways of Seeing*. Baltimore: Penguin, 1972.
Birrell, Anne M. "The Dusty Mirror: Courtly Portraits of Woman in Southern Dynasties Love Poetry." In *Expressions of the Self in Chinese Literature*, ed. Robert E. Hegel and Richard C. Hessney, pp. 33–69. New York: Columbia University Press, 1985.
———, trans. *New Songs from a Jade Terrace*. London: Allen & Unwin, 1982.
Bodman, Richard Wainwright. "Poetics and Prosody in Early Mediaeval China: A Study and Translation of Kūkai's *Bunkyō Hifuron*." Ph.D. dissertation, Cornell University, 1978.
Cahill, James. *The Compelling Image: Nature and Style in Seventeenth-Century Chinese Painting*. Cambridge, Mass.: Harvard University Press, 1982.
Cao Xueqin 曹雪芹. *Hong lou meng bashi hui jiaoben* 紅樓夢八十回校本, ed. Yu Pingbo 俞平伯. Beijing: Renmin wenxue 人民文學, 1958.
Chang, Kang-i Sun. *The Evolution of Chinese Tz'u Poetry from Late T'ang to Northern Sung*. Princeton: Princeton University Press, 1980.
Chaves, Jonathan. "The Tz'u Poetry of Wen T'ing-yun." M.A. thesis, Columbia University, 1966.
Chen Shangjun 陳尚君. "Wen Tingyun zaonian shiji kaobian" 溫庭筠早年事迹考辨. *Zhonghua wenshi luncong* 中華文史論叢 18 (May 1981): 245–67.

———. "Ye tan Wen Tingyun shengping zhi ruogan wenti" 也談溫庭筠生平之若干問題. *Nankai daxue xuebao* 南開大學學報 1982, no. 6 (Nov. 1982): 22–28.

Ding Fubao 丁福保. *Qing shihua* 清詩話. Shanghai: Shanghai guji 上海古籍, 1963.

Downer, G. B., and A. C. Graham. "Tone Patterns in Chinese Poetry." *Bulletin of the School of Oriental and African Studies* 26 (1963): 145–48.

Du Mu 杜牧. *Fan chuan shi ji zhu* 樊川詩集注, ed. and comm. Feng Jiwu 馮集梧. Shanghai: Shanghai guji 上海古籍, 1978.

Fang Yu 方瑜. *Zhong wan Tang san jia shi xilun* 中晚唐三家詩析論. Taipei: Mutong 牧童, 1975.

Frodsham, J. D., trans. *The Poems of Li Ho (791–817)*. Oxford: Oxford University Press, 1970.

Graham, A. C., trans. *The Book of Lieh-tzu: A Classic of Tao*. New York: Columbia University Press, 1990.

———, trans. *Poems of the Late T'ang*. Harmondsworth, Eng.: Penguin, 1965.

Gu Xuejie 顧學頡. *Wenxue lun ji* 文學論集. Beijing: Zhongguo shehui kexue 中國社會科學, 1987.

Guo Maoqian 郭茂倩, ed. *Yuefu shi ji* 樂府詩集. Beijing: Zhonghua 中華, 1979.

He Wenhuan 何文煥. *Lidai shihua* 歷代詩話. Beijing: Zhonghua 中華, 1981.

Holcombe, Charles. "The Exemplar State: Ideology, Self-Cultivation, and Power in Fourth-Century China." *Harvard Journal of Asiatic Studies* 49, no. 1 (June 1989): 93–139.

Hu Zi 胡仔. *Tiaoxi yuyin conghua* 苕溪漁隱叢話. Beijing: Renmin wenxue 人民文學, 1962.

Huang Kunyao 黃坤堯. *Wen Tingyun* 溫庭筠. Taipei: Guojia 國家, 1984.

Hung, William. *Tu Fu: China's Greatest Poet*. Cambridge, Mass.: Harvard University Press, 1952. Reprinted—New York: Russell & Russell, 1969.

Ji Yougong 計有功. *Tang shi ji shi* 唐詩紀事. Beijing: Zhonghua 中華, 1965.

Jin shu 晉書. Beijing: Zhonghua 中華, 1974.

Jiu Tang shu 舊唐書. Beijing: Zhonghua 中華, 1975.

Knechtges, David R., trans. *Wen Xuan, or Selections of Refined Literature*, vol. 1, *Rhapsodies on Metropolises and Capitals*. Princeton: Princeton University Press, 1982.

Kūkai 空海. *Bunkyō hifuron* 文鏡秘府論, ed. Wang Liqi 王利器. Beijing: Zhongguo shehui kexue 中國社會科學, 1983.

Legge, James, trans. *Li Chi: Book of Rites, An Encyclopedia of Ancient Ceremonial Usages, Religious Creeds and Social Institutions*. 2 vols. Reprinted—New Hyde Park, N.Y.: University Books, 1967.

Li He 李賀. *Li He shi ji* 李賀詩集, ed. and comm. Ye Congqi 葉蔥奇. Beijing: Renmin wenxue 人民文學, 1984.

Li Shangyin 李商隱. *Li Shangyin shi ji shuzhu* 李商隱詩集疏注, ed. and comm. Ye Congqi 葉蔥奇. Beijing: Renmin wenxue 人民文學, 1986.
Liang shu 梁書. Beijing: Zhonghua 中華, 1973.
Liezi jishi 列子集釋 ed. and comm. Yang Bojun 楊伯峻. Beijing: Zhonghua 中華, 1979.
Lin Bangjun 林邦鈞. "Lun Wen Tingyun he tade shi" 論溫庭筠和他的詩. *Wenxue yichan* 文學遺產 1981, no. 4 (Dec. 1981): 132–44.
——. "Wen Feiqing 'Huyin ci' xu bian" 溫飛卿湖陰詞序辨. *Zhonghua wen shi lun cong* 中華文史論叢 19 (Aug. 1981): 194.
Lin Shuen-fu. *The Transformation of the Lyrical Tradition: Chiang K'uei and Southern Sung Tz'u Poetry*. Princeton: Princeton University Press, 1978.
Liu, James J. Y. *The Poetry of Li Shang-yin*. Chicago: University of Chicago Press, 1969.
Liu Sihan 劉斯翰, ed. *Wen Tingyun shi ci xuan* 溫庭筠詩詞選. Zhongguo lidai shiren xuan ji 中國歷代詩人選集. Hong Kong: Sanlian 三聯, 1986.
Liu Xie 劉勰. *Wen xin diao long zhu shi* 文心雕龍注釋, ed. Zhou Zhenfu 周振甫. Beijing: Renmin wenxue 人民文學, 1981.
Liu Yiqing 劉義慶. *Shishuo xinyu jiao jian* 世說新語校箋, ed. and comm. Xu Zhen'e 徐震堮. Beijing: Zhonghua 中華, 1987.
Lu Qinli 逯欽立, ed. *Quan xian Qin Han Wei Jin Nan Bei Chao shi* 全先秦漢魏晉南北朝詩. Beijing: Zhonghua 中華, 1983.
Luo Genze 羅根澤. *Zhongguo wenxue piping shi* 中國文學批評史. 4 vols. Shanghai: Shanghai guji 上海古籍, 1984.
Mather, Richard B. "A Note on the Dialects of Lo-yang and Nanking During the Six Dynasties." In *Wen-lin: Studies in the Chinese Humanities*, ed. Chow Tse-tsung, pp. 247–56. Madison: University of Wisconsin Press, 1968.
——. *The Poet Shen Yüeh (441–513): The Reticent Marquis*. Princeton: Princeton University Press, 1988.
——, trans. *Shih Shuo Hsin Yü: A New Account of Tales of the World*. Minneapolis: University of Minnesota Press, 1976.
Miao, Ronald C. "Palace-Style Poetry: The Courtly Treatment of Glamour and Love." In *Studies in Chinese Poetry and Poetics*, vol. 1, ed. Ronald C. Miao, pp. 1–42. San Francisco: Chinese Materials Center, 1978.
Mou Huaichuan 牟懷川. "Wen Tingyun shengnian xinzheng" 溫庭筠生年新証. *Shanghai Shifan Xueyuan xuebao* 上海師範學院學報 1984, no. 1 (Mar.): 48–53.
Murakami Tetsumi 村上哲見. "On Hikyō no bungaku" 溫飛卿の文學. *Chūgoku bungaku hō* 中國文學報 5 (1956): 19–40.
——. *Sō shi no kenkyū: Tō Godai Hoku Sō hen* 宋詞の研究:唐五代北宋篇. Tokyo: Sōbunsha 創文社, 1976.
Nan shi 南史. Beijing: Zhonghua 中華, 1975.

Nienhauser, William H., ed. *The Indiana Companion to Traditional Chinese Literature*. Bloomington: Indiana University Press, 1986.
Owen, Stephen. *The Great Age of Chinese Poetry: The High T'ang*. New Haven: Yale University Press, 1981.
———. "Place: Meditation on the Past at Chin-ling." *Harvard Journal of Asiatic Studies* 50, no. 2 (June 1990): 417–57.
———. *The Poetry of Meng Chiao and Han Yü*. New Haven: Yale University Press, 1975.
———. *The Poetry of the Early T'ang*. New Haven: Yale University Press, 1977.
———. *Traditional Chinese Poetry and Poetics: Omen of the World*. Madison: University of Wisconsin Press, 1985.
———, trans. *Readings in Chinese Literary Thought*. Cambridge, Mass.: Harvard University, Council on East Asian Studies, 1992.
Qian Zhongshu 錢鐘書. *Guan zhui bian* 管錐編. Beijing: Zhonghua 中華, 1979.
Quan Tang shi 全唐詩. Beijing: Zhonghua 中華, 1960.
Quan Tang Wudai ci 全唐五代詞. Shanghai: Shanghai guji 上海古籍, 1986.
Ren Bantang 任半塘. *Tang sheng shi* 唐聲詩. 2 vols. Shanghai: Shanghai guji 上海古籍, 1982.
Ripley, Stephen. "Some Findings on Tone Patterns in Tang Regulated Verse." *Journal of Chinese Linguistics* 8, no. 1 (Jan. 1980): 126–47.
Schafer, Edward H. *Mirages on the Sea of Time*. Berkeley: University of California Press, 1985.
Shih, Vincent Yu-chung, trans. *The Literary Mind and the Carving of Dragons: A Study of Thought and Pattern in Chinese Literature*. Hong Kong: Chinese University Press, 1983.
Sima Guang 司馬光. *Zizhi tongjian* 資治通鑑. Beijing: Zhonghua 中華, 1956.
Sima Qian 司馬遷. *Shi ji* 史記. Beijing: Zhonghua 中華, 1962.
Stimson, Hugh M. *Fifty-five T'ang Poems*. New Haven: Far Eastern Publications, 1976.
———. *T'ang Poetic Vocabulary*. New Haven: Far Eastern Publications, 1976.
Su Shi 蘇軾. *Su Shi shi ji* 蘇軾詩集, ed. Wang Wen'gao 王文誥, comm. Kong Fanli 孔凡禮 et al. Beijing: Zhonghua 中華, 1982.
Tang ren xuan Tang shi 唐人選唐詩. Beijing: Zhonghua 中華, 1958.
Twitchett, Denis, ed. *The Cambridge History of China*, vol. 3, *Sui and T'ang China, 589–906, Part I*. Cambridge, Eng.: Cambridge University Press, 1979.
Uchida Sennosuke 內田泉之助, trans. *Gyokudai shin'ei* 玉臺新詠. 2 vols. Shinshaku kambun taikei 新釈漢文大系, vols. 60–61. Tokyo: Meiji Shoin 明治書院, 1974–75.

Bibliography 245

Valéry, Paul. *Poésies*. Paris: Gallimard, 1978.
van Zoeren, Steven. *Poetry and Personality: Reading, Exegesis, and Hermeneutics in Traditional China*. Stanford: Stanford University Press, 1991.
Wagner, Marsha. *The Lotus Boat: The Origins of Chinese Tz'u Poetry in T'ang Popular Culture*. New York: Columbia University Press, 1984.
Waley, Arthur, trans. *The Book of Songs*. New York: Grove Press, 1960.
Wan Man 萬曼. *Tang ji xulu* 唐集紋錄. Beijing: Zhonghua 中華, 1982.
Wang, C. H. *The Bell and the Drum: Shih Ching as Formulaic Poetry in an Oral Tradition*. Berkeley: University of California Press, 1974.
Wang Dajin 王達津. "Wen Tingyun shengping zhi ruogan wenti" 溫庭筠生平之若干問題. *Nankai Daxue xuebao* 南開大學學報 1982, no. 2 (Mar. 1982): 48–53.
Wang Li 王力. *Hanyu shilü xue* 漢語詩律學. Shanghai: Xin zhishi 新知識, 1958.
Wang Yi 王易. *Yuefu tong lun* 樂府通論. Taipei: Guangwen 廣文, 1961.
Watson, Burton. *Early Chinese Literature*. New York: Columbia University Press, 1962.
———, trans. *Records of the Grand Historian of China*. 2 vols. New York: Columbia University Press, 1961.
Wen Tingyun 溫庭筠. *Wen Feiqing shi ji jian zhu* 溫飛卿詩集箋注, ed. and comm. Zeng Yi 曾益, Gu Yuxian 顧予咸, and Gu Sili 顧嗣立. Shanghai: Shanghai guji 上海古籍, 1980.
Wu Diaogong 吳調公. *Li Shangyin yanjiu* 李商隱研究. Shanghai: Shanghai guji 上海古籍, 1982.
Wu Dunsheng 吳遁生. *Wen Tingyun shi xuan* 溫庭筠詩選. Hong Kong: Daguang 大光, 1973.
Wu Fuxing 吳复興. "Tang shi yu yinyue" 唐詩與音樂. In *Tangdai wenxue conglun* 唐代文學叢論, 5th series, pp. 131–54. Xi'an: Shaanxi renmin 陝西人民, 1984.
Wu Gengshun 吳庚舜. "Lüe lun Tangdai yuefu shi" 略論唐代樂府詩. *Wenxue yichan* 文學遺產 1982, no. 3 (Sept. 1983): 64–74.
Xia Chengtao 夏承燾. *Tang Song ciren nianpu* 唐宋詞人年譜. Shanghai: Shanghai guji 上海古籍, 1979.
Xiao Tong 蕭統 (Zhaoming taizi 照明太子), ed. *Wen xuan* 文選. Beijing: Zhonghua 中華, 1977.
Xin Tang shu 新唐書. Beijing: Zhonghua 中華, 1975.
Xin Wenfang 辛文房. *Tang caizi zhuan jiao zheng* 唐才子傳校証. Nanjing: Jiangsu guji 江蘇古籍, 1987.
Xu Ling 除陵, ed. *Yutai xinyong jian zhu* 玉臺新詠箋注, comm. Wu Zhaoyi 吳兆宜. Beijing: Zhonghua 中華, 1985.
Yan Yu 嚴羽. *Canglang shihua* 滄浪詩話, ed. and comm. Guo Shaoyu 郭紹虞. Beijing: Renmin wenxue 人民文學, 1983.

Yang Haiming 楊海明. *Tang Song ci shi* 唐宋詞史. Nanjing: Jiangsu guji 江蘇古籍, 1987.
Ye Jiaying 葉嘉瑩 (Chia-ying Yeh Chao). "The Ch'ang-chou School of Tz'u Criticism." *Harvard Journal of Asiatic Studies* 35 (1975): 101–32.
————. *Jialing lun ci conggao* 迦陵論詞叢稿. Shanghai: Shanghai guji 上海古籍, 1980.
Yong Tao 雍陶. *Yong Tao shi zhu* 雍陶詩注, ed. Zhou Xiaotian 周嘯天 and Zhang Xiaomin 張效民. Tang ren xiao ji 唐人小集, 2nd series. Shanghai: Shanghai guji 上海古籍, 1988.
Yu, Pauline. "Formal Distinctions in Chinese Literary Theory." In *Theories of the Arts in China*, ed. Susan Bush and Christian Murck, pp. 27–53. Princeton: Princeton University Press, 1983.
————. *The Reading of Imagery in the Chinese Poetic Tradition*. Princeton: Princeton University Press, 1986.
Zeitlin, Judith. "Objects of the Boudoir in the *Yutai xinyong*." Unpublished manuscript.
Zhao Chongzuo 趙崇祚, ed. *Huajian ji* 花間集. Sibu beiyao 四部備要 ed.
Zhou Chengzhen 周誠真. *Li He lun* 李賀論. Hong Kong: Wenyi 文藝, 1971.
Zhou Zhenfu 周振甫. *Shi wen qian shi* 詩文淺釋. Beijing: Shifan xueyuan 師範學院, 1986.

Index of Titles

ENGLISH

Only poems translated in the text (completely or partially) are included. For other titles mentioned in the text, see the Index of Subjects. In this index an "f" after a number indicates a separate reference on the next page, and an "ff" indicates separate references on the next two pages. A continuous discussion over two or more pages is indicated by a span of page numbers, e.g., "57–59." *Passim* is used for a cluster of references in close but not consecutive sequence. Entries are alphabetized letter by letter, ignoring word breaks, hyphens, and accents.

POEMS BY WEN TINGYUN

Autumn Rain, 192
The Buddhist Temple at Mawei, 154–55
Carefree Wanderings, 21–22
Composed at Random, 196–97
A Dancer's Robe, 86–89, 94, 125, 196
Dawn Immortal Song, 49–50, 139
Early Autumn, Dwelling in the Mountains, 4, 5–6
Early Autumn: Sent to a Friend, 191–92
Encountering Rain in Xianyang, 192–93, 209
"Genglou zi" (sixth of six), 66–67

The Grave of Secretary Cai, 167–68
Huaqing Palace: Matching Secretary Du [Mu], 144–46
Huaqing Palace: Two Poems, 149–51
The Imperial Secretariat Possessed a Poem of Secretary He's . . . , 164–66
I Went to Visit Master Zhixuan [Knowledge-of-Mystery] . . . , 205–7
Lament for Spring, 62–64
Lotus Bank Song, 47–48, 62
Matching a Friend's Poem: "Country Villa by a Stream," 193–94

248　Index of Titles

Matching Zhao Gu: "Written on the Peak Temple," 23–25
Mawei Station, 151–52, 156
A Night Banquet, 82–85, 89–94 *passim*, 125, 196
On West River, Seeing off a Fisherman, 210–11
On Willows, 194–95
Painting of a Woman Seen at Longwei Station, 158
Peonies: Two Poems, 195–96
Presented to a Close Friend, 197–98
"Pusa man" (second of fourteen), 64–65
"Pusa man" (twelfth of fourteen), 64
Rain on a Spring Day, 168, 185
Randomly Composed on a Spring Day, 208–9
Recalling True Pearl Pavilion, 3–4, 22
The Reflection, 79–80, 87
Seeing off Retired Scholar Lu on His Travels to Wu and Yue, 212
Sent to Magistrate Yan of Xiangyun: Begging for a Fishing Reel, 201–2
Sent to Secretary Xiao of the Hanlin Academy, 188–89
Setting out Early from Mount Shang, 18–19, 229
Song: Cock-crow Dike, 118–23, 125ff, 137
Song: Duke Xie's Villa, 129–31, 133, 135, 141, 199
Song: Naval Battle on Kunming Lake, 134–38, 141
Song: Night of Spring Rivers and Flowered Moons, 123–28
Song of Huyin, 131–34, 135f
Song of Wu Garden, 17–18, 21, 62, 65
Song: Retired Scholar Guo Strikes the Musical Bowls, 54–60, 65, 82, 229
Song: The Han Emperor Welcomes Spring, 139–41
The Southern Ferry at Lizhou, 207–8
Spending the Night by a Friend's Pool, 190–91
Spring Dawn Song, 81–82
Su Wu's Temple, 161–62
Taking Leave of Master Sheng at Dawn at the Temple of Right Seeing, 203
Two Poems Sent to Supernumerary Retainer Li of Yuezhou (no. 1), 198–99
Visiting Chen Lin's Grave, 166–67
Visiting Huaqing Palace: Twenty-two Rhymes, 144–49
Visiting New Feng, 160–62
Visiting Wuzhang Plain, 163–64
While Dwelling in the Imperial Suburbs . . . , 209–10
With a Swift-Flowing Brush I Playfully Thank Retired Scholar Li Yu . . . , 200–201
Written Offhand on a Forest Pavilion, 20–21, 193
Written on Gazing Garden Post Station, 155–56
Written on the Duanzheng Tree, 157
Written on the Monk's Courtyard at West Brightness Temple, 203–4
Written on the Shrine to the Bamboo Valley Spirit, 22–23, 192
Zhang Jingwan Gathers Lotus, 89–94

POEMS BY OTHER POETS

Anonymous: Song of New Green, 30–31, 32
Bai Juyi: Lady Li, 157; Newly Cut Bamboo, 182
Cui Hao: Seventh Night Song, 42–43

Index of Titles 249

Du Mu: Egrets, 181; Mooring on the Qinhuai, 123; Passing by Huaqing Palace, 36–39, 109, 150; Red Cliff, 112–13; The Southern Tower at Kaiyuan Temple in Xuanzhou, 184–85; Visiting Mount Li, 114–15, 137; Written on the Water Pavilion of the Kaiyuan Temple ..., 208
Fu Zai: Song of Ganzhou, 33–34
Gao Shi: Song: Old Daliang, 39–41, 43, 108
Han Yu: Listening to Master Ying Play the Lute, 52
Jia Dao: After Rain, Spending the Night at the Pool of Adjutant Liu, 178; After Snow, Gazing Afar in the Evening, 178; On Adept Tongzhen, 178–79; Passing the Night at a Mountain Temple, 177; Playfully Sent to a Friend, 175; Seeing off Tang Huan on His Return to Fu River Village, 175–76; Sent to Master Mo of Baige Mountain, 178; Spending the Night at Jingye Temple ..., 178
Li Bai: In the Qingping Mode (third of three), 31–32; Meditation on the Past: Ascending the Old Battlefield ..., 103–5; Observing Antiquity at Yue, 137; Song of Roosting Crows, 105–6
Li He: The Ballad of Li Ping and His Harp, 51–54; Dreaming of Heaven, 45–46, 139; Song: Hearing Master Ying Play the Lute, 53; The Terrace of Liang, 44–45, 107
Li Shangyin: Frosty Moon, 181–82; Imitating Xu Ling's Style: Presented to a Serving Maid, 69–70, 196; Mawei (second of two), 152–54; On History, 115–16; Song: Qi Palace, 111–12;

Southern Dynasties, 116–17; The Sui Palace, 109–11, 112, 115, 123
Liu Yuxi: Black Robe Lane, 127; Gusu Terrace, 113–14; Meditation on the Past: Western Pass Mountain, 108–9, 116
Lu Zhaolin: Thoughts of Old on Chang'an, 100–102, 107–8, 121, 127
Meng Haoran: Matching Magistrate Lu's "Seeing off Zhen the Thirteenth ...," 41–42
Nie Yizhong: Crows Cry at Night, 34
Shen Yue: Written for a Newly Wedded Youth, 76–77
Sikong Tu: Twenty-Four Categories of Poetry, 172–73
Su Shi: First Day of the Twelfth Month, I Travel to Gushan ..., 205
Valéry, Paul: César, 137–38
Wang Taiqing: Moon on the High Tower of a Wanderer's Wife, 74
Wang Wei: Reply to Secretary Guo, 186–88; Written Offhand While Living in the Mountains, 4–5
Wang Yun: Spring Month (first of two), 80–82
Wei Zhuang: Xianyang: Meditation on the Past, 113
Xiao Gang: Matching a Poem by the Prince of Xiangdong ..., 75–76; New Swallows, 87–88; On a Beauty Surveying a Painting, 78–80; Song: Night After Night, 74
Xiao Yan: Autumn Song (first of four), 31–32
Yong Tao: Autumn Dwelling, While Ill, 180–81; Matching Six Poems by Liu, Rectifier of Omissions ..., 183; Recalling the Mountains, I Send This to a Monk,

179–80; Recluse Wei's Dwelling in the Suburbs, 180–81; Seeing Someone off on His Return to Wu, 183–84; Visiting the Former Dwelling of Du Fu, 180–81

Zhang Shuai: Distant Appointment, 74

CHINESE

The first section below lists poems by Wen Tingyun only, ordered first by stroke count and then by radical number. The second section lists poems by other authors and is ordered by stroke count of the authors' names.

▶ 溫庭筠

五畫

正見寺曉別生公, 203

六畫

早秋山居, 4, 5–6
西江上送漁夫, 210–11

七畫

初秋寄友人, 191–92
利州南渡, 207–8
吳苑行, 17–18, 21, 62, 65
投翰林蕭舍人, 188–89
更漏子(玉鑪香), 66–67
李羽處士寄新醞走筆戲酬, 200–201
牡丹二首, 195–96

八畫

和友人溪居別業, 193–94
和趙嘏題岳寺, 23–25
夜宴謠, 82–85, 89–94 *passim*, 125, 196
昆明治水戰詞, 134–38, 141

九畫

咸陽值雨, 192–93, 209
春日雨, 168, 185
春日偶作, 208–9
春江花月夜詞, 123–28
春曉曲, 81–82
秋雨, 192
郊居秋日有懷一二知己, 209–10

十畫

秘書省有賀監知章草題詩筆力遒勁風尚高遠拂塵尋玩固此有作, 164–66
送盧處士游吳越, 212
馬嵬佛寺, 154–55
馬嵬驛, 151–52, 156

十一畫

偶遊, 21–22
偶題, 196–97
偶題林亭, 20–21, 193
商山早行, 18–19, 229
宿友人池, 190–91
寄岳州從事李員外二首之一, 198–99
寄湘陰閻少府乞釣輪子, 201–2
張靜婉采蓮曲, 89–94
惜春詞, 62–64
訪知玄上人遇暴經因有贈, 205–7
郭處士擊甌歌, 54–60, 65, 82, 229

十二畫

湖陰詞, 131–34, 135f
菩薩蠻(夜來皓月), 64
菩薩蠻(水精簾裏), 64–65
華清宮二首, 149–51
華清宮和杜舍人, 144–46

十三畫

照影曲, 79–80, 87
經五丈原, 163–64
過陳琳墓, 166–67

Index of Titles   251

過華清宮二十二韻, 144-49
過新豐, 160-62
　　　　十四畫
漢皇迎春詞, 139-41
舞衣曲, 86-89, 94, 125, 196
　　　　十五畫
蓮浦謠, 47-48, 62
蔡中郎墳, 167-68
　　　　十六畫
曉仙謠, 49-50, 139
龍尾驛婦人圖, 158
　　　　十七畫
謝公墅歌, 129-31, 133, 135, 141, 199
　　　　十八畫
雞鳴埭歌, 118-23, 125ff, 137
題竹谷神祠, 22-23, 192
題西明寺僧院, 203-4
題柳, 194-95
題望苑驛, 155-56
題端正樹, 157
　　　　十九畫
懷眞珠亭, 3-4, 22
贈知音, 197-98
　　　　二十畫
蘇武廟, 161-62

▶ 他人

　　　　四畫
王筠:春月二首之一, 80-82
王維:山居即事, 4-5; 酬郭給事, 186-88
王臺卿:蕩婦高樓月, 74
　　　　五畫
白居易:李夫人, 157; 新裁竹, 182
司空圖:二十四詩品, 172-73

　　　　七畫
李商隱:南朝, 116-17; 效徐陵體贈
　更衣, 69-70, 196; 馬嵬二首之二,
　152-54; 詠史, 115-16; 隋宮,
　109-11, 112, 115, 123; 齊宮詞,
　111-12; 霜月, 181-82
李白:烏棲曲, 105-6; 清平調三首之三,
　31-32; 登廣武古戰場懷古, 103-5;
　越中覽古, 137
李賀:李憑箜篌引, 51-54; 梁臺古意,
　44-45, 107; 夢天, 45-46, 139;
　聽穎師彈琴歌, 53
杜牧:赤壁, 112-13; 泊秦淮, 123;
　宣州開元寺南樓, 184-85; 過華清宮
　絕句三首, 36-39, 109, 150;
　過驪山作, 114-15, 137; 宣州開元
　寺水閣閣下宛溪夾溪居人, 208;
　鷺鷥, 181
沈約:少年新婚為之詠, 76-77

　　　　八畫
孟浩然:和盧明府送鄭十三還京兼
　寄之什, 41-42

　　　　九畫
韋莊:咸陽懷古, 113

　　　　十畫
高適:古大梁行, 39-41, 43, 108

　　　　十一畫
崔顥:七夕詞, 42-43
張率:遠期, 74
符載:甘州歌, 33-34

　　　　十二畫
無名士:青陽歌曲, 30-31, 32

　　　　十三畫
賈島:雨後宿劉司馬池上, 178; 送唐環歸
　敷水莊, 175-76; 宿山寺, 177;
　寄白閣默公, 178; 淨業寺與前鄠縣
　李廓少府同宿, 178; 雪晴晚望, 178;
　戲贈友人, 175; 題童眞上人, 178-79
雍陶:和劉補闕秋園寓興六首之三, 183;

秋居病中, 180-81; 送人歸吳, 183-84; 經杜甫舊宅, 180-81; 韋處士郊居, 180-81; 憶山寄僧, 179-80

十五畫
劉禹錫:西塞山懷古, 108-9, 116; 姑蘇臺, 113-14; 烏衣巷, 127

十六畫
盧照鄰:長安古意, 100-102, 107-8, 121, 127

十七畫
蕭綱:和湘東王名士悅傾城, 75-76; 夜夜曲, 74; 詠美人觀畫, 78-80; 新燕, 87-88
蕭衍:秋歌四首之一, 31-32
韓愈:聽穎師彈琴歌, 52

十八畫
聶夷中:烏夜啼, 34

二十畫
蘇軾:臘日遊孤山訪惠勤惠思二僧, 205

Index of Subjects

In this index an "f" after a number indicates a separate reference on the next page, and an "ff" indicates separate references on the next two pages. A continuous discussion over two or more pages is indicated by a span of page numbers, e.g., "57–59." *Passim* is used for a cluster of references in close but not consecutive sequence. Entries are alphabetized letter by letter, ignoring word breaks, hyphens, and accents.

Account of the An Lushan Affair (An Lushan shi ji), 142
Account of the Imperial Music School (Jiao fang ji), 32
Allusions (*diangu*), 98–99, 104–5, 141
An Lushan, 37f, 109, 143–48 *passim*
Autobiography, *see under Shi* (lyric poetry)

Bai Juyi, 52, 144, 150, 172; *Pipa xing*, 52; "Song of Lasting Pain" (*Chang hen ge*), 142, 149, 157. See also Index of Titles
Bamboo, 5
Ban Gu, 55
Ban Jieyu, 43, 81
Bao Zhao, 110
Berger, John, 232n9
Bing Han, 24f
Birrell, Anne, 232n8
Blason, 233n16

Bo Ya, 52
Buddhism, *see* Monasteries and monks
Bunkyō hifuron, 172

Cahill, James, 231
Cai Yong, 167–68
Caidiao ji, 230n52
Canglang shihua, 2
Cao Cao, 97, 112, 166f
Cao Pi, *see* Emperor Wen (Wei)
Cao Zhi, 97
Chang, Kang-i Sun, 65, 229n40
Chang'an, 12, 100ff, 154, 174, 191
Chang'e, 33, 181
Changxin Palace, 43, 81
Chao, Chia-ying Yeh, 61, 65–66
Chen dynasty, 30, 110–11, 118, 122f, 125–26, 128
Chen Hong, 142
Chen Houzhu, 109f, 115, 118–19, 120–26 *passim*, 194; "Jade Trees

254   Index of Subjects

and Rear Court Flowers" (*Yushu houting hua*), 110, 120, 123, 126
Chen Lin, 166–67
Chen Xuanli, 148
Cheng Palace, 75
Chi You, 148
Chu (Warring States), 87, 192
Chu ci: "Nine Songs," 50, 51–52; "Li sao," 102; "A Summons to the Recluse," 212
Ci (song lyrics), 16, 33, 60–62, 89; differences from *shi*, 34
Classic of Poetry (*Shi jing*), 27; "Mao's Great Preface" (*Mao shi daxu*) 27; "Odes of Wei" (*Wei feng*), 76; no. 62, 80; no. 275, 40
Contrafactual, 112
Couplet craft, 174–75, 177–78
Courtesans and brothels, 2ff, 15, 66, 83, 195–97

Dingling Wei, 165
Dong Jiaorao, 3, 194
Dong Qichang, 231
Dongfang Shuo, 154f
Dongting Lake, 42, 192
Du Fu, 7–8, 16, 18, 25, 172, 180, 237n47
Du Mu, 15f, 38f, 68, 184, 190, 192, 208; attitude toward history, 112, 117, 128, 142, 157, 169; status as a Late Tang poet, 171, 181–82; "Huaqing Palace: Thirty Rhymes" (*Huaqing gong sanshi yun*), 144. See also Index of Titles
Duan Anjie, 12
Duan Chengshi, 12, 225n23
Duling, 18

Early Tang, 39, 69, 77, 100, 127, 187, 227n1
Emperor Cheng (Han), 43, 96, 140f
Emperor Dezong (Tang), 128, 174
Emperor Fei (Southern Qi), 111
Emperor Gaozong (Tang), 198

Emperor Gaozu (Han), 24, 96, 102–5, 133, 159–60, 162
Emperor Gaozu (Tang), 87
Emperor Guangwu (Han), 210
Emperor Huai (Jin), 52
Emperor Jianwen (Liang), 69, 231. See also Index of Titles (under Xiao Gang)
Emperor Ming (Jin), 131–34, 138
Emperor Suzong (Tang), 143–44
Emperor Taizong (Tang), 148
Emperor Wen (Han), 96
Emperor Wen (Wei), 97
Emperor Wu (Han), 31, 51, 75, 96, 134–38, 140, 154–61 *passim*, 193
Emperor Wu (Liang), 23, 111, 118. See also Index of Titles (under Xiao Yan)
Emperor Wu (Southern Qi), 79, 116, 121
Emperor Wuzong (Tang), 12, 55
Emperor Xuan (Han), 18, 161
Emperor Xuanzong (Tang; r. 712–56), 31f, 37f, 142–45, 148–58 *passim*
Emperor Xuanzong (Tang; r. 846–59), 13
Emperor Yang (Sui), 109f, 115, 123–28 *passim*
Emperor Yizong (Tang), 14
Emperor Yuan (Liang), 75, 117
Empress Lü (Han), 87, 159
Empress Wu (Tang), 100
"Empty words" (*xu ci*), 20, 178
Eremitism, *see* Reclusion

Fan Li, 165, 183, 207–8
Fan Ning, 206
Fangcheng (Hubei), 14
Five Dynasties, 68, 174
Fu Jian, 128f, 131
"*Fu* on the Western Capital" (*Xi jing fu*), 55
Fugu (return to antiquity), 231
Fuxi, 148

Index of Subjects

Ganhuai, 102, 235n12
Ganxing (reaction to stimulus), 52
Gao tang fu, 31
"Geng louzi," 62
Gong Yun, 119
Gongyuan (palace lament), 70
Gou Jian, 95–96, 137
Gu Sili, 61, 140
Gu Xuejie, 11, 14, 24
Guangwu, 103–4
Guo Maoqian, 28
Gushi (old-style poetry), 16, 29, 39, 41, 216
Gusu Terrace, 105–6, 113

Han dynasty, 27–28, 96–97, 100ff, 104, 140f
Han Feizi, 114
Han shu, 136
Han Wo, 228n37, 229n48
Han Xin, 103
Han Yu, 9, 172, 175, 182–83. See also Index of Titles
Hangu Pass, 114
He Zhizhang, 164–66, 167, 212
Hengtang, 63
Herd Boy, see Weaver Girl and Herd Boy
Hermits, see Reclusion
High Tang, 39, 42, 70, 95, 99, 102, 127, 172f, 182, 227n1
Historical song, 99, 106–7, 128, 141–42
Hong lou meng, 228–29
Hou Jing, 119
Hou Ying, 40
Huaigu (meditation on the past), 22, 95, 101f, 107–10, 115, 117–18, 134, 136–37, 234–35n12
Huainan zi, 140
Huajian ji, 60ff, 229–30
Huantou (stanza-break in ci), 60, 65, 68
Huaqing Palace, 37, 143–50 passim
Huineng, 206

Huiyuan, 24f, 204, 206
Hung, William, 7

Irony, 114–15, 125–26, 142, 235n21

Jia Dao, 9, 182; attitude toward composition, 9, 175–79, 184; poetry compared with Wen Tingyun's, 190ff, 203. See also Index of Titles
Jiang Kui, 89
Jiang Ziwen, 22–23
Jiankang, see Jinling
Jin dynasty, 29, 128, 200
Jingyang Palace, 79, 119, 156, 188
Jinling (Jiankang), 116–29 passim
Ju Mang, 140

King Mu (Zhou), 151f, 156ff
"King of Qin Wraps a Robe" (Qin Wang juan yi), 88
Kuai Tong, 103
Kuaiji, 165
Kūkai, 172
Kunming Lake, 134, 136

Lady Kong, 119
Lady Li, 31, 151, 157, 193f
Lady Pan, 111
Lady Qi, 87
Lady Sheng, 152, 156f
Lady Sun, 148
Lady Xun, 131
Laozi, 160
Late Tang, 23, 33, 36, 38–39, 83, 99, 166, 169, 184, 223n1, 229n48; later attitudes toward, 4, 9f; craftsmanship of poetry, 9–10, 19, 172–73; ci development during, 62, 229n49; attitudes toward palace-style poetry, 70, 231n4; attitudes toward history, 99, 108, 113, 117–18, 137–38, 159, 162; characteristics of poetry, 171, 173–74

256 Index of Subjects

Li Bai, 38, 42, 165–66, 172; and historical poetry, 99, 102, 105f. *See also* Index of Titles
Li Deyu, 12–13
Li He, 15, 17, 42, 43–44, 50, 57ff, 63f, 68, 85, 127f; and historical song, 106–7, 141; and *yuefu*, 44, 121; "The King of Qin Drinks Wine" (*Qin Wang yin jiu*), 45, 106, 125, 128; "Lord, Don't Dance" (*Gong mo wu ge*), 106; "The Bronze Immortal Takes Leave of the Han" (*Jintong xianren ci Han ge*), 55, 106, 122. *See also* Index of Titles
Li Linfu, 143
Li Shangyin, 12–13, 15f, 68ff, 184, 189f; attitude toward history, 109f, 117f, 142, 157, 169; status as a Late Tang poet, 171, 181–82. *See also* Index of Titles
Li Si, 113
Li Yannian, 31
Li Yu, 2
Liang dynasty, 30, 69–70, 72, 99, 111
Linghu Gao, 13
Linghu Tao, 12–15 *passim*
Liu An, 140
Liu Bang, *see* Emperor Gaozu (Han)
Liu Bei, 97, 162
Liu Changqing, 42
Liu Han, 14
Liu Ling, 200
Liu Lingxian, 232
Liu Song dynasty, 29
Liu Yiqing, 128
Liu Yuxi, 108, 113–14, 235n17; "Gathering Water Chestnuts" (*Cai ling xing*), 90. *See also* Index of Titles
Longwei, 158
Lord Xinling, 40
Lotus, 5; puns associated with, 32, 48, 87, 91

Lotus-picking poems, 32, 48, 91, 93
Lu Ji, 188
Lu Tong, 172
Luo Yin, 182
Luoyang, 71, 81
Lüshi (regulated verse), 16, 149, 170

Madame Wen (Wen Tingyun's sister), 1–2
Maoling, 135f
"Master Dengtu the Lecher" (*Dengtu zi haose fu*), 75, 232n9
Mather, Richard, 130
Mawei Station, 143, 151–56 *passim*
Meng Haoran, 173. *See also* Index of Titles
Meng Jiao, 172, 175
Meng Zhu, 168
Metalepsis, 112
Miao, Ronald C., 231n2
Mid-Tang, 9, 52, 62, 99, 108, 137, 172, 174–75, 182, 227n1
Mochou, 153
Monasteries and monks, 16, 23–25, 184, 203–5, 207
Mount Li, 37, 143
Mount Lu, 24, 204
Mount Shang, 18
Mount Wu, Goddess of, 31, 56, 80, 87
Mount Zhong, 22, 116, 120, 206
Music and poetry, 27–35 *passim*, 66, 229–30n51. *See also* Quatrain songs; *Yuefu*
Musical Poetry of the Tang (*Tang sheng shi*), 32

Nan Zhao, 183
New Feng (Xin Feng), 159–60
New Verses from the Jade Terrace (*Yutai xinyong*), 30, 71, 73f, 231n2
Nineteen Old Poems, 74, 101
Niu Sengru, 12–13
Nongyu, 33, 50
Nü Wa, 52

Index of Subjects   257

"Objectivity," 21, 65–66, 81, 106, 127
Owen, Stephen, 100

Pailü, 16, 144–45
Palace-style poetry (*gongti shi*), 30, 57, 69, 72–77, 82–89 *passim*, 93–94, 194, 230–31n2
Pei Wei, 200
Penglai, 49
Peonies, 195–96
Picasso, Pablo, 70
Poems on music, 52–53
"Poetry selection" (*cai shi*), 90
Prince Runan (Jin), 3
Prince Xiao of Liang (Han), 45
Princess Pingyang (Han), 75
"Pusa man," 13, 62–67 *passim*

Qiao sisters, 112
Qiao Zhou, 164
Qin Ershi, 124
Qin Shihuang, 96, 113ff, 120, 135
Qing dynasty, 8, 61f
Qu Yuan, 128, 204, 206
Quatrain songs, 29–30, 42, 77; tonality of, 30ff; conventional imagery of, 34–35; and poem sequences, 35–38
Queen Mother of the West (*Xi Wang Mu*), 3, 151f

Reclusion, 5, 16, 186f, 202, 207–12 *passim*
Record of Rites (*Li ji*), 27, 139
Red Cliff, Battle of, 97, 112
Ren Bantang, 32–36, 42, 68
Renjian cihua, 62
Ruan Ji, 102, 104f

"Safe space," 182–85 *passim*, 190, 194
Se (sensuous appearance), 75
Self-expression, *see under Shi* (lyric poetry)

Seven Masters of the Jian'an Era, 97, 166
Seven Sages of the Bamboo Grove, 97, 201
Sexuality and poetry, 72–76, 229n48, 232n9
Shan Jian, 20
Shang dynasty, 147
Shanglin Park, 140, 161
Shangyang Palace, 198
Shao Weng, 151
Shaopi Lake, 55
Shen Manyuan, 232
Shen Xun, 14
Shi (lyric poetry): morality of, 3–4, 10, 77; as autobiography, 6–10; as self-expression, 71, 73, 99, 159, 172f, 177
Shihua, 4
Shi ji, 100, 103
Shishuo xinyu, 128, 130, 199–200, 202, 207
Shitou, 108
Shu (Five Dynasties), 61
Shu (Three Kingdoms), 97, 162–63
Shun (sage ruler), 51–52, 147
Sikong Tu, 172
Sima Guang, 118
Sima Qian, 141
Sima Xiangru, 85, 96, 110, 140
Sima Yi, 163
Song dynasty, 2, 11, 61, 205
Song Yu, 31, 75, 232n9
Song Zihou, 3
Sou shen ji, 52, 156
Southern Qi dynasty, 30, 72, 111
Stanzaic poetry, 39; defined by rhyme changes, 39–46 *passim*; confusion with quatrain songs, 42–43
Stimson, Hugh, 217
Stravinsky, Igor, 70
Su Wu, 160–62, 167
Sui dynasty, 30, 77, 110, 118, 122f, 125–26, 128

Index of Subjects

Taiyuan, 11
Tang dynasty, 1, 29f, 32, 70, 83, 144. See also Early Tang; High Tang; Late Tang; Mid-Tang
Tang Yin, 2
Tao Qian, 42, 97–98, 182, 189, 201
Taoist immortals, 46, 49f, 139ff
Tian Dan, 147
Tonal regulation, 29, 39, 41, 215–19, 226n4, 226n5, 227n21

Valéry, Paul, 136–37
Voyeurism, 74–76, 198

Wang Can, 167
Wang Changling, 35
Wang Dun, 131–34
Wang Fuzhi, 9
Wang Guowei, 62
Wang Ji, 200
Wang Jun, 108
Wang Li, 39
Wang Mang, 141
Wang Wei, 25, 35, 172f, 184, 189, 204; poetry compared with Wen Tingyun's, 4–6, 186–89; "Wang Stream Collection," 32. See also Index of Titles
Wang Zhihuan, 35
Weaver Girl and Herd Boy, 43, 87f, 153
Wei (Warring States), 39–40
Wei dynasty, 97, 162–63, 164
Wei Zhuang, 61, 113, 182, 230n52. See also Index of Titles
Wei Zifu, 230
Wen (style, ornament), 71
Wen Tinghao, 12, 14f
Wen Tingyun: poetry compared with Wang Wei's, 4–6, 186–89; biography, 11–15; status as a Late Tang poet, 16, 170–71, 225n23; and stanzaic yuefu, 42f, 46–47; and tonal poetry, 47, 215–19; poetry compared with Li He's, 51–60;

and poetry collections, 60–61, 228n34, 228n35; reputation as a ci poet, 60–62, 67–68, 228–29; ci style, 62, 67; ci compared with yuefu, 62–65; erotic yuefu compared with palace-style poetry, 78–82, 83–94 passim; attitude toward history, 128, 137–38, 141–42, 157ff, 168–69, 199–200; attitude toward public service, 185–86; attitude toward reclusion, 186, 207–11; and Buddhism, 203–7. See also Index of Titles
Wen Xian, 12
Wen xuan, 98
Williams, William Carlos, 177
Willow Branch Songs (Yang liu zhi), 36
Wu (Three Kingdoms), 48, 108
Wu (Warring States), 17, 48, 94–95, 96, 106, 113, 183
Wu Diaogong, 116
Wu Gang, 52ff
Wuzhang, 163

Xi Shi, 96, 113, 117, 165
Xia dynasty, 114
Xia Chengtao, 11
Xian Zhengse, 118
Xiang River, Goddesses of, 50ff, 56–57
Xiang Yu, 96, 102–5
Xiangyang, 14, 20
Xianyang, 192, 197
Xiao Gang, see Emperor Jianwen (Liang)
Xiao Shi, 33
Xiao Tong, 98
Xiao Yan, see Emperor Wu (Liang)
Xie An, 128–31, 136, 138, 199
Xie Lingyun, 98, 200, 206
Xie Shi, 128
Xie Xuan, 129
Xiongnu, 160ff

Xu Chi, 231
Xu Fu, 113
Xu Hun, 182
Xu Ling, 69f, 231
Xu Shang, 14
Xu Zhaopei, 117
Xuanwu Lake, 116
Xue Neng, 36
Xue Xue, 8, 18

Yan Guang, 210
Yan Yu, 2, 223
Yang Guifei, 31, 37f, 142–58 passim
Yang Guozhong, 143, 148, 158
Yang Kan, 89, 91–94 passim
Yang Shou, 15
Yang Xiong, 101–2, 141, 200
Yangzhou, 14–15, 110, 125
Yao (sage ruler), 51
Yao Xu, 1–2, 11
Ye Congqi, 51
Ye Jiaying, see Chao, Chia-ying Yeh
Yellow Emperor, 148
Yong Tao, 179–84, 190, 192. See also Index of Titles
Yonghuai (Ruan Ji), 102
Yongshi (poem on history), 95, 107–8, 109, 115, 117f, 234–35
Yongwu (poem on things), 73, 77f, 85–89 passim, 194f, 202
Yu Pingbo, 62
Yu quan zi, 2
Yu Xin, 17–18, 72
Yu Xuanji, 15, 195
Yuan Zhen, 172
Yue (Warring States), 94–95, 96, 106, 137, 165, 183
Yuefu (Music Bureau), 27, 90

Yuefu (kind of poetry), 10, 16f, 29, 57; folk origins of, 27; elite imitations of, 28, 72–73, 99; fictionality of, 28, 99, 102. *See also* Music and poetry; Quatrain songs
Yuefu shiji, 28, 88, 91
Yuefu zalu, 12
Yuyang, 37, 143

Zhang Heng, 167
Zhang Hu, 35
Zhang Hua, 204
Zhang Huiyan, 61, 65
Zhang Jingwan, 89–94 passim, 194
Zhang Liang, 24–25
Zhang Lihua, 110, 119
Zhang Ruoxu, 126
Zhang Yue, 164
Zhang Zhan, 206
Zhao Chongzuo, 60f
Zhao Feiyan, 43, 75, 92, 96, 140f
Zhao Gu, 24f, 182
Zhao Zhuan, 1
Zhaoyang, 148
Zheng Jiaofu, 76
Zhongzi Qi, 52
Zhou dynasty, 114
Zhou Yafu, 163
Zhou Yu, 112
Zhou Zhenfu, 231n2
Zhu Hai, 40
Zhuangzi, 13, 42
Zhuge Liang, 97, 116, 162–64, 167, 237n47
Zhuo Wenjun, 85
Ziye ge (Ziye songs), 73
Zou Yan, 153
Zuo zhuan, 100

Library of Congress Cataloging-in-Publication Data

Rouzer, Paul F.
    Writing another's dream: the poetry of Wen Tingyun / Paul F.
Rouzer.
    p.   cm.
    Includes bibliographical references and index.
    ISBN 0-8047-2165-3 (alk. paper):
    1. Wen, T'ing-yün, 812–ca. 870—Criticism and interpretation.
I. Title.
PL2677.W45Z87   1993
895.1′13—dc20   92-33907
                                                                             CIP

∞   This book is printed on acid-free paper